BREACHING THE PEACE

Sarah Cox

BREACHING THE
PEACE

The Site C Dam and a Valley's
Stand against Big Hydro

on
point
PRESS

VANCOUVER | TORONTO

27 26 25 24 23 22 21 20 19 18   5 4 3 2 1

Printed in Canada on paper that is processed chlorine- and acid-free, with vegetable-based inks.

Library and Archives Canada Cataloguing in Publication

Cox, Sarah, author
Breaching the Peace : the Site C Dam and a valley's stand against big hydro / Sarah Cox.

Includes bibliographical references and index.
Issued in print and electronic formats.
ISBN 978-0-7748-9026-7 (softcover). – ISBN 978-0-7748-9027-4 (PDF). – ISBN 978-0-7748-9028-1 (EPUB). – ISBN 978-0-7748-9029-8 (Kindle)

1. Dams – Environmental aspects – Peace River Valley (B.C. and Alta.).
2. Water resources development – Environmental aspects – Peace River Valley (B.C. and Alta.). 3. Protest movements – Peace River Valley (B.C. and Alta.).
4. Farmers – Peace River Valley (B.C. and Alta.). 5. Peace River Valley (B.C. and Alta.). I. Title.

TD195.D35C69 2018   333.91'4140971187   C2018-901334-6
                                                   C2018-901335-4

Canadä

UBC Press gratefully acknowledges the financial support for our publishing program of the Government of Canada (through the Canada Book Fund), the Canada Council for the Arts, and the British Columbia Arts Council.

Printed and bound in Canada by Marquis
Set in Univers and Minion by Artegraphica Design Co. Ltd.
Copy editor: Matthew Kudelka
Proofreader: Kristy Lynn Hankewitz
Indexer: Sergey Lobachev
Cover designer: Jessica Sullivan
Cartographer: Eric Leinberger

On Point Press, an imprint of UBC Press
The University of British Columbia
2029 West Mall
Vancouver, BC V6T 1Z2
www.ubcpress.ca

For Arlene and Ken Boon

Contents

Foreword

Alex Neve

Secretary-General, Amnesty International Canada

The irony that such an epic struggle for rights and justice has had to be waged to save a river and a valley called "Peace" has been particularly bitter.

Much has been written about the economic folly of Site C, about the burden that will be created for future generations by sinking billions into old technologies for power that is not demonstrably needed and when other more forward-looking alternatives are available. The environmental cost of Site C has also energized opposition throughout British Columbia and across Canada among those who are deeply moved by the thought of the unnecessary destruction of such a rich and unique ecosystem. But ultimately what is most shocking about the construction of the Site C dam is the irreversible and irreparable human cost that will be borne by the families and communities who live on this land.

The Peace Valley has more than ten thousand years of human history. For all these generations, the ancestors of the Dunne-Za people travelled the river and hunted and gathered plants and medicines on its banks. Their bones are part of the land. Today, their descendants, and the Cree and the Métis as well, maintain these traditions. When the Dunne-Za and Cree of the Peace River region entered into Treaty 8, they sought to protect this way of life for all time. But those treaty commitments, made by and binding on the Canadian Crown, have been casually pushed aside and disingenuously ignored by provincial and federal governments.

The rights of non-Indigenous farmers and other landowners have also been unjustly ignored. They may be relatively new arrivals to the Peace, but many families have now sunk deep roots into the valley. At the very least, they deserved to have all other alternatives properly considered before being asked to give up their homes. But that basic sense of justice was denied them.

The determined campaign to stop Site C, so evocatively captured in Sarah Cox's timely and important book, has always been much bigger than a fight about one dam in one river valley. So many people and communities from so many different backgrounds and points of view – living in the valley, nearby, elsewhere in British Columbia, and around the world – have come together and devoted their effort, time, resources, heart, and soul to this enormously consequential struggle. Why? Because what is at stake has been a critical test of the willingness and prepared- ness of federal and provincial governments to act with honour and uphold human rights, reconcile with Indigenous peoples, commit to core principles of justice for farmers and landowners, and protect the environment.

That is why such an incredible diversity of people has found com- mon cause, determined to stop Site C. They believe passionately in being true to rights, reconciliation, justice, and the environment. They recog- nize that those values go to the very heart of how we absolutely must live, with one another and with our increasingly imperilled natural world. Sarah Cox richly captures the amazing strength, staying power, and resilience shown by grassroots community members from the Peace who have been (and still are) the engine, spirit, and conscience of this fight.

All of this explains why the campaign to stop Site C became such a priority for Amnesty International. Over the past several years, we have spent many weeks in the Peace, hearing first-hand from First Nations leaders and community members, landowners, and environmental campaigners. We have joined forces with the remarkable women and men who inspired and drove this campaign forward. We have gone to court, provincial and federal government offices, and the United Nations to press for resolution. Along with many partners in the Peace region and the rest of BC, we have submitted more than 120,000 petition signatures to the federal and provincial governments. We have mobilized members and supporters – across Canada and around the world – who have written imploring letters to provincial and federal leaders, signed and circulated petitions and postcards, and sent heartfelt images and messages of solidarity to the people and communities of the Peace.

Some people were surprised to see that Amnesty International was so committed to this campaign, thinking of Amnesty's work as being limited to prison cells and war zones. But there's nothing to be surprised about. We showed up because this is a human rights struggle of enormous consequence, one that goes to the very core of the most vitally important human rights challenge we face in Canada: reconciliation and respect for the rights of Indigenous peoples. The longer we have stayed – paddling the waters of the Peace, hearing and learning from First Nations elders, walking the land, and listening to the birds – the urgency of putting a stop to this travesty has become ever more apparent.

That is why we showed up, and we are certainly not going away. Quite the contrary. The deeper the disregard for human rights, the greater our indignation and persistence.

Since plans to construct Site C and destroy a sizable tract of the Peace River Valley were announced in 2010, two Canadian prime ministers, three BC premiers, and numerous provincial and federal ministers responsible for Indigenous affairs, the environment, waterways, and other relevant portfolios (from three different parties of widely varying political ideologies) have had the precious responsibility and clear opportunity to intervene and do the right thing. Yet they have all abjectly and disgracefully failed to do so. That is why this campaign and this book are so necessary.

It comes down to accountability. That could not have been clearer than when BC Premier John Horgan sought to deflect criticism of his crushing December 2017 announcement that construction of the Site C dam would proceed, with the perverse justification that his was not the first government to disappoint Indigenous peoples.

That cannot stand. Past injustice does not excuse more of the same; rather, it makes it imperative to break with that disgraceful history.

In the pages of this book, we read of the shameful litany of excuses offered up for government failures to uphold Treaty 8, respect human rights, and protect the environment. Federal officials pretend it is out of their hands and up to the province. The Horgan government now asserts it is hamstrung by the money already invested by its predecessors. Indeed, the overarching calculus comes down to money. Too expensive to turn back, says Premier Horgan. But the truth really is that he and all other political leaders before him have been unwilling and unable to accept their responsibility to treat the Peace River Valley and its people as something more than a resource to be exploited for the benefit of the rest of the province.

And as goes Site C and the Peace River Valley, so goes the rest of the country. Too expensive. Too entrenched. Too cowardly. Too shortsighted. Sarah Cox tells us a story that points to a history that defines more than 150 years of failure to respect the rights of First Nations, Inuit, and Métis in Canada. She shows us how failing once again to commit to reconciliation is also inextricably tied up with disregard for the rights of non-Indigenous families and communities and the prospect of devastating environmental destruction. These are stories and histories of injustice and harm that are so often intertwined in Canada.

The title of Sarah Cox's book, *Breaching the Peace*, means so much. It speaks to the looming risk that the flowing waters of this majestic river will be brutally disrupted. It is an indictment of government disregard of binding treaties, international law, and constitutional provisions. And it reminds us that "peace" ultimately must be grounded in rights, reconciliation, and our environment.

The Peace region has contributed much to BC's provincial economy, but its own needs have been badly neglected. Sarah Cox's insightful book makes it clear that stopping Site C is an opportunity for meaningful investment in the BC northeast, investment made in partnership with Indigenous peoples that respects the rights of all.

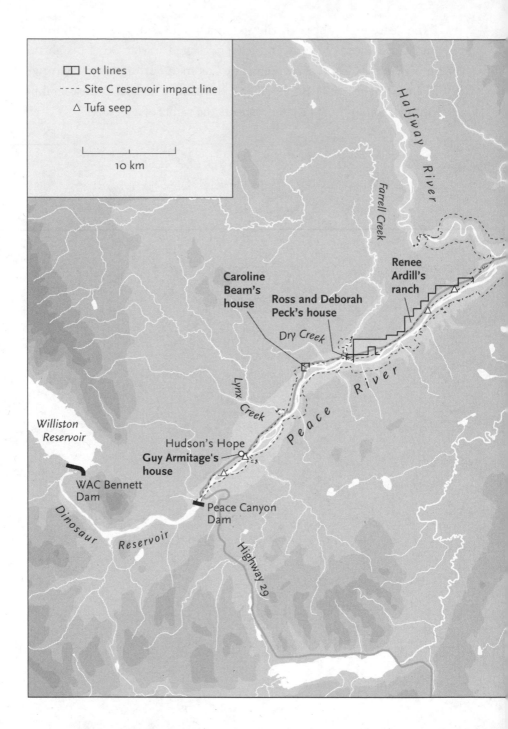

Legend

☐☐ Lot lines
- - - - Site C reservoir impact line
△ Tufa seep

10 km

Halfway River

Farrell Creek

Renee Ardill's ranch

Caroline Beam's house

Ross and Deborah Peck's house

Dry Creek

Peace River

Lynx Creek

Williston Reservoir

Hudson's Hope

Guy Armitage's house

WAC Bennett Dam

Dinosaur Reservoir

Peace Canyon Dam

Highway 29

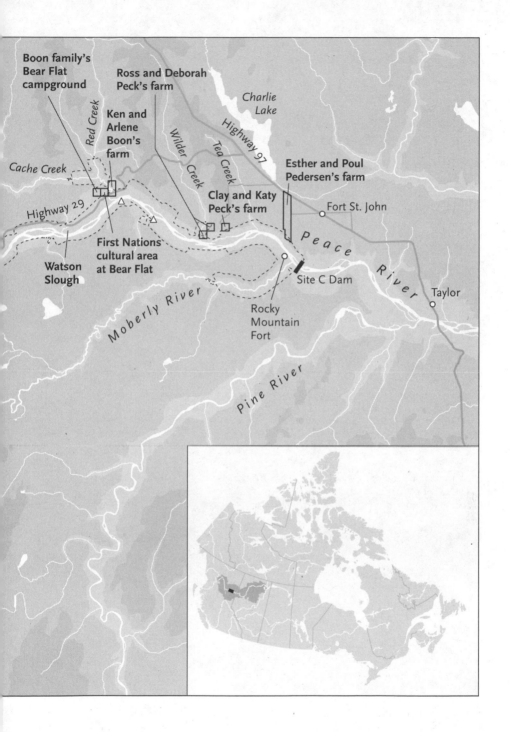

Boon family's
Bear Flat
campground

Ross and Deborah
Peck's farm

*Charlie
Lake*

Red Creek

Ken and
Arlene
Boon's
farm

Wilder Creek

Highway 97

Tea Creek

Cache Creek

Esther and Poul
Pedersen's farm

Highway 29

Clay and Katy
Peck's farm

Fort St. John

First Nations
cultural area
at Bear Flat

P e a c e

Watson
Slough

R i v e r

Moberly River

Site C Dam

Taylor

Rocky
Mountain
Fort

Pine River

BREACHING THE PEACE

Ken and Arlene Boon holding yellow stakes on the front steps of the house built by Arlene's grandfather | *Photo by Louis Bockner*

Prologue

On the rare days she felt disheartened, Arlene Boon gazed at the rows of yellow stakes outside her kitchen window. They sprouted from the earth like hundreds of sunflowers in a field, each marked with the name of a well-wisher in indelible black ink. Volunteers had painted the stakes by hand and pounded them into the ground at gatherings reminiscent of barn raisings.

Arlene lived with her husband, Ken, in a bungalow on the crest of a sun-drenched bank of the Peace River in northern British Columbia. She loved to garden. Normally, she cultivated everything from watermelon and tomatoes to artichokes and corn. But this year, in 2017, Arlene had planted little more than potatoes and three solitary rows of green beans. Her future was far too uncertain. Seven months earlier – the week before Christmas – the BC government had expropriated the bulk of the Boons' agricultural land and the bungalow that Arlene's grandfather had built. The couple had been ordered to leave their home by May 31.

But by the end of June, the Boons had yet to move. Arlene had boxed up only her sewing and quilting supplies, along with the extra linen, and had stored them in a mini log cabin that Ken had hastily converted into a storage shed. She refused to dismantle anything else. Her grandson Caleb's toys, the china cabinet in the kitchen, and living-room wall trophies from Ken's hunting and trapping days (a stone sheep and lynx among them) remained in place. The refrigerator door continued to

Arlene Boon in her garden, behind the farmhouse built by her grandfather.
BC Hydro planned to run the new Site C highway right through her garden |
Photo by Garth Lenz

sprout family photographs. "We're still here," Arlene told anyone who
called or texted.

A petite woman with a pixie cut, powder blue eyes, and a heart-
shaped face, Arlene had grown up, the second oldest of five children,
on a cattle ranch next door to her grandfather's homestead. She had
lived in the Peace River Valley for most of her fifty-five years. Arlene
knew where to find prickly-pear cacti in yellow bloom: on the slopes
of the Cache Creek Valley that cut through the undulating hills behind
the farmhouse. She knew the best places to pick purple Saskatoon berries and red chokecherries for pie, syrup, and jam. She knew where the
black bear denned, halfway up the creek bank, emerging most springs
with a small furball of a cub and sometimes two. She and Ken tracked
Red-Tailed Hawks and Golden Eagles that nested high in the forest that
cloaked the creek valley. They described walking through the Cache
Creek woods, freckled with old-growth cottonwoods and lively with
birdsong, as "akin to a tour through the Sistine Chapel."

For seven years, Arlene had been having trouble sleeping. She would wake in the quiet of the night, needled by the injustice of her situation. Her family had been the caretakers of their forest and farmland for seventy years, and they had looked after it well. They had preserved habitat for wildlife and forged a respectful relationship with local First Nations members, who continued to gather regularly, just as their ancestors had for millennia, at this serene spot near the confluence of Cache Creek and the Peace River, known locally as Bear Flat.

The defining issue in Arlene's life, the one causing her insomnia, was a large hydro project known as the Site C dam. BC Hydro, a provincial Crown corporation, planned to build the dam across the Peace River, a designated heritage river that was the heart and soul of Treaty 8 First Nations territory. The river's low-elevation valley supported rare and precious ecosystems, more than one hundred species vulnerable to extinction, some of Canada's richest farmland, and hundreds of protected heritage and archaeological sites, including Indigenous burial grounds. All would be flooded by the dam's extensive reservoir.

BC Hydro had asserted that the Site C dam would produce clean electricity at a time when concern about global warming was mounting. The former BC government, backed by Canada's federal government, had insisted that the project needed to be built "for the public good," but Arlene didn't believe that rationale for an instant. BC didn't need Site C's electricity, and BC Hydro planned to sell the power on the spot market at far less than it would cost to produce it. Even if the province pledged to slash greenhouse gas emissions further, clean energy options such as wind and geothermal could provide the same amount of electricity at the equivalent or a lower price tag and without deep cultural and environmental sacrifice.

The Site C project had seemed unstoppable. But now, defying all odds, its future hung in the balance, largely because of resistance led by the Boons and other Peace Valley landowners and First Nations. Two years into clear-cutting and bulldozing in preparation for the dam's construction, a series of extraordinary events had finally led to an independent review of the project. The Boons and their immediate neighbours had been given a four-month reprieve from eviction – Arlene called it her "stay of execution" – while the review, ordered by a new provincial government, was hastily convened.

The Boons had begun a Herculean task equipped only with dial-up Internet, an aging desktop computer, and no cell reception. They had no experience using social media, being interviewed by media, or giving public talks, and they knew no more about legal matters than your average Canadian homeowner. Yet as accidental activists, they played a game-changing role in propelling the Site C dam project into the public spotlight and finally garnering the critical scrutiny it deserved. "Someone's got to hold BC Hydro accountable," explained Arlene as she reflected on their struggle. "We're going to be a thorn in their side for as long as we can stand it."

At the eleventh hour, Arlene clung to a brightening beacon of hope that the dam could still be stopped. By day, she and Ken farmed fields that no longer legally belonged to them. By night and day, they fought Site C. Theirs was a war of principle, of sheer grit. Standing on her three front steps in the fall of 2017, waiting for the final verdict on her family's future, Arlene could see a gleaming stretch of the Peace River far below. The river often changed colour like a chameleon, sometimes blue, sometimes silver, mocha with the spring melt, pink in the setting sun.

Arlene had already witnessed the disfigurement of some of the valley for the dam, including the clear-cutting of the Cache Creek forest immediately below her home. But even now, two years into a planned nine-year construction project, almost 90 percent of the Peace River Valley remained untouched. When Arlene turned her head to look downstream, where the Peace River curved like a fish hook and disappeared, her vista of old-growth forest and terraced slopes remained unchanged.

Arlene grappled with a weariness that could not be lightened by a good night's sleep. The journey had been long and fraught. But there was nothing – neither rest nor money – that would persuade her to surrender now.

1

The Announcement

On a warm, breezy day in April 2010, British Columbia's premier, Gordon Campbell, and a large entourage flew to a short airstrip in the province's northeast. Campbell's London Air Service Learjet, filled with politicians and hand-picked supporters, landed just outside Hudson's Hope, an old-world town perched on the cliffs of the Peace River. Four more chartered planes touched down in quick succession at the airstrip that morning, one of them circling to avoid a moose that threatened to wander onto the runway.

Along with reporters, the aircraft delivered 120 people, many of them silver-haired men. Decades earlier, these same men had toiled on the construction of two large hydro dams upstream from Hudson's Hope. BC Hydro, the publicly owned corporation that built the dams, dubbed the retired cohort the "Power Pioneers." It had taken considerable effort to herd the former workers together for the trip, but a substantial budget existed for the announcement that Campbell planned to make, and the government had spared little expense. BC Hydro shelled out more than $360,000 for expenses that day, including flights and hotel accommodation. The Crown corporation deemed appearance so important that it thought nothing of spending $1,000 for lanyards and name badges.

The lavish spending from the public purse brought swift rebuke from John Horgan, BC's opposition energy critic, who seven years later would be sitting in Campbell's chair as premier. "How do you justify sending five planes full of people for a two-page press release?" Horgan asked during Question Period. "You announced an environmental review, not the second coming of Christ." Campbell's press secretary, Bridgitte Anderson, had a ready answer: "It was a significant announcement for the region, and it was important to make the announcement in the region where people would be directly affected."

As the outsiders disembarked from their aircraft, sixty Peace Valley residents, fenced into a small section of the gravel runway with yellow tape, chanted "No Site C" and waved placards that said "Damn That Dam" and "Site C Is an Unnecessary Evil." Two of the protesters were Ken and Arlene Boon. Two years earlier, the Boons and owners of 105 other impacted properties along the Peace River had received a letter from BC Hydro confirming that plans for Site C, a third dam on the Peace River, were well under way. "Oh my god, not again," thought Arlene. "You've got to be kidding." Site C had threatened the valley community before, but it had always been rejected, and for good reason.

BC's renowned premier William Andrew Cecil (W.A.C.) Bennett had first proposed Site C in the 1950s, as the third in a string of five dams along the Peace River. Over the ensuing decades, once the W.A.C. Bennett and Peace Canyon dams were completed, provincial governments of various political stripes returned again and again to the idea of erecting a third dam. In 1983, a government led by Bennett's youngest son, Bill, reluctantly rejected the idea following a review by an independent watchdog called the BC Utilities Commission. The review – which lasted almost two years and heard testimony under oath – found that the province did not need Site C's electricity at the time, that the dam would have negative social and environmental impacts, and that geothermal power should be investigated to meet future energy needs. As the commission noted in a report that proved to be still relevant decades later, "The evidence does not demonstrate that construction must or should start immediately or that Site C is the only or best source of supply."

The second time a government proposed Site C, in the early 1990s, BC Hydro's own board of directors discarded the project. "Site C is dead for two reasons," explained Marc Eliesen, BC Hydro's president and CEO at the time. "The fiscal exposure is too great ... the dam is too costly. Also, it is environmentally unacceptable." Eliesen added that Site C's energy was not needed domestically, and with that – along with the dam's significant impact on First Nations – the door to Site C appeared to shut for good. Years later, Eliesen recalled that the board had known that if BC ever needed additional power, other options would be less costly and much preferable: "The Board determined that there were no grounds upon which the project should ever be advanced in the future."

Less than two decades later, Campbell's flashy arrival in Hudson's Hope signalled a new opening for Site C. This cast a dispiriting shadow over the valley residents who gathered that morning in the designated protesters' corral. The path that lay ahead for Site C – from its revival in 2010 to final approval in 2014 to a construction jump-start in 2015 to a review by an independent watchdog commission in 2017 – would be strewn with contradictions and disinformation and marked by a repeated failure of due process. The megaproject flew in the face of Canada's commitments to an international declaration on the rights of Indigenous peoples and international human rights standards, including justification for forced evictions. The province still had no need for Site C's energy, and the project's cost, to be bankrolled by BC Hydro customers, climbed from $6.6 billion in 2010 to $10.7 billion in January 2018 – which was only two years into a minimum nine years of construction. Yet Site C was propelled along post-haste by a provincial Liberal government that many believed had lost its moral compass. At every step of the way, the government seemed far more interested in securing its own political future than in the repercussions of saddling hydro customers with a cripplingly expensive project that, as the months ticked by, assumed many characteristics of a boondoggle. Eliesen called Site C a "white elephant," a term coined after the King of Siam gave rare and holy albino elephants to courtiers he disliked, a gift they could not dispose of and whose upkeep ruined them financially.

ON THE DAY THAT Campbell and his coterie arrived in Hudson's Hope, more than 80 kilometres of the Peace River Valley remained relatively intact. It was this stretch of valley that BC Hydro hoped to flood, but most visitors that day saw little of its scenery, nor did they meet the Boons or the other people who would be forced from their homes and property if the project moved ahead. Had they travelled downstream, up and down the valley's rolling uplands, they would have seen dozens of farms and ranches, each a different size, shape, and contour, giving the delightful appearance of a landscape both thoughtful and unplanned. Across the river, on the valley's cooler, north-facing slopes, they would have encountered sandstone cliffs, wheaten in colour, that gave way to a mosaic of forests that included old-growth white spruce, cottonwood, and balsam poplar. They might have heard the trill of a Canada warbler, a yellow songbird in sharp decline, as it arrived back from its South American wintering grounds to nest in the valley. Or perhaps they would have glimpsed a Trumpeter Swan, whose restricted BC breeding territory includes the Site C flood zone. Local birders could have told them that the low-elevation Peace River Valley, an integral part of North America's boreal "bird nursery," hosts three-quarters of the province's bird species and is a flyway of continental importance for migrating songbirds, woodpeckers, and waterfowl. As many as thirty thousand songbirds and woodpeckers breed in the reservoir impact zone, and eleven thousand shorebirds have been observed in a single month during migration.

They would have passed river islands of varying shapes and sizes, ranging from low-lying ovals that are leafy havens for elk, moose, mule deer, and white-tailed deer to calve away from predators, to the teapot islands near Hudson's Hope that look like two-storey top hats. They might have glimpsed a red fox, marten, fisher, beaver, muskrat, or black bear or one of the elusive wolverines or grizzly bears that travel through the valley, a vital connection route for wildlife in the Rocky Mountains.

This Rocky Mountain corridor, one of the planet's last intact mountain ecosystems, stretches all the way from Yellowstone National Park to Yukon Territory. The Peace forms its narrowest point.

AT A 2017 LUNCHEON address to the Prince George Chamber of Commerce, Brad Bennett, the chair of BC Hydro's board of directors (and the son and grandson of former premiers Bill Bennett and W.A.C. Bennett) referred to Site C as a seemingly inconsequential "widening" of the Peace River. Playing down the project's impacts, Bennett, a real estate developer with close ties to the governing BC Liberal Party, warned his attentive audience composed of local business people to be wary of "fake news" about the dam. "We do have to build Site C," declared Bennett, whose credentials included an Order of British Columbia and service on an array of public and private boards, including that of the Fraser Institute, a Conservative think tank based in Vancouver. "I take issue with the fake news crowd, talking about Site C and whether it's needed or not." Site C, Bennett continued, in an attempt to bolster the project's environmental cachet, would use "basically recycled water" from the other two Peace River dams.

The Boons and other residents knew otherwise. Site C would destroy their valley's farming and ranching community and with it the traditional rural way of life that they had forged over many decades on a landscape that had been home to Indigenous peoples for millennia. The dam would directly affect thirty-four farms, destroying some entirely while rendering the chopped up pieces of the others unfit for viable cultivation. It would also inundate the last portion of the Peace River Valley available to First Nations for traditional practices like hunting, fishing, trapping, and teaching children Native languages on the land that had helped shape them. The right to continue such practices had been guaranteed to them in a treaty their ancestors had signed in 1900.

Site C's earthen-filled structure would rise 7 kilometres upstream from Fort St. John, a small oil and gas city near the north bank of the Peace River. The dam's reservoir would flood 83 kilometres of the remaining valley, to the Peace Canyon dam just beyond Hudson's Hope.

It would also inundate 45 kilometres of valley bottoms along seven of the Peace River's tributaries, including Cache Creek, where the Boons live, and the Halfway River further upstream, spawning grounds of bull trout populations vulnerable to extinction. In total, 128 kilometres of the Peace River Valley and its tributary valleys would be covered by up to fifteen storeys of water. Imagine if the area between Vancouver and Whistler, Victoria and Nanaimo, Calgary and Banff, or Toronto and Niagara Falls were flooded.

The district of Hudson's Hope, the third-oldest European settlement in the province and home to a thousand people, would lose sixty-eight properties to Site C, along with its water intake, pumping station, and treatment plant. To prevent more of the town from sloughing into Site C's reservoir, BC Hydro planned to build a berm 14 metres high, 7 metres wide, and 2.5 kilometres long that would take two years to construct and erase much of the town's scenic views.

From the residents' perspective, BC Hydro's maps make Site C's reservoir look innocuous, even pretty. You can barely tell which land the reservoir will subsume. Its outline is superimposed on satellite maps of the valley, in a dark-blue cross-hatch that blends in with the bluish-grey of the river and the brown of the land. The reservoir will initially widen the Peace River by an average of 2 to 3 kilometres, the equivalent of twenty-five to thirty-eight city blocks. After that, what engineers refer to as the "unstable banks" of the Peace River will weaken and collapse under the weight of the water, and the reservoir's girth will expand in fits and starts. The best guess at Site C's true reservoir borders is referred to as the erosion impact line. The line is neon green, but unless you peer closely at the maps it is not easy to reach the visual conclusion that the land within its borders will become part of the blue cross-hatch of the reservoir.

A blue line on BC Hydro's maps is called the flood impact line. As the banks of the Peace fall into the reservoir, close to four thousand landslides could ensue, according to a document prepared for BC Hydro. Many landslides will be small. But some will be large enough to generate mini tsunamis. These will wash over properties, stripping away rich topsoil from remaining farm fields. Wind-generated waves, when combined with high reservoir levels, will cause additional land to disappear inside the flood impact line.

And then there is the stability impact line. Coloured purple on the maps, it marks the farthest area that might crumble into the reservoir. BC Hydro will not permit any new residential structures to be built on remaining private property within the stability impact line, although existing homes can remain "for a period of time," provided they undergo regular geotechnical assessment. The Boons and others understood the implications. Once the land within all the different impact lines had been merged – and coloured blue instead of green and brown – Site C's reservoir looked far more like a substantial blight on the landscape than a picturesque "widening" of the river.

Renee Ardill, a long-time valley rancher, summed up the community's reaction to BC Hydro's maps and other Site C promotional materials, which marketed the project as clean energy for BC homes, even though there were no existing or anticipated homes in BC that lacked hydro power. "They'll sing you a song and tell you that everything will be lovely, but it won't," said Ardill, who lives on a riverside ranch with 350 Hereford and Angus cows, a bullmastiff, a border collie, and four generations of her cattle-raising family. "Those impact lines are a guess at best. They don't have a clue, and neither do we. They say it will be a lovely recreational lake but we know it will be a mud hole. These are some of the best soils in the world, and they're just going to rot."

Ardill was in the middle of calving season the day that Campbell visited, and she did not attend the protest. She would later attend most of the many BC Hydro meetings that would send residents scurrying up and down the valley to get the latest information about how, exactly, Site C would affect their homes, properties, and community. "I have a business to run," Ardill explained. "You either give up or keep going. You can't just sit and do nothing."

ON THE DAY OF Campbell's visit, his invited guests climbed aboard chartered buses and drove several kilometres west to the Bennett dam visitors' centre, where a room overlooking the dam had been set up with

Renee Ardill and a family member at their fourth-generation cattle ranch on the banks of the Peace River | *Photo by Garth Lenz*

a half-moon of chairs and a podium for the premier. Campbell's office had invited the media and local governments to a "clean energy workshop" at the Bennett dam. But most people knew they were really there for an announcement about Site C. At the podium, strategically positioned to offer the best view of the semicircular Bennett dam and the grey waters of the reservoir it held in check, Campbell made the statement everybody was waiting for: BC Hydro would seek regulatory approval for the Site C dam, starting with an environmental review. The new dam, the premier told the carefully screened audience, would be an important part of the province's energy, economic, and social future. He promised it would have lasting benefits for northern communities and First Nations. And, Campbell vowed, it would be the last big dam BC would ever build.

Because only vetted guests could enter the visitors' centre, third-generation Peace Valley rancher Leigh Summer decided to crash the gathering, and he bushwhacked along a shoulder of Portage Mountain for about an hour to get to the centre, where the first person he encountered was a security guard. Summer's family of eight had lost their farm to the Bennett dam when he was just fourteen, and now his ranch near Hudson's Hope stood to be carved up for Site C. Like many locals, he felt that the Peace Valley had already forfeited enough to send electricity to the rest of the province. Summer wanted to address the gathering to present the valley's point of view, and he told the security guard, "Either you let me in or arrest me." Moments later, he was surrounded by police, handcuffed, placed in the back of a police cruiser, and driven back to the airstrip, where he had left his tractor with a large sign that said "Keep the Peace." Other valley residents had waited for him there, and Arlene soon went home to transplant tomato seedlings in her greenhouse.

That same day, in an exchange that foreshadowed the troubled relationship that would ensue between BC Hydro and many Peace Valley residents, BC Hydro officials delivered a letter to Summer and his family. It invited them to start negotiations with BC Hydro to determine where a provincial highway would cross their land once it had been relocated from the Site C flood zone. Also the same day, the Boons and other landowners received hand-delivered letters from BC Hydro with an "update" on Site C. The letter stated that BC Hydro was committed to consultation with property owners and gave them contact information for Hydro's property representative – a thinly veiled reminder that they could sell their properties to BC Hydro for Site C at any time. In response, Summer uttered three words that many people faced with the loss of their homes, farms, and community might use, words that quickly became a rallying cry for the Boons and other valley residents: "I say no."

VALLEY RESIDENTS HAD been saying no to Site C for decades. Arlene's grandfather, Lloyd Bentley, had chased BC Hydro representatives off his property when they first came knocking in the 1970s to talk about the dam. An infuriated Bentley scribbled a warning letter to BC Hydro. "I will not give you permission to come on my land for anything regarding your dam for it is going to flood the best pieces of my ranch," it said. "I have three hired men and if I can will get some more help to put you off ... Two of your surveyors say when the water comes up my house will tumble into Cache Creek ... I have been in the Peace for 64 years and this is the worst thing that is happening. You should go up further north where no-one lives."

In the fall of 1976, as work on the Peace Canyon dam progressed and BC Hydro began drawing up detailed plans for Site C at the behest of the government led by Bill Bennett, three hundred people flocked to a public meeting in Fort St. John to discuss the project. The mood at the gathering was "dramatic" and hostile, according to one BC Hydro official. There were three reasons for the hostility, opined the official in an internal hydro memo. Many valley residents objected to flooding the rich soils of the lower Peace Valley, which were among the most fertile in the country. They also objected to the prospect of relocation and did not "trust Hydro to be fair or reasonable in compensation." The third reason, the official wrote, was that people in the region "resent being exploited for the benefit of the Lower Mainland ... without direct benefit to the region, and are opposed to further similar development."

Bentley was hardly the only large landowner voicing fierce opposition to the Site C project in the 1970s. In the words of a senior BC Hydro official, the project was becoming "bogged-down." A confidential BC Hydro memo reported that surveyors for the dam were encountering opposition from landowners along the Peace River "by way of threatening gestures & verbal warnings to stay off their land." Flags marking a new route for a provincial highway in the flood zone had mysteriously disappeared, and one surveyor vehicle had the distribution wire removed from its engine and placed on the hood. "We have a somewhat irate and anxious group of owners and environmentalists who refuse to give Hydro permission to enter and survey," wrote a senior official in BC Hydro's Properties Division in an inter-office memo. The same memo compared the situation of valley ranchers and farmers to a scenario in which BC Hydro informed an employee that he would likely be fired or terminated but without giving any indication as to when. "The effect is dramatic and depressing for all involved," this official noted.

The week following Campbell's announcement at the Bennett Dam visitor centre, his government changed the law to remove Site C from being scrutinized by the BC Utilities Commission, a public guardian that would have determined whether the project was in the best interests of BC Hydro customers. BC's Liberal government intended to forge ahead even if Site C's power was not required and no matter the ultimate cost.

I TRAVELLED TO THE Peace River Valley for the first time in July 2013 to speak to locals and hear their perspectives on Site C. At the time, I was working for Sierra Club BC, focusing on wilderness and wildlife protection through the lens of climate change. Most of BC's environmental groups did not seem overly concerned about the dam – not enough, anyway, to dedicate time or resources to trying to stop it. The dam would generate clean energy, after all, and taking action to slow global warming was a top priority for many organizations, including mine. I expected to see just another pretty BC valley, another threat to what, at the time, I had mistakenly perceived to be a relatively small sliver of the natural world. I was much more accustomed to thinking of conservation as the protection of large, relatively pristine landscapes rather than the preservation of other values as well: traditional ways of life, human history, the smaller green spaces that connect protected areas for wildlife, how everything fits together.

I had lived in BC since I was a teenager and had travelled throughout much of the province, but like most British Columbians, I had never visited the Peace. I knew the region mainly as a split-second weather update on the morning radio from my home in BC's capital city of Victoria, on Vancouver Island. I had little conception of just how far from most of the province it was, in so many ways, and how difficult it would be for the Boons, First Nations members, and other valley residents to bridge that yawning gap. I had no idea I would encounter something of a biological curiosity in the valley, a northern Garden of Eden with outlier species that intrigued scientists, especially as evidence

mounted that the valley might have escaped glaciation during the last
Ice Age. They believed that the valley's flood zone – a mixing area for
species from four different ecoregions – could hold important clues to
how species might adapt to global warming.

By car or truck, the Peace River Valley is fourteen hours from Vancouver, about the same amount of time it takes to drive to Saskatchewan from the Lower Mainland. By plane from Vancouver or Calgary,
the flight north is only ninety minutes. From Vancouver, my flight rose
over the snowy Coast Mountains and skirted north over Prince George,
tucking low over the serpentine Peace River in the final descent before
landing just outside Fort St. John. I wasn't immediately endeared to
the place; a glass display case in the airport contained an exhibit called
"Mosquitoes of the North."

From the plane, I had seen roads crisscrossing the landscape all around
Fort St. John, many ending in a square gas well pad, even in the middle
of a farm. I knew that the region surrounding the valley supported
widespread industrial logging, open-pit coal mining, and vastly expanded
natural gas fracking, one of the most water-intensive fossil fuel extraction methods on the planet. The result was a landscape splintered by
development, its wildlife in sharp decline. The pace of industrial development in BC's Peace region had been so rapid that it exceeded even the
rate of development in Alberta's booming Oil Sands. And that was *before*
the price of oil plummeted and forest fires ravaged Fort McMurray. By
the time I visited, there were 45,000 kilometres of roads in the Peace.
If you added the adjoining pipelines and seismic lines in the region, the
linear disturbances were long enough to wrap around the planet four
and a half times.

The Peace River Valley was easy to spot from the air: an oasis of green
amidst development, anchored by a broad river that looped and twirled
invitingly. Once I landed, I drove by rental car twenty-five minutes
southwest from Fort St. John, where I slowed to navigate a stretch of
highway that coiled down a precipitous hill. To my right as I descended,
stretching deep into the foothills of the distant Rocky Mountains, un-
folded the valley about which I had heard so little on BC's coast. It was

much broader than I had expected, and a patchwork of farmers' fields sprawled out in dappled shades of green. The fields curled tight against the banks of the Peace River, which jogged through the valley and disappeared around a bend. The fields rose and fell with the contours of the land, coming to rest at the foot of hills that sloped to the horizon: patchy green, silver, and brown. It looked as if someone had ploughed the hills into wide furrows, shaping the earth into uneven, bumpy rows. Far below, I could see the land belonging to the Boons, the family I had come to visit. A loose cluster of weathered wood-plank and log buildings marked the centre of their grain and hay farm.

I angled down the hill, made a hairpin right turn, and moments later found myself at the Boons' steep gravel driveway. A hand-stencilled wooden sign said, "Site C Sucks. Feed Oats and Barley for Sale." Near the top of the extended driveway was another sign, a marker. It had a graphic of wavy blue lines like the sea and the words, "Flood Reserve Level." About a kilometre away from the Peace River and 40 metres above it, the sign marked the height to which the Site C flood waters would rise. Much of the family's farmstead lay squarely in Site C's inundation zone, in the cold company of dozens of other properties that would be lost, completely or in part, to flood waters or to the provincial highway that would be relocated for the dam.

I found Arlene in the garden beside her house, picking green beans and the season's first carrots in the tropical heat. Barn and cliff swallows pitched overhead, scooping insects from the air while they chirped and tweeted. Handmade birdhouses, painted cheerful colours like a row of asymmetrical Newfoundland houses, sat on top of wooden poles that anchored the garden fence. Already, the tall grass outside the garden was turning to golden straw.

Arlene's corn was shoulder-high, and green cantaloupes crawled along the ground. "We can grow anything here," she said, handing me a carrot. She wore a blue baseball hat and dirt-stained jeans. "Broccoli, watermelon, tomatoes, corn, strawberries, asparagus, you name it." She brought out a framed photograph of her grandfather, posing on the same front steps where she sometimes stood looking out. In the photo,

Arlene's grandfather held a half-grown black lamb. A sprinkling of snow cloaked the fields behind him. He wore Wellington boots, muddy brown overalls that didn't quite reach his ankles, and a Humphrey Bogart–style fedora hat.

"Every day we get to walk up the same steps that my grandpa walked up and we live in the same house that he built with his blood, sweat, and tears," Arlene told me as she showed me the farm. Its buildings included a renovated log cabin – the original Bear Flat schoolhouse – where her elderly mother resided, and a guest cabin that had been the first post office in Hudson's Hope and still had the original mail slot. Another log cabin housed a family museum, visited by hundreds of schoolchildren from Fort St. John. The museum displayed fossils and arrowheads that the Boons had unearthed on their property, along with old-time household and farm wares.

"All the money in the world is not going to replace what we get to enjoy physically and emotionally every day when we sit in the same kitchen as my grandfather," explained Arlene. "We can't be bought out. We cherish every morning that we can get up and look out and see that river flowing by. And we'll continue to do that forever, as long as we live. I'll be damned if I'm going to walk away without a fight."

The Boons, and many people like them, were determined to take on Big Hydro. But did they truly know what they were up against? Little did the couple and other locals, including First Nations members, know that they would become the target of an unprecedented civil lawsuit, launched against them by BC Hydro and sanctioned by their own government. While other major conflicts over resource development in BC involved multinational corporations like Kinder Morgan, Shell, and Enbridge – companies that had reputations and brand names to bolster and shareholders to please – the Site C dissidents faced a much more challenging adversary: their own government and power company. Those two would prove to be far more formidable than many multinational corporations and – as the Boons and others would soon learn – very deep-pocketed, resourceful, and litigious.

Chief Roland Willson of West Moberly First Nations standing in front of the Peace River | *Photo by Garth Lenz*

Before my visit, seventy landowners who would be impacted by Site C had formed a group called the Peace Valley Landowner Association (PVLA) and started speaking as one voice. The group, which met over potluck dinners salted with farming chitchat, elected Ken Boon as president and Ardill as vice-president. Meanwhile, the Peace Valley Environment Association (PVEA), created during the 1970s and loosely based in Fort St. John, was dusted off and reactivated. Local volunteers raised money to hire a part-time coordinator, which was all they could afford, and together with the landowners' association, they launched a "hearts and minds" grassroots campaign in an uphill effort to draw province-wide attention to some of the little-known damage that Site C would cause and to the folly of its finances. Each year, on the second Saturday in July, the environmental association and First Nations staged a Paddle for the Peace, which drew up to eight hundred people to canoe a magical stretch of the Peace River that would be lost to Site C. West Moberly First Nations Chief Roland Willson referred to the paddle collaboration as "the cowboys and Indians, working together."

In preparation for the Site C environmental review announced by Campbell, BC Hydro and a battalion of lawyers and contractors had spent years amassing more than fifteen thousand pages of documents, including detailed technical reports. As BC political columnist Vaughn Palmer quipped, "not for nothing does the giant utility have a reputation for suffocating its critics in a blizzard of paper."

In August 2013, after the federal and provincial governments deemed BC Hydro's five-volume Environmental Impact Statement satisfactory, a panel was appointed to shepherd the review process. The Joint Review Panel, as it was called, was chaired by Harry Swain, a former federal deputy minister with project-financing expertise who would go on to become one of Site C's thorniest and most outspoken critics. Under new environmental assessment regulations introduced by the Stephen Harper government, only thirty days of public hearings were allotted. The strict time limitation meant that the panel could convene hearings only in Fort St. John and other northern communities, even though Site C would affect all British Columbians. The ill-timed hearings began in mid-December and continued into January, with a break for the Christmas holidays, prompting Joe Foy, national campaign director for the Wilderness Committee, to protest that "Ottawa and Victoria are behaving like old Mister Grinch."

The Joint Review Panel in May 2014 delivered its much-awaited report, in which it gave a stark account of Site C's impact on the environment and First Nations. The phrase "significant adverse effects" appeared throughout. The panel noted that it had neither the time nor the resources to scrutinize BC Hydro's cost projections for Site C, or to verify projections of future energy needs or the cost of clean energy alternatives. It concluded that BC did not need Site C's energy in the time frame BC Hydro had presented. It also recommended that the project be reviewed by the watchdog BC Utilities Commission with an eye to its price tag, which at that point in time stood at $7.9 billion.

By the time the panel's report was released, Campbell had resigned as BC's premier and as leader of the BC Liberal Party – an informal coalition of political parties on the right of the political spectrum that, despite its name, had no formal ties to Canada's federal Liberal Party. Into Campbell's place had stepped Christy Clark, a bubbly former radio show host with a perpetual smile. Clark, who enjoyed posing for media photos wearing a hard hat and other work gear, such as a safety vest and goggles, had won an election in 2013 during which she campaigned on a platform of job creation and the promise of one hundred thousand new jobs in BC's embryonic liquefied natural gas (LNG) industry. Just one LNG plant, Clark later mused to the media, could consume every watt of Site C's energy (overlooking that LNG plants worldwide eschew grid electricity in favour of burning their own gas).

While campaigning for re-election in the spring of 2017, Clark said it was urgent to build Site C "to literally keep the lights on" for BC families. The declaration echoed information BC Hydro had submitted to the Joint Review Panel, claiming that Site C's electricity was required for domestic use. Several months after that, Clark changed her tune again and said that Site C's energy would be needed for electric cars. Even while Clark raised the spectre of a future electricity shortage so severe that British Columbians might not have enough power to flick on their kitchen lights, BC was swimming in so much extra electricity that hydro customers were paying independent power producers millions of dollars a year not to produce power, in much the same way that the US government had paid farmers not to produce hogs when the pork market was glutted.

Clark's "big news" announcement took place in Victoria just before the Christmas holidays in 2014. Standing beside Clark that day was BC Hydro's new president and CEO Jessica McDonald, who had served as Campbell's deputy minister and the head of BC's public service. This time, there was not a whisper about delivering the announcement in the region most affected by the project. For the Boons and other Peace Valley residents, it was not a happy holiday message. Clark, standing by a wall-sized backdrop with an artists' rendition of the Site C dam and its reservoir – which looked like a blue alpine lake in a rather drab and uninhabited valley – said her government had made a decision that would make "a real difference" in the lives of British Columbians.

The Site C dam would proceed, said the premier, smiling but also properly serious, considering that she was about to embark on a financial gamble far riskier than the fast ferry scandal that in 2001 had booted a BC New Democrat government from office. The Site C project had undergone a "thorough and independent multi-year environmental assessment process," Clark informed British Columbians. She said Site C would provide "clean, reliable and affordable energy" for more than one hundred years (later, the figure was quietly changed to seventy years). In case anyone missed Clark's message, a blue sign fastened to the podium repeated it for the television cameras and for photographers who had gathered at the legislature to receive the news.

Seven months later, in July 2015, as Clark's promised LNG industry failed to materialize and it was revealed that the sector had created virtually no jobs, the premier authorized the start of preliminary clearing and bridge-building work for Site C. She cheerily stated that the project would create ten thousand construction jobs. It was a dubious pledge given that when Site C was proposed in the early 1990s, BC Hydro said the dam would create 2,182 construction jobs, and the considerably larger Bennett Dam had employed 3,500 people at peak construction in the 1960s. But Clark's upbeat job-creation message stuck and would be repeated for many years to come as a key justification for the project.

In green-lighting Site C, Clark ignored the major recommendation of the Joint Review Panel – backed by calls from organizations such as the Royal Society of Canada, the Union of BC Municipalities, and the Union of BC Indian Chiefs – that the project be dispatched to the BC Utilities Commission for a thorough independent review to determine if it was in the best interests of British Columbians.

Before different phases of Site C construction could proceed, BC Hydro was required to obtain a raft of legal permits. Federal government permits would allow BC Hydro to build bridges over navigable rivers, including Peace tributaries, and to alter and destroy fish habitat, including habitat for at-risk bull trout and thirty-one other Peace River fish species. Provincial government permits would allow the destruction of protected heritage and archaeological sites; the denuding of old-growth forests in the reservoir area; the eradication of beaver dams, muskrat houses, and eagle nests; and the capture and relocation (it was not revealed to where) of amphibians.

The first fourteen federal permits for Site C were quietly issued in the dying days of the Harper government. In a highly irregular departure from convention, which normally saw only routine and uncontested permits issued during an election campaign, the Harper administration delivered the Site C permits after the writ had been dropped for the fall 2015 election, which Harper subsequently lost. These early permits included permission to cause "serious harm" to fish habitat, including the destruction of spawning habitat for mountain whitefish, a salmonid species of cultural value to First Nations.

So many provincial permits were legally required that BC Hydro instituted weekly meetings with the provincial Ministry of Forests, Lands, and Natural Resource Operations to prod civil servants along when the pace of authorizations lagged. In an astonishing case of the proverbial fox guarding the hen house, BC Hydro, representing one arm of the provincial government, simply applied to another arm of the government for permits for a project that the government had already approved. Some of the permits legally required public consultation, and the natural resource ministry duly posted opportunities for comment. The process, in the words of Ken and Arlene Boon, was "a farce." It didn't matter how many comments were filed expressing concern about BC Hydro's plans to clear-cut old-growth forest, bulldoze rare and ancient wetlands, destroy protected heritage and archeological sites, and eradicate endangered species habitat – the requisite permit never failed to arrive in BC Hydro's inbox.

Three months into preliminary construction, in November 2015, BC Hydro issued a press release outlining its progress on Site C. Contractors working for the Crown corporation had transported hundreds of pieces of heavy machinery to the dam site. They had felled 520 hectares of boreal forest – an area much larger than all of Stanley Park. They had dredged more than 1,000,000 cubic metres of earth, gravel, and rock

The Peace River Valley before and after initial clearing work near the dam site |
Photos by Garth Lenz

from the Peace River. The Boons and other valley residents noted that
contractors had also dragged unmillable wood and vegetation into
huge brush piles to burn, logged a Peace River island that had provided
a haven for moose and elk to calf, retrieved an excavator from the river
where it had overturned, destroyed a beaver dam that was at least
three decades old, and toppled two eagle nests. BC Hydro called it one
hundred days of construction. Valley residents referred to it as one
hundred days of destruction. "We're mad as hell about it," noted Ardill.
"They didn't have to flatten the island and wreck the eagles' nests. Their
whole strategy is a bully tactic."

As 2015 drew to a close, Site C's logging operations approached an
area, at the confluence of the Peace and Moberly rivers, that was a
designated BC heritage site and a protected old-growth forest of great
cultural importance to First Nations. The Boons and other valley residents, including First Nations members, secretly set up a winter camp
at the Rocky Mountain Fort heritage site on the remote south bank of
the Peace River, where the next phase of clear-cutting would take place,
and settled in to stay.

Treaty 8 Stewards
of the Land

The camp consisted of a plywood shack, a canvas hunting tent, and a lean-to covered with a yellow tarp. Along with a pile of split logs, a fire pit, and three snowmobiles, the makeshift dwellings were tucked just out of sight in a spruce and poplar forest on the Peace River's wilder side. The camp was on Crown land that First Nations members were entitled to use for traditional practices, such as prayer, ceremonies, and gathering medicinal plants and fungi. If challenged, they would explain that it was a coincidence that their activities happened to be in the path of Site C logging, logging that would become part of one of the largest modern clear-cuts in the province.

Only a metal sign and a few depressions on the snowy forest floor hinted at the campsite's consequential past. In 1793, explorer Alexander Mackenzie, travelling west in a birchbark canoe with six voyageurs, had selected this spot, on a raised bank of the Peace River with clear sight lines upstream and down, for the first European fort in mainland BC. The site was "an excellent situation for a fort or factory," opined Mackenzie, "as there is plenty of wood, and every reason to believe that the country abounds in beaver." Mackenzie also noted the abundance of bison and other wildlife: so thick were these on the landscape, he said, that parts of the valley resembled a farmyard. The Rocky Mountains towards which he headed shimmered on the horizon, and the site was named Rocky Mountain Fort.

The rough outpost became not just a fur-trading post but also a rudimentary factory for making pemmican, meat preserved in rendered grease for the voyageurs' long journeys by canoe. Described by archaeologists as a "significant piece of western Canadian history," the fort was the strategic gateway for corporate fur trade expansion and for European exploration of BC's interior, as well as an early meeting place for Europeans and Beaver Indians, who traded animal pelts there for iron, weapons, beads, and other goods. Explorers like David Thompson and John Finlay later bunked down in the fort's log buildings, which were likely arranged in a U facing the fast-flowing river, with a view of what Mackenzie called the valley's "exuberant verdure."

In the mid-1980s, almost two centuries after the fort site was abandoned, archaeologists unearthed more than twenty thousand artifacts ranging from glass beads, brass cufflinks, and a glass bottle (originally containing "Essence of Peppermint") to fish hooks, razors, axes, and awls. Traditional Indigenous bone and antler tools, as well as Mi'kmaw-style stone pipes, were also found, along with the remains of a fireplace built of stones hauled from the Peace River and prodigious quantities of animal bone waste, an indicator of the importance of the post's provisioning function. In the prevailing custom of the day, however, only portions of the two remaining fort buildings and their immediate surroundings, where the traders and voyageurs had lived, were ever excavated. Archaeologists had neither the time nor the resources (the dig had been funded by the now defunct Heritage Resources BC) to search for any remains of the five or more First Nations lodges that had been raised near the fort.

First Nations encampments were far more difficult to find and interpret than fort structures, according to Scott Hamilton, a specialist in fur trade archaeology and ethnohistory, who, as a PhD student, had spent two summers as the "pit boss" overseeing the dig. As the Rocky Mountain Fort camp took root, Hamilton pointed out that much would be lost to history if the fort site was destroyed for Site C before it could be thoroughly studied from a First Nations perspective. "What about all those hard-to-find, hard-to-interpret, widely scattered Aboriginal camps that represented the Aboriginal side of the ledger in the fur trade?" he asked. "They will be gone forever if this project proceeds."

The Rocky Mountain Fort site would be flooded by the Site C reservoir. But first it was slated to become something else in service to the dam: part of a 2.2 kilometre-long dump for 7 million cubic metres of waste rock that would cover an area more than half the size of Stanley Park. The construction waste rock might well be acid generating – that is to say, laden with sulfide materials that, when exposed to air and water, react to form sulfuric acid. Sulfuric acid can dissolve other harmful metals from the rock, such as arsenic, making the rocks highly toxic to animals, plants, and fish. To prevent arsenic and other heavy metals from leaching into the river during Site C construction, BC Hydro planned to build a giant berm, or retention dike, around the fort site. The berm would eventually be submerged by the reservoir, providing, according to BC Hydro, new habitat for fish.

When I stood at the fort site and squinted, I could see far across the Peace River to a farm owned by Esther and Poul Pedersen, high on a grassy bluff. The Pedersens were certified Equine Canada riding coaches who bred horses. Esther, a former milk inspector for the BC Agriculture Ministry, ran a popular equestrian centre, only a ten-minute drive from an expanding clientele in Fort St. John; Poul commuted to a job in the oil patch. The couple loved to watch the wildlife that crisscrossed their land: a large elk herd swimming back and forth across the river, whitetail and mule deer, moose, coyotes, black bears, foxes, muskrats, and what Esther called an "amazing variety" of birds, including songbirds, corvids, waterfowl, seabirds, great horned and snowy owls, and birds of prey ranging from tiny sparrow hawks to kestrels.

A narrow strip of Crown land overgrown with purple crocuses, wild strawberries, and berry bushes separated the Petersen's hayfields from the steep and ragged riverbank. Gazing downstream from a grassy point that sloped steeply down to the river, the Pedersens had a clear view of the Site C construction site. For the next two years, the promontory by the couple's farm would be the only place where valley residents could view the site, which was guarded from the public eye.

In the fall of 2015, as preliminary construction work for Site C hastily advanced, First Nations members and other valley residents hoisted a small shack onto a trailer and trucked it to the Pedersen's farm. They set the plywood shack down on Crown land and affixed a sign that said, "Property of Treaty 8: Say No to Site C." The reddish-brown shack, about the size of two garden sheds, had windows overlooking the construction site, a scope with which to view construction activity, an old patterned couch, a bed, and a wood stove. A striking photograph of the valley, taken from the Pedersens' point before Site C construction began, hung above the window. The photo, taken by local photographer and mill worker Don Hoffmann, showed the Moberly River estuary on the opposite side of the river, the forest slopes above it crowned with autumn amber and gold. The Moberly zigzags through forest to Moberly Lake, where West Moberly First Nations has a reserve. On the Peace River between the estuary and the Pedersens' point sat the island, thick with trees, that was in the process of being cleared and excavated for dam construction. Eventually, the entire island would disappear. Upstream from the Moberly River, near the shapely bank of the Peace, the same photo showed a spruce tree whose unusually tall peak stuck up like a spire, marking the Rocky Mountain Fort site.

The Pedersens could hear the Site C construction, quite loudly at times, as blasting took place and pilings were pounded. Logging machinery advanced along both sides of the river, mulching old-growth cottonwoods and spruce and carving an access road into the sandstone bluff below them. The racket of machinery running twenty-four hours a day, and bright lights shining into their windows at night, ensured that the couple and their neighbours were routinely sleep deprived. "It sounds like an airport," commented Esther, "with beep, beep, beep all night long." She fretted that Poul might fall asleep at the wheel while driving to his job as a gas field operator, endangering not just his own life but the lives of other people on the road.

Back in the 1990s, when the Pedersens purchased their property and built a house, they hadn't known that Site C would strip away their

Cook shack at the Rocky Mountain Fort camp | *Photographer unknown*

land. The couple only learned of it by chance one day, about a year after Campbell's announcement, when they were attending the annual Fort St. John trade show and stopped to look at a booth run by the Peace Valley Environment Association. Glancing at the association's maps, they were shocked to discover that Site C would claim about half their land, including the sheltered spot they had chosen to build an indoor riding arena, along with nearby riding trails developed by a local club and located on Crown land. They had built the large, modern house (their "dream house," Esther called it) for themselves and their two daughters. It and the forest that surrounded it would be lost to the reservoir. If the dam proceeded, the Pedersens would be left with only disjointed pieces of their land and a highly uncertain future as a horse-breeding and riding facility. Esther, a frank, dark-haired woman, minced no words: "We're expendable. This is a really crappy way to live."

As the 2015 Christmas holidays approached, Ken Boon and several other valley residents trucked a second small survival shack to the Pedersen's land. A local rancher and welder named Mark Meiers owned the three-bunk shack. He had wired it for electricity and fabricated a small wood stove with a pipe that jutted out from one of the walls. A

former North American rodeo circuit rider, Meiers ranched just outside the valley at Charlie Lake, where he also grew premium oats, pearl
barley, wheat, and grasses.

Earlier that month, Meiers had become the first person arrested in an
act of civil disobedience against Site C. The farmer, small and broad-
chested like a bulldog, had planted himself in the middle of the Old
Fort Road leading to the dam construction site, blocking trucks from
moving past. He did it, he said, to show local residents they would not
be physically harmed if they demonstrated against Site C. "You're not
going to shoot me, are you, Officer?" Meiers asked the RCMP inspector
who arrested him.

The previous summer, an RCMP officer had fatally shot a Cree–Métis
man named Jimmy McIntyre outside a BC Hydro Site C Open House
in Dawson Creek, an hour's drive south of Fort St. John. The police had
received a call saying that a Hydro protester was overturning tables at
the Fixx Urban Grill in the Stonebridge Hotel, where the event was taking place in the banquet room. Outside the hotel, officers encountered
McIntyre, who was carrying a knife and wearing the signature Guy
Fawkes mask of the hacktivist group Anonymous. They shot him in the
leg when he did not put down his knife, hitting a major artery. McIntyre
quickly bled to death on the pavement. To further the intrigue, and
amidst growing local fears of potential consequences for protesting
Site C, it was quickly revealed that McIntyre was not, in fact, the person
who had disrupted the Site C meeting.

One month after Meiers' first arrest, the rancher again blocked a road
to the Site C worksite while dozens of other Fort St. John residents
demonstrated with placards calling for an immediate halt to dam construction. Meiers and two other demonstrators (Penny Boden, a Fort
St. John art teacher, and Arthur Hadland, a farmer and former director
of the Peace River Regional District) refused to budge when asked to
move. The three were arrested and charged with mischief. They spent
six hours in the same jailhouse where Meiers had worked as a welder.
One condition on the release form Meiers signed was that he had to
stay 150 feet away from any BC Hydro operation. He pointed out that

it was not an easy thing to do in Fort St. John, where BC Hydro maintained a prominent office on the main street adjacent to a major intersection, directly across the street from one of Canada's biggest banks. The office was sometimes guarded, and the doors were locked shut unless residents had an appointment.

Meiers had a message for the Fort St. John RCMP inspector who drove to his ranch to discuss the charges against him. "We're ordinary people," he told the officer. "Ordinary people that you never see in your course of duties. And you have to ask yourself, 'Why are these people out there doing this?' There's something terribly wrong when ordinary people take a stand against what is happening here. After this is over, we'll disappear, looking after our ranches, looking after our farms, and you'll never see us again." Meiers had no issue with the second condition on his release form. It ordered him to Keep the Peace.

In late November, before the Peace River chilled to mid-winter temperatures and boat motors seized, Meiers and Bob Fedderly, a Fort St. John oil and gas contractor, travelled to the fort area on Meiers' 6-metre jet boat. There, they met up with Bud Napoleon, an elder and former chief of Saulteau First Nations, and Ken. Both men arrived on a quad. The quartet cleared a few small trees and bushes and set up a large canvas hunting tent that belonged to Meiers. They covered it with a blue tarp and then left, knowing they could quickly return if crews hired by BC Hydro came to clear-cut the forest.

By the time Ken delivered the second shack to the Pedersens' field, BC Hydro contractors had logged right up to the slopes beside the Moberly River. During the Christmas holidays, with the requisite federal permit in hand – a parting gift from the outgoing Harper government – BC Hydro finished constructing a temporary winter bridge across the Moberly estuary. Contractors moved a feller buncher and other heavy logging equipment over the bridge and into a grove of rippled cottonwoods so old they might have predated Mackenzie's arrival. When work crews began to level the forest leading to the fort site – a forest so ecologically unique it carried four protective designations – the Boons, Esther Pedersen, Meiers, and many other valley residents, including members of five different Treaty 8 First Nations, decided they had finally had enough.

At the time, five legal actions involving Site C were still waiting to be heard. Prophet River First Nation and West Moberly First Nations had jointly filed three lawsuits, challenging the federal and BC environmental approval of the project as well as the provincial permits that had been issued. The First Nations argued that Site C had been green-lighted without due regard for the "significant adverse" impacts on their traditional practices that had been highlighted by the Joint Review Panel – practices guaranteed to them by Treaty 8 – and that alternatives to Site C, including geothermal and smaller hydro, had not been adequately considered. A fourth ongoing legal case, filed by Treaty 8's Blueberry River First Nations, claimed that unprecedented industrial disturbances on their traditional territory – including Site C – meant that band members could no longer practise the way of life guaranteed to them by the treaty.

Four months earlier, in August 2015, the landowners' association had lost a sixth Site C lawsuit in federal court. Association members had decided not to appeal. That suit, too, sought to overturn federal permission for Site C, on the grounds that Ottawa had not taken the findings of the Joint Review Panel into consideration before issuing project permits. The BC Supreme Court had dismissed a second suit filed by the association, which had attempted to overturn BC's environmental certificate for Site C on similar grounds. What was the point of conducting an expensive environmental assessment, asked Ken, if BC's environment minister could "turn a blind eye and not consider its recommendations?" The Boons, the Ardills, and other landowners had decided to appeal the BC decision and were waiting for their court date.

Also in August 2015, West Moberly First Nations and Prophet River First Nation had lost their application to the Supreme Court of BC for an injunction to prevent BC Hydro from clear-cutting an initial 1,600 hectares of forest for Site C – the rough equivalent of forty-five thousand logging trucks of timber, they said, which would be milled, mulched, or burned. The initial area BC Hydro planned to destroy encompassed what the nations called "some of the most spiritually and culturally significant areas in all of Treaty 8 territory." It included the land around the Rocky Mountain Fort site; the banks of the Moberly River, a waterway that supports the most diverse array of fish species in any Peace River tributary; and trees with eagle nests, a bird revered in First Nations culture. The nations argued that logging the area around the fort site would cause them "irreparable harm."

On the eve of the injunction hearing, BC Hydro had agreed to delay clearing of the lower Moberly and a few other areas of interest to First Nations – but only for one year. The nations subsequently lost their application for an injunction. (A BC Supreme Court judge concluded that they had not established irreparable harm and that BC Hydro would suffer irreparable harm if the injunction were granted.) Faced with the arduous task of raising tens of thousands of dollars for an appeal in a short amount of time, the nations had decided to focus their energies and fundraising efforts on the other Site C court cases.

Against this backdrop, the valley residents secretly took up a collection to charter a helicopter (at a cost of $22,000) to ferry the survival shack and supplies to the Rocky Mountain Fort site. During the Christmas holidays a call went out on Facebook: "All those who want to protect the Peace River Valley, come to Rocky Mountain Fort. Be prepared for winter camping." At ten thirty in the morning on New Year's Eve, a helicopter lifted the shack, dangling from a cable, from the Pedersens' hayfield and carried it across the river to the fort site.

Two days earlier, Ken had driven up the valley in his grey Chevy pickup truck, pulling a snowmobile. Green-eyed and dark-haired, Ken was a self-described fiscal conservative. To others, he was a portrait of equanimity. Even during the worst of the legal and personal travails that he and Arlene confronted in their battle against Site C, Ken never lost his cool. When BC Hydro contractors and representatives drove up the couple's long access way, almost always bearing problematic news, Arlene typically sent Ken outside – friendly and unflappable, wearing his customary baseball cap or cowboy hat – to deal with them, in case she herself said something she might later regret.

Ken crossed the valley on a highway bridge near Hudson's Hope and drove for almost two hours through a maze of snow-crusted resource roads until the last one dwindled out into a clearing. He piled his shipment onto the snowmobile – sleeping rolls, sweaters, a coffee pot, thermoses, and cardboard boxes of fresh and frozen food – and motored the final 6 kilometres to the fort site, where he chopped firewood and hooked up a small generator. He spent the afternoon of New Year's Eve ferrying campers from the clearing to the fort site. Ken summed up the motivation of the people who gathered, as the temperature dropped to minus eighteen degrees Celsius and hovered there before continuing to fall. "There comes a time when you just have to step up. That time is now."

One of the people who travelled to the camp that day was Helen Knott of Prophet River First Nation. She arrived with two young friends, each from a different Treaty 8 First Nation in the Peace. Knott, a twenty-eight-year-old social worker, poet, and mother of a young son, descends from a line of chiefs. Her great-great-grandfather, Chief Makannacha, also known as Chief Bigfoot, was one of the last signatories to Treaty 8. A century earlier, the treaty had given the Crown a vast tract of land in BC's northeast, a path to Yukon gold. That land included the entire Peace River Valley.

Ever since, Knott said, they had been clinging to their cultural survival. So much industrial development had taken place on her people's once bounteous territory that by 2017 it was almost unrecognizable, with one clear exception: the stretch of the Peace River Valley from Hudson's Hope to Fort St. John that had been slated for the Site C reservoir. Knott said her great-great-grandfather would never have signed the treaty (like other chiefs, he did not read or write and marked it with an X) had he known what would happen to the valley that had sustained his people for untold thousands of years and that contains places so sacred they remain to this day a secret from the outside world.

Knott had taken time off from her job helping disadvantaged families in Fort St. John. She had left her eight-year-old son with her mother and her younger brother and driven her jeep for almost four hours to the clearing. By the time she arrived at the fort site, the hunting tent – its open floor to be strewn with cardboard and fragrant spruce boughs – had been set up with cots, and a fire was soon crackling in the shack's tiny stove. A determined band of campers prepared to settle in. They hauled water in ice cream buckets from a hole in the river ice amidst a willow thicket and organized food donated by businesses and families in the Peace. The following day, they hiked through the snow along a winding forest path for one and a half kilometres to the place where the Peace greets the smaller Moberly, where the rivers intertwine, and where Knott made tobacco offerings. For the next two months, the fort site and the frozen flats where the two rivers converge set the scene for a standoff that would change the lives of people, especially Knott and the Boons, in ways they never imagined.

IN MID-JANUARY, I visited the Rocky Mountain Fort camp, travelling from my home by plane, truck, and snowmobile. In Fort St. John, I met up with Ken, who had driven into town to pick up supplies. Arlene, a workhorse who never seemed to rest, texted me after I had called her to ask about the camp: "You go in with Ken Monday. Safe travels. Ken will have your winter gear." That week, Arlene had lost a granddaughter, who died shortly after birth. She had left the camp for a few days to be with her son and daughter-in-law and was looking after her three-year-old grandson Caleb when I flew in, wearing a winter coat and boots that Arlene, despite her preoccupations, somehow knew would be no match for the rugged backcountry of the Peace. The week before, the camp thermometer had parachuted down to minus twenty-four degrees Celsius, even colder with the wind chill. A second text message from Arlene told me I was in luck; it was getting warmer. Only minus eleven now, she said.

At a First Nations reserve near the valley, we rendezvoused with Yvonne Tupper, a member of Saulteau First Nations, one of six BC Nations belonging to the Treaty 8 Tribal Association. Almost a decade earlier, tribal association members had begun Site C consultations with a single voice. But fissures had formed in their united front largely because of the multimillion-dollar deals and employment opportunities

BC Hydro was offering in return for acquiescence to the project. Tupper, who had left her car with relatives on the Saulteau reserve, was returning to the camp for a second week-long stint to help "hold down the fort," as she put it with a tempered laugh. She did not agree with the direction that her newly elected band council and chief had taken with Site C, following a contentious online vote in which four out of five eligible voters did not participate. Chipper and talkative, Tupper carried a clear plastic container stuffed with fleece blankets and a bag of food cooked by members of a church in Chetwynd, the mill town where she lived and worked in community health.

Behind Boon's truck, in a closed trailer stuffed with fresh and frozen food, we pulled a third snowmobile, donated to the camp by Meiers. As a condition of his release, Meiers was prohibited from stepping foot anywhere near the Site C project area, but he remained firm in his conviction that Site C was wrong in every way. When the resource road petered out, we parked in the clearing beside Knott's jeep and several other vehicles, all of them coated in a fine dust of snow. Dusk was fast approaching, and we loaded up the snowmobile and sled. The snowmobile growled along a narrow trail, shadows from the winter forest growing deeper all around us. The path twisted and descended. We flew past fallen trees that had blocked the trail until Ken and others cleared openings with a chainsaw, giving the impression, as we whizzed past, of arboreal gates opening to let us through. In the near dark, the snowmobile descended an abrupt hill to a terrace on the bank of the Peace River, where wood smoke puffed from a slender stovepipe in the shack wall. The shack was painted forest green and yellow. Boon parked near a metal sign that said, in bold black letters, "No Trespassing, Treaty 8 Territory."

Inside the shack, three women cooked dinner. They were squeezed between a two-burner propane hot plate, with one working unit, and a tiny stove that warmed a chipped metal bowl of water for washing. I recognized Knott from a selfie she had taken. It had garnered many favourable comments in the media and on the Internet, especially among groups fighting for Indigenous land rights. In the photo, she was wearing an orange toque and standing in front of the large "Rocky Mnt Fort" sign that Meiers and other valley residents had brought to the site by boat the previous fall after requests to the BC government to mark the historic fort location were ignored. Knott had shoulder-length black hair and black-brown eyes, partly hidden by stylish thick-rimmed glasses. She was wearing the same orange hat.

Knott stood in front of three narrow wooden bunks. The top bunk overflowed with plastic plates and mugs, coffee and tea supplies, cookies and Timbits, and an assortment of canned food, as well as bags of apples, celery, and carrots. The two lower bunks housed neatly rolled up sleeping bags and pillows. A mishmash of winter jackets, snow pants, hats, and mitts and a hopeful bunch of plastic daisies dangled from hooks and rafters. The windowsill held a two-way radio and a cell reception booster in a metal box. A handful of phone chargers sprouted from an extension cord, while an outside generator powered the cabin's dangling light bulbs. A calendar tacked to the plywood wall showed a picture of a silver river in the snow. The first thirteen days of January had been crossed off with smiley faces, marking the number of days at the camp.

One of the women in the shack, Rhoda Paquette, a professional archivist and herbalist, was also from Saulteau First Nations. Quiet and introspective, Paquette brewed remedies and salves from herbs and fungi, such as the mottled gray *chaga*, which grew on the birch trees that surrounded the camp like tall, ghostly sentries. Paquette called it "poor man's medicine." The volunteer camp cook, Lynn Chapman, a retired community health worker and new grandmother from BC's Sunshine Coast, had flown up to the Peace to volunteer when she heard about the camp. Chapman had curly grey hair, a lively laugh, and a metal rod in her right shoulder from an accident. She was almost seventy and had never camped in wintertime before. The only toilet was outside, a hole in a piece of plywood with a seat of purple styrofoam, screened by spruce branches. Chapman had been at the camp for ten days, and the younger women fondly called her Mom. "Yes, Mom ... No, Mom ... Thanks, Mom."

Over bowls of thick meat stew, Knott explained why she had travelled to the winter wilderness to try to stop Site C. A self-described warrior, she was no shrinking violet, although later press conferences for Amnesty International would always put her nerves on edge. Her poised maturity hinted at a past that at times had been anything but smooth. She had been valedictorian for her bachelor of social work class at the Nicola Valley Institute of Technology in Merritt, BC. As a student at the Coady International Institute at St. Francis Xavier University, in a leadership program sponsored by the Imperial Oil Foundation and ExxonMobil Foundation, she had travelled to the UN offices in Geneva as an Indigenous youth ambassador. She had helped build a school in Bella Vista, Nicaragua. Knott was quite candid about her struggle with alcohol as a youth and had embraced total abstinence four years earlier. Later, she would write that being at the Rocky Mountain Fort camp, as tough as it was, had brought her joy: "Waking up to stoke the woodstove in the shack or in the canvas tent in the frigid winter air actually made me happy. It was the purpose of being there and the confrontation that weighed heavy on my spirit."

Knott had been living in the Okanagan when she heard that Site C had been approved. One night she couldn't sleep and saw a shooting star, a message in the dark. She knew then that she must move back to the Peace, to defend her people's treaty land. "We're fighting for the right to existence," she explained. "This is my home. This is where I want to raise my children and my grandchildren. This is where my people are from. What will we have left? That's the part that scares me. The home that I know won't be there anymore."

At that point in time, and for many weeks to come, the camp at Rocky Mountain Fort had not been ruled illegal. BC Hydro representatives had tacked a note to the door of the survival shack on the day it was airlifted in, demanding that the encampment and all its materials be removed within twenty-four hours. If they were not, BC Hydro would take them away and deliver them to the Fort St. John RCMP – a threat that Knott described as little more than "a big scare tactic from a corporate bully." The public utilities company had no authority to remove First Nations members from Crown land they were using for traditional practices, including prayer and gathering chaga from the trees around the camp. Knott and the others were not deterred. Tupper said the land had never been for sale. "For them to say that BC Hydro owns this land is an insult to us."

The campers called themselves the Treaty 8 Stewards of the Land. They had three demands, which they put forward in a press release they had written in the shack: (1) Clear-cut logging in the Rocky Mountain Fort area must stop until all court cases against the dam were resolved. (2) The federal government must suspend Site C approvals and permits until an open and transparent review of the project's infringement on First Nations treaty rights could take place. (3) The project must be independently reviewed by the BC Utilities Commission – the same independent commission that the BC government had legally stripped of its mandate to determine whether Site C was in the best financial interests of BC Hydro's customers.

The campers had no money, no lawyer, and no communications expertise. They did, though, have a handout from a BC Civil Liberties Association workshop called "Know Your Rights," which they passed around the shack. Knott read it and said she knew her rights: "I do not believe in the right of people to forcibly remove me from my traditional territory."

ORION WAS STILL SPARKLING in the night sky when the campers awoke just after six a.m. A second, slightly larger survival shack was scheduled to arrive later that morning, insulated and outfitted with five bunk beds, a newly welded stove, and wiring for electricity. The new hut would be delivered by helicopter, along with a dozen daytime visitors. They included some dignitaries: Canadian scientist and author David Suzuki, as well as Grand Chief Stewart Phillip, the passionate and outspoken president of the Union of BC Indian Chiefs.

Lawyers for Prophet River First Nation and West Moberly First Nations had advised the chiefs and councils that any involvement in the Rocky Mountain Fort camp could jeopardize their court cases. The two chiefs had subsequently made it clear, in a letter BC Hydro later presented as evidence in court, that they and their councils (along with band

David Suzuki and Grand Chief Stewart Phillip stand on the lookout point by the Pedersen's farm | *Photo by Don Bain, Union of BC Indian Chiefs*

employees) did not condone the camp. But Grand Chief Phillip was under no such restrictions.

More Peace Valley residents arrived by truck and snowmobile that morning to join the gathering and tour the camp and bridge. BC Hydro officials knew that Suzuki and the grand chief were on their way since a few stories had appeared in the morning media. But they were surprised to see a second survival shack dangling from the blue Bell 205 helicopter – a special delivery package for the campers. The following month, when BC Hydro went to court seeking an injunction and enforcement order to remove the campers, a video clip of the flying shack was presented in the courtroom as Exhibit A.

Over a quick breakfast of coffee and oatmeal sprinkled with nuts and seeds, the campers divvied up the chores. Ken said he would make a landing pad for the helicopter, in the willows at the river's flat edge. He would also level the frozen ground for the arrival of the second tiny bunkhouse, which would be lowered onto logs. Affable and extroverted, Ken was a jack of many trades. He had been a bush pilot and had guided in the backcountry for many years. He could hunt a moose, skin a cougar, and snare a snowshoe hare. Also handy with machinery, he coddled the camp generator and coaxed the snowmobiles up hills when their motors threatened to give out. When he was out of earshot, Knott and Tupper affectionately called him the Ken Barbie Doll, Bush Edition.

Paquette had her own powers of alchemy. There, in the middle of winter, with no refrigerator, no oven, and no grocery store, she said she would make a moose meat stew for eighteen visitors and fry golden bannock on the tiny wood stove. Outside in the lean-to, she sifted through frozen food supplies, which would soon be discovered by a brazen thief – a weasel that left its lacy footprints in the snow.

As the sky hinted at a purple dawn, Boon ferried Knott and Tupper to the new Moberly River bridge on his snowmobile. Knott stood on the sled's back skids, clinging to a metal bar as Boon wove among the trees. Thick clumps of snow stuck to spruce and cottonwoods. The snowmobile's headlamp illuminated hand-painted signs hung from trees. "Breach against Treaty 8." "No Cutting." "Treaty 8 Territory." "Court Cases Pending."

Boon dropped Knott and Tupper off beside a fresh pile of tree trunks close to the mouth of the Moberly River, where the bridge arched over the water from the dam construction site. The women coaxed a fire to start in a pit of ashes from the previous day, feeding flames with waste wood left by the loggers. A feller buncher, backhoe, and excavator sat unattended, big and yellow in the flicker of the fire. The grind of machinery and pounding of pilings from the dam construction site could be heard in the distance. Constellations winked out one by one while, across the Peace River, dust rose like puffs of breath in the cold air.

A large grey pickup truck waited on the new bridge, lights illuminated like two watching eyes, motor running. Boldly, because BC Hydro's security guards had warned them to stay on their side of the bridge, Knott and Tupper decided to strike some yoga poses on the bridge's closest flank. They discussed, with equal parts laughter and derision, Premier Clark's attempt the previous summer to shut down Vancouver's Burrard Bridge for "Om the Bridge," a massive yoga class she planned to lead at a cost of $150,000 to taxpayers. Clark's public relations stunt had backfired when the main sponsors, YYoga and AltaGas, pulled out and another potential sponsor, the global yoga clothing company Lululemon, declined to participate after First Nations groups pointed out that the premier had unwisely (and even more to the point, perhaps unknowingly) chosen National Aboriginal Day for her downward dogs.

Knott and Tupper, bulky in their winter garb, stretched into their own downward dogs on the bridge. Security guards filmed them from the warm comfort of the running truck as the sky slowly blued. Later, they posted photos of the yoga exercise on social media: "One bridge that should be shut down."

The bonfire kept the loggers at bay. It signalled that the Treaty 8 Stewards of the Land were firmly in possession of the riverbank. Not one balsam or spruce had been levelled for a week, not since a logging crew had slipped in one frigid day at noon when the campers retreated to the shack for food. They had felled two-hundred-year-old cotton-woods in a 60-metre strip starting near the bridge, but since then the logging had stopped. Tupper had been at the camp that day with Beatrice Harding, an elder from Doig River First Nations, whose grandfather, Chief Attachie, had also signed Treaty 8. The diminutive Harding im-mediately commanded the attention of seven strapping loggers wearing bright safety vests and hard hats. Instead of telling the men to leave, she gathered them in a line and welcomed them to her traditional ter-ritory. Then she scolded them, saying, "We will be here in the future because this is our home. If my grandfather knew that this land would be flooded 116 years later, he would not have signed the treaty."

That afternoon, another Doig River elder, Jack Askoty, stepped in front of the feller buncher. Askoty, a stooped craftsman who makes birchbark canoes, drums, snowshoes, moose antler carvings, and lamps, had a message for the loggers: "I live off the land. This hurts me so much, to see all this that has been damaged. Look at these big trees here; they're over 250 years old. I'm a trapper, a hunter, and I go out there and I study animals. We are the worst animal on this planet."

After that, the logging crew left. The machines sat idle. The bonfire burned.

KNOTT HEARD THE helicopter before she saw it. It settled down, in a froth of wind, in the clearing Boon had cut among the willow bushes along the river's frozen edge. Holding back tears, Knott waited by the shack with other campers and a half-dozen visitors from the community who had arrived that morning by snowmobile. She had been toughing it out in the bush for the better part of two weeks and had to leave that afternoon to pick up her son from school and return to her job. But first she wanted to meet Suzuki and the grand chief. Later, she recalled that "to be up there, isolated in camp, and to see big names like Suzuki and the grand chief come up, it was a relief, an exhale moment. I started crying and cried again later on. It really solidified that what we were doing out there was right. We had no other way forward for our voices to be heard."

Suzuki arrived first, stepping up a slippery path in the steep embankment. He wore big white snow boots, a grey overcoat, and a long black hat. He was somewhat incognito in his winter clothing and dark glasses, but Knott identified him instantly. Before she could greet him, however, the reporters and camera men and women who had flown over with Suzuki recognized Knott, from her selfie in front of the fort sign, and peppered her with questions. "*You're* the one who is famous," Suzuki joked to her.

In a scenario that had become all too familiar to valley residents, the reporters were from local and alternative media, with the notable exception of the national Aboriginal Peoples Television Network. The mainstream media's fleeting attention to the camp reinforced the growing perception of valley residents that British Columbians paid far more attention to destructive resource projects when they threatened the collective coastal backyard, where most people live. The Burnaby Mountain protests against the Kinder Morgan pipeline garnered provincial headlines day after day; the annual Paddle for the Peace to stop Site C, which had brought together four to eight hundred people for more than ten

straight years to canoe a stretch of the threatened Peace River, had been
virtually ignored.

Knott accompanied Suzuki, the grand chief, and the media through
the woods to the logging equipment, where Tupper had maintained a
solitary vigil by the fire. When Suzuki expressed interest in approaching the security truck on the bridge, Knott told him they had been forbidden to walk over the structure. "Let's go," said Suzuki, and a dozen
campers and guests walked slowly to the centre of the bridge. They
included the grand chief, who wore a large, beaded pendant over his
coat that said "Stop Site C" in symbolic red and white. Slowly, the security truck backed up. The two truck passengers filmed the procession.
The attending media filmed the two passengers who were filming the
campers and their guests. Suzuki approached the truck and motioned,
smiling, that he wanted to speak to its occupants. They knew who he
was. A woman in the front seat smiled back and rolled down her window. But no one got out.

IN THE UPSIDE DOWN world of Site C, BC Hydro had obtained all the
provincial permits it needed to clear cut the protected forest around
the Rocky Mountain Fort site. The logging, however, could only take
place during winter. In a perverse nod to the spectacularly diverse birdlife
all around the fort site, BC Hydro was not legally permitted to log after
March 31, the date set in law for the return of migrating birds.

By early April, tens of thousands of songbirds such as the Canada
Warbler, a yellow-breasted boreal bird whose population has dropped
by 75 percent in its namesake nation, had started to land in the Peace
River Valley to nest. The warbler's distinctive call, heard around the
fort site in the spring and summer, sounded like someone sweetly
singing, over and over, *suey de swee-ditchety, suey de swee-ditchety*. The
leafy valley was also the only place in the entire province where two
other warbler species threatened with provincial extinction hatched
their young: the Black-Throated Green Warbler, a small songbird with
a bright yellow face and black bib, and the little-known and mysterious
Connecticut Warbler, yellow, green, and grey. The BC government's

Conservation Data Centre, established to map the locations of at-risk species and ecological communities so that they can be preserved, lists known nesting sites for the Black-Throated Green Warbler and the Connecticut Warbler right around the fort site.

The international Migratory Birds Convention Act, of which Canada is a signatory, prohibits the destruction of active nests. One of its goals is to protect songbirds, which are vanishing around the world at unprecedented rates. In the Peace Valley, this meant that the cottonwood, spruce, poplar, and other trees and bushes that graced the area around the fort site could not be touched if songbirds sat on eggs or their young were still helpless in the nests. As soon as the fledglings could fly away to safer ground, out of the path of logging machinery, the trees could all come down legally.

Similarly, BC's Wildlife Act protected nesting migratory birds, along with their eggs and flightless young, from injury, displacement, harassment, or destruction. It was illegal under provincial law for BC Hydro to clear-cut the forest near the Rocky Mountain Fort site in the spring and early summer. It was not illegal, though, for BC Hydro to strip the forest of trees and other vegetation during the winter or fall, after the songbirds' young had fledged. Nor was it illegal for BC Hydro to chop down well-established eagle nests during the fall and winter months, when no young were flightless in their homes of sticks.

If the campers could stall clear-cutting between the Moberly River bridge and the Rocky Mountain Fort site until March 31, logging would be over for the season. They would buy themselves and others months of time to fight Site C, a project still largely unknown to most British Columbians. If the public could see BC Hydro's destruction, said Ken, people would soon realize that Site C made a "mockery" of clean energy. He told a local television station, "We are used to their bully tactics, and y'know there is just too much at stake here to worry about that."

MALE SECURITY PERSONNEL walked over the BC Hydro bridge twice a day to film Helen Knott and the other campers. I had been told about their visits, yet I was still startled when I looked up from interviewing

campers at the fire and saw two men wearing hard hats, black winter
coats, and fluorescent safety vests standing directly in front of us. I had
not heard them coming. One pointed a video camera at me. I was new
fodder for their tapes.

The men identified themselves only as Sten and Glen. They said they
were security investigators. With the camera running, they asked for
our full names. Tupper and Knott gave their first and last names, as they
had done many times already, in response to the same question. They
were on Crown land and it was not illegal for them to be there, at least
not yet, although BC Hydro would later prove in court that the campers
had failed to obtain a permit from the provincial government to set up
the shacks.

The video camera held by Glen slowly panned our faces and bodies.
Sten, the tall one, asked the questions. "Do you intend on allowing or
preventing timber harvesting in this area?" "How long do you intend
on staying?" Knott and Tupper were growing weary of answering repeti-
tive questions twice a day. They answered politely but with some exas-
peration in their voices, as they filmed all the interactions on their cell
phones. Tupper told them she was serving notice to them "and whomever
you work for" that there were other people engaging in traditional
practices in the area BC Hydro planned to log. She told them she had a
right to be here. "I'm exercising my treaty rights. There are court cases
pending and I find it an insult that this is happening. There was no prior
consent to Site C from any First Nations band in the area for this construction." When Sten pressed Tupper to say how long she would be
staying, she looked directly into his camera, "As long as the sun shines,
the grass grows, and the river flows." The phrase, which originated in
the United States when treaties were first signed, is often cited by First
Nations in Canada to underscore that commitments made in treaties
have no end date.

After the investigators grilled the campers by the fire, Glen and Sten
walked for twenty minutes along the trail through the woods to question
people near the shack. Some of the campers did not want to be filmed.
They hid inside the cookhouse, listening through its thin walls. One

Indigenous woman ventured out of the shack to hover on the outskirts of a late afternoon questioning. She had a scarf wrapped around her face, showing only her eyes. Over and over, the campers asked Glen and Sten not to come inside the camp where women were sleeping, eating, bathing, and using an outdoor toilet. They said they would meet them at the bridge to answer any questions. But the investigators continued to walk through the camp twice a day, often at different times, in the morning and late afternoon.

Later, Knott recounted the typical response when she asked investigators to stop filming her. "They say, 'This is what we were instructed to do.' And we say, 'Well, it's not okay.'" One day in early January, several days after the camp had opened, Knott was alone in the bush when three male security guards suddenly appeared with cameras and started to film her. "It was intimidating ... as a young Indigenous woman coming into daily contact with men with cameras in the middle of nowhere." Tupper observed that the security men asked more questions "and intimidate[d] more" when they encountered a single female standing by the fire or at the camp. She said that BC Hydro and its security detail were not listening to the resounding "no" of Indigenous women who were willing to answer questions but who did not wish to be filmed.

According to Craig Benjamin, who was Amnesty International's Campaigner for the Rights of Indigenous Peoples in Canada, filming and questioning Indigenous people is "very much par for the course" when First Nations communities oppose large resource projects in Canada. It happened to members of Indigenous communities who took issue with the Enbridge Northern Gateway Pipelines project. And the RCMP monitored and surveilled members of the Lubicon Cree in Alberta who objected to the rest of their lands being covered by new oil and gas wells and oil sands development, after much of their traditional territory had already been affected by the oil and gas industry.

There are only two reasons to ask the same questions over and over again, according to Benjamin. Either it is purely to pester, or it is done in the hope that people will get so annoyed that they will say something incriminating that can be used against them in court. Benjamin cut BC

Hydro and its security contractors no slack: "I don't doubt that part of the harassment was trying to deliberately be provocative." It was in the corporate interest, said Benjamin, to portray the campers, "or anybody engaged in any sort of assertion of rights that stands in the face of a project," as a threat to public safety and as radicalized and unreasonable. "I think there's a real effort to try and get those 'gotcha' moments on tape."

As BC Hydro's security investigators collected information on the Rocky Mountain Fort campers, lawyers in the downtown Vancouver offices of the international business law firm Fasken Martineau were gathering evidence for BC Hydro's case against the protesters. Fasken Martineau had a long history of representing governments and resource companies in legal cases against First Nations. The firm had already represented BC Hydro in legal proceedings launched by First Nations and the landowners' association against Site C, as well as during the Joint Review Panel hearings and with regard to what the firm referred to as undisclosed "Aboriginal matters" relating to Site C. Among the company's seven hundred lawyers was Mark Andrews, one of Canada's top corporate and commercial litigators. Andrews, on behalf of BC Hydro and the BC government, would lead the courtroom battle against the Rocky Mountain Fort campers.

3
Slapped by Lawsuits

One week after Suzuki and the grand chief visited the camp, BC Hydro filed an injunction and enforcement order to remove the encampment and proceed with logging. The campers had fully expected an injunction. But they were unnerved when BC's Liberal government, in an unprecedented turn of events, allowed BC Hydro to launch a civil lawsuit against five of the campers and a camp supporter.

The thirteen-page civil suit was astonishing in its audacity. It accused the Rocky Mountain Fort campers of conspiracy, intimidation, trespass, creating a public and a private nuisance, and intentionally interfering with economic relations by unlawful means. Those charges, one unaffiliated lawyer said, placed their peaceful protest on par with the occupation of the Oregon Wildlife Reserve by armed militants, which was taking place almost at the same time. Knott, Tupper, and the Boons were all named in the suit. Coastal resident Lynn Chapman, who had spent more nights at the camp than either Knott or Arlene Boon, was not named. Nor were the many First Nations members who had stayed at the camp or visited during the day, including all the elders and two former Saulteau First Nations chiefs, Bud and Art Napoleon.

Knott and Tupper were the only First Nations members to be singled out. The suit seemed carefully thought out: it appeared to be an attempt to target and punish those residents who were most likely to be among

Site C's most vexing opponents and whose names would not generate headlines. Knott wrote eloquently: "In this moment I am heartbroken, stunned, angry, confused, mildly numb, utterly perplexed, and unsure of how to proceed. I had to take myself away from reading my grad-school texts in order to write because the feelings I needed to process kept pestering me much like northern bush mosquitos that can pene-trate through thick clothing. I couldn't block it out. Helen: court case."

The fifth person named in the suit was local resident Verena Hofmann, the red-haired, freckled mother of a two-year-old boy. Hofmann had only stayed at the camp for one or two nights at a time. But she had helped transport people to it, including First Nations elders, and she had advertised it widely on social media. Later, she explained that she was motivated by "feeling helpless and feeling frustrated" about the impending destruction of the valley and the lack of "weight or bearing" given to the fact-based case against Site C, pointing out that "people's voices were not being heard." The Rocky Mountain Fort camp, Hofmann said, was the only step left for Peace residents to try to stop the dam: "We were backed into a corner and people needed to do something."

Esther Pedersen, who had visited the camp only once, for fifteen minutes, was the sixth person targeted. Pedersen had used an outdoor freezer to collect food for the camp from community members. She had also permitted the use of her farm for the three chartered helicop-ter flights that ferried survival shacks, fire extinguishers, supplies, and visitors to the fort site. And she had allowed First Nations members and many other community members to access her land to reach the Treaty 8 shack, which she described as "a place where people can come out and watch the destruction of the valley." On the day that Suzuki and the grand chief flew to the camp from the Pedersen farm, there had been an extra seat in the helicopter, and Pedersen had jumped in for a fleet-ing visit, zipping back to her farm and business duties when the heli-copter returned to pick up the shack.

One lawyer characterized the inclusion of Hofmann and Pedersen in the suit as a warning shot across the bow for anyone who hoped to sup-port the camp with food and financial donations or who might post

Esther Pedersen clears snow from her "$420 million appliance," the freezer used for Rocky Mountain Fort camp food donations for the community | *Photo by Louis Bockner*

information about the camp on social media. If that were not already enough of a deterrent, BC Hydro included the names of John Doe and Jane Doe in the suit, leaving the door wide open to naming future campers and other supporters even if they never visited the site.

And that was far from all. BC Hydro also sued the campers named in the civil suit for damages, contending that the camp had caused it irreparable harm and considerable expense. The Crown corporation claimed general damages, punitive damages, costs, and interest. The bill, lawyers later suggested, could total as much as $420 million. At that point, Esther Pedersen started referring to the outdoor freezer as her $420 million appliance. Notably, BC Hydro refused to divulge the amount of money that hydro customers would pay for filing the civil suit or the total amount of what were undoubtedly hefty legal fees related to Site C.

The civil suit was accompanied by hundreds of pages of affidavits that unnerved the campers. They had fully expected an eventual injunction and enforcement order. But they did not anticipate being sued by their own government. The campers had no idea that BC Hydro's lawyers had been monitoring their personal Facebook pages, Twitter feeds, Instagram accounts, blogs, and other social media, and even collecting information about their family businesses. They had written freely about the peaceful camp on social media and engaged with BC Hydro's security investigators in good faith, and now everything they said was being used against them in the civil suit.

On New Year's Day, by the Moberly River bridge, Knott had had the first of many uncomfortable encounters with the security guards and investigators hired by BC Hydro contractors. She wrote about that day in a blog:

> I went to where they built the bridge, where they crossed the Moberly River, because I wanted to see where they had cleared the land and offer tobacco for the trees and the loss of the living forest and animal homes. I was told not to cross the bridge to where they cleared so I went to the frozen river to pray. As I stood there in prayer the security man got out to film me and record my "doings." I prayed for him too. He got back in the vehicle by the time I was done praying but apparently a Native in prayer is something to be feared and to record.

In the civil suit, the interaction was recorded as "helen knott incursion into operational area" at 13:25. The names of some of Knott's Facebook friends who liked her post, and their written comments about it, were included in the affidavit – another legal sortie that might deter other people from any kind of involvement in opposition to Site C.

The day before Knott prayed, a security guard had notified the campers that they were being evicted from BC Hydro land. "I told him I have a right to be here," Knott had written on her Facebook page, in a post used by BC Hydro as legal evidence against her. "I'm exercising my inherent right and as a Treaty 8 member I have a right to camp and be on the land within my territory ... They hadn't the right to be clearing on crown land while there are court cases pending."

BC Hydro's affidavits for the civil suit contained, as exhibits, screenshots of Facebook pages. Some campers now discovered that their pages were not personal and private. Evidence against Arlene Boon, who had a public Facebook page, included a February Facebook posting in which she stated: "Day 45. I may have froze my feet off, but I am still here at the Rocky Mountain Fort!" Evidence against Tupper included a GoFundMe.com fundraising page that she had set up to collect non-food donations for camp supplies, along with the names of some of the people around the province who had donated to the page, the amount each contributed, and their supportive comments.

Print, radio, and TV interviews with the campers had been transcribed by a company contracted by BC Hydro and included in the affidavit. In one CBC interview, Tupper had told security guards, "We're having a peaceful protest to identify our lands and post that this is Treaty 8 territory, and you're trespassing." Another of Tupper's postings that made it into an affidavit, though intended to incriminate her, summed up the protective spirit of the winter camp. "No injunction, no civil suit will ever take away 44 days of no destruction."

When BC Hydro filed the civil suit, injunction application, and enforcement order against the campers, the visit by Grand Chief Phillip and Suzuki was conspicuously absent from its extensive testimony. Yet that testimony documented the other helicopter flights to and from the camp, and it recorded details about the surveillance of the campers and other visitors on that very same day, January 12, 2016.

Details from the security investigators, included in BC Hydro's affidavits, were striking:

On the way to the camp on the snowmobile trail we passed a woman with her face covered, believed to be Christine (Inu). She was heading towards the 2nd fire. Did not stop. Upon arrival the lone occupant at

the camp was line [Lynn Chapman]. Introductions were made and at
10:47 Ken Boon drove in on a snowmobile with three others. The others
were a female Caucasian, unidentified, wearing a mask, a younger
maybe 10-12 years old also wearing a mask and Reg Whiton [the cor-
rect name was Reg Whiten] a reporter with his media credentials. I
started to ask the usual questions about their purpose there ... Lynn
[Chapman] said they were camping and would be there indefinitely.

Some campers and supporters clearly did not want to be identified.
Others, though, were wearing scarves and snowmobile masks to shield
themselves from the wind and freezing temperatures, especially while
travelling by snowmobile. One affidavit filed as part of the civil suit
stated that Pedersen used the "alias" Rachel Blatt. Rachel Blatt was the
name Pedersen used on her Facebook page, which BC Hydro lawyers
had monitored and from which they had taken excerpts to demonstrate her opposition to Site C. In fact, Pedersen's Facebook page had
previously been hacked, so she had switched to her middle name, Rachel,
and a maiden name, Blatt: hardly the sinister-sounding "alias" recorded
in documents BC Hydro filed in court.

Sten, one of the security investigators who had filmed the campers,
also served some of them with civil suits. Arlene was at the fire by the
Moberly River when Sten placed the papers at her feet. Ken was at
home looking after the farm when he was served. Tupper could not
easily be located, so the man who called himself Glen, which court
documents revealed to have been a fake name, stuffed the papers under
the door of her Chetwynd home and left a message on her cell.

Hofmann was indignant to discover that Glen had delivered the papers
to her babysitter. When she spoke to him on the phone, she asked for
his name, and he refused to give it. Knott was surprised, and a little sus-
picious, when one of the security investigators from the Rocky Mountain
Fort camp served her the papers while she was unlocking gates on the
Pedersens' farm. She felt like she was being followed. Pedersen was so
angry when the papers were dropped off with her husband, Poul, who

was at home between stints working in the oil patch, that she phoned
the investigators and informed them in no uncertain terms that she
would not accept the documents. They would go into the muck in the
chicken coop where they belonged, she said.

The papers for the injunction were served separately. Arlene was alone
in her farmhouse when her two healer-cross dogs, Buster and Shiloh,
alerted her to visitors approaching the door. The man called Sten handed
her a huge stack of papers while a second man wearing a white baseball
cap filmed the interaction. "These are all the documents that you need
to give to your legal counsel," Sten informed her, "so you can formulate
your defence." When the two men lingered in the Boons' yard, Arlene
marched out and told them, "Never mind gawking around. Just hop in
your vehicle and get out of here."

Colleen Brown, a former Wall Street attorney living in Fort St. John,
referred to BC Hydro's civil suit as a SLAPP suit – a strategic lawsuit
against public participation. SLAPPs, which were mainly an American
phenomenon until the 1990s, have one primary goal: to discourage
people from engaging in public discussion and protest on issues of public
interest. SLAPP suits were once banned in BC, as they are in other jurisdictions, but the Liberal government overturned the short-lived law
forbidding them shortly after it came to power in 2001.

As Brown surmised, in an opinion piece she wrote for a Peace region
newspaper, "There is no question that the lawsuit brought against the
campers by BC Hydro has served to intimidate some of its opponents,
deplete the resources of the campers and reduce their ability to participate in public debate, while deterring others from speaking freely on
matters of public importance." Filing the civil suit in a Vancouver court
far from the campers' homes, making public their home addresses, and
gathering personal information about them from their Facebook pages
and other social media served as warnings to anyone who might think
about voicing public opposition to Site C: be careful what you say, or
you may risk financial and personal ruin. As if on cue, the morning
after the civil suit was filed, Knott awoke at her home in Fort St. John,

in between stints at the camp, to find that her jeep window had been smashed while she and her young son slept.

Three months later, BC Hydro filed a second civil suit. This time, the Crown corporation targeted a group of people, mainly in their twenties, who had been camping outside BC Hydro's high-rise office tower in downtown Vancouver for more than a month to draw public attention to Site C. The group's key media spokesperson was Kristen Henry, a Simon Fraser University graduate, who held what became a life-threatening hunger strike in a personal effort to stop Site C. Climate scientist Andrew Weaver, at the time the BC Green Party's only MLA, visited Henry at the camp and described her as an "articulate, passionate and highly educated young woman who has literally put her life on the line in an attempt to draw attention to the reckless folly of proceeding with Site C." Weaver had stood beside Campbell at the 2010 announcement at the Bennett Dam, believing that Site C would help address global warming, but he soon changed his mind about the project, becoming one of its loudest opponents and calling it "fiscally reckless" given that cheaper alternatives such as wind power could generate new and clean electricity if needed.

Like the Rocky Mountain Fort campers, the Vancouver camp participants expected that BC Hydro would eventually file an injunction and enforcement order to remove them. The camp was bothersome to BC Hydro employees and some locals, and according to BC Hydro it had caused thousands of dollars in damage to its corporate grounds. One BC Hydro statement claimed that "BC Hydro's security team has witnessed spray painting and vandalism on BC Hydro structures and signage, fire hazards such as gasoline tanks, an open pit fire, propane stoves, an enclosed camp with several tents and tarps surrounding the camp, the use of our fountains and water features for bathing and other activities, and the construction of make-shift structures such as a latrine." The statement also noted that "there have also been reports of individuals climbing streetlights in the immediate area to cover the lights with bags."

While the camp was no doubt vexatious for BC Hydro employees, the people associated with it insisted that BC Hydro's claims of vandalism were "incredibly exaggerated." As Julia Ratcliffe, a Vancouver resident and frequent visitor to the camp, explained, "They're saying there's graffiti ... I don't know what they're talking about – there's sidewalk chalk. The exaggerations they are stirring up, it's a big problem for us. It's a bullying tactic."

PARTICIPANTS IN THE ongoing Vancouver protest also did not anticipate that BC Hydro would launch a civil suit in which it claimed "hundreds of thousands" of dollars in damages. An expense list in legal documents included $30,000 to replace BC Hydro's looped door handles with new handles (to which protesters could not chain themselves) even though none of the campers had shown any inclination to lock themselves to Hydro's doors. BC Hydro also said it had already spent close to $230,000 in increased security measures and would need to dole out up to $60,000 a month to hire a company called Xpera Risk Mitigation (the same company it had hired to help keep tabs on the Rocky Mountain Fort camp) to monitor the campers. Furthermore, the Crown corporation said it would require $35,000 a month to boost general security measures.

Henry, who was admitted to hospital for kidney and heart issues related to her three-week hunger strike, said that the civil suit catapulted her dangerously close to a nervous breakdown, especially after three weeks without food, which she described as "quite a traumatizing experience." On top of her kidney and heart issues, she suffered from anxiety attacks and chest pains after the civil suit was launched. Henry railed at the charges against her – mischief, damages to the corporation's grounds, and trespassing among them – which had been levelled at the same time as BC Hydro clear-cut the valley's old-growth forest. As she posed to BC Hydro, "You just killed how many animals and took down how many acres in the Peace River Valley today and you're worried about us [messing] up your lawn? It was infuriating, the injustice of it all."

Ten days after the suit was filed, the Vancouver campers packed up, saying they had neither the money nor the inclination to fight the deep-pocketed public utility in court. "It was too stressful," recalled Henry. "The idea of having to go to court with them for god knows how many years, for a shitload of money, I just couldn't handle the stress of it."

Just as Pedersen had been included in the civil suit against the Rocky Mountain Fort campers, Ratcliffe was named in the Vancouver civil suit even though she had not actually stayed at the camp overnight. She had, however, helped collect tens of thousands of signatures, including from passersby, on a petition calling for a halt to Site C construction, and had sent them to the federal government.

University of Victoria law professor Chris Tollefson, an expert on SLAPP suits, said he had never heard of a Crown corporation seeking damages from an individual for lawfully and peacefully exercising the right to protest on a matter of public interest – not in BC "or anywhere else for that matter." Ultimately, Tollefson said, determining whether a legal suit is a SLAPP suit is up to the courts. "I would say it [the Site C civil suit] has some of the hallmarks of a SLAPP suit." Regardless of what the civil suits were called, however, Tollefson was clear about their consequences. "If the end result is that they [the campers] face financial or personal ruin, a key implication is that others won't want to follow in their footsteps and take that risk. Then free speech becomes a luxury that only those who have nothing, or those who are incredibly rich, can afford."

One of the organizations watching the BC Hydro civil suits with growing disquiet was the BC Civil Liberties Association, a not-for-profit group dedicated to protecting human rights in Canada. Josh Paterson, the association's executive director, called the civil suits a matter "of grave concern" because, as he put it, they could cause others "to think twice before they talk about their political opinion." The association's unease was heightened, said Paterson, because BC Hydro is a Crown corporation. "What it does is send a message, perhaps deliberately, that 'you'd better be careful if you plan to oppose these kinds of developments' ...

BC Hydro as a public institution should be very cautious about making these kinds of claims for damages it would impose."

After the civil suits were launched, some valley residents who supported the fight against Site C were reluctant to have any dealings with the Boons, concerned that they might be targeted by BC Hydro themselves if they associated too closely with their marked neighbours. The Boons, who already stood to lose their family home, farm, land, and livelihoods to Site C, now faced the prospect of personal bankruptcy for their role in the camp. Only half-jesting, Knott said she would have to sell a kidney or her womb, becoming a one-kidneyed surrogate mother, to pay her legal fees. Along with the other campers, she was worried. But that was clearly the intention of the civil suits, as the BC government upped the ante in the fight over the future of the Peace River Valley.

BC HYDRO'S INJUNCTION application against the Rocky Mountain Fort campers was heard in a windowless Vancouver courtroom on a bluebird-sky day in late February 2016. By that time, the Boons, Knott, Tupper, and dozens of other people had occupied the winter camp for almost two months, taking turns to stay overnight and visit during the day in between their work, farm, and family duties. Knott, who spent three days every week at the camp, three days working and parenting, and one full day dedicated to her son, was physically and emotionally worn out. She had contracted Giardia (an intestinal parasite) from drinking the river water and was feeling weak and vulnerable. Her troubles worsened when she suffered a personal heartbreak, and she wrote about her state of mind in a blog that mentioned a craving for chocolate. The next time she returned to the camp, a box was there with her name on it, full of chocolate from an anonymous sender. For Knott, it was a turning point. She had been feeling alone and vulnerable; now she felt supported. One woman knitted warm socks for all the campers. So many people sent food that the campers had far more than they could ever eat, including ready-cooked stews that only required thawing.

Among the speakers at an impromptu press conference on the court-house steps were Suzuki and Grand Chief Phillip, the camp visitors not mentioned by BC Hydro in its affidavits, even though the grand chief had stated publicly that he was willing to break the law to stop Site C. Suzuki spoke passionately about the immeasurable loss of prime farm-land to Site C, while Grand Chief Phillip zeroed in on the lawsuits, saying that "the action of BC Hydro in court today is to purposefully target, censor, intimidate and silence the peaceful camp of Treaty 8 members and landowners at Rocky Mountain Fort Camp ... This is a complete abuse of power, democratic process, and treaty and legal rights of all the parties involved."

Tupper had just completed a three-week medic course, returning to stay at the camp on weekends. She had volunteered to represent the Rocky Mountain Fort campers at the courthouse and had driven alone all night, through slick rain and slippery snow, only to be stranded near Hope at four in the morning with an open car window that refused to roll back up. She called an auntie who lived nearby, and her uncle drove her the rest of the way to the courthouse, where she arrived breathless, wearing jeans and a black fleece, a few minutes after the press conference concluded. Holding her head high, Tupper linked arms with the grand chief and Suzuki and, shaking slightly, walked up the courthouse steps feeling slightly apprehensive but secure in the knowledge that the grand chief and the famous scientist were standing right beside her.

Poised and collected, the lawyers for the campers mounted an impres-sive case that kept BC Hydro's heftier legal team, led by Mark Andrews, on the defensive. Andrews, wearing a charcoal-grey suit and a striped, blue-and-grey tie, told the judge that the case had nothing to do with the evidence contained in four expert-witness affidavits, filed by lawyers Jason Gratl and Lara Tessaro in support of the campers' request for a one-year moratorium on Site C. Those affidavits, including one from Eliesen, who was also the former chair and CEO of Ontario Hydro and the former chair of Manitoba Hydro, questioned the validity, time frame, and cost projections of Site C. (Eliesen called BC Hydro's claim that postponing clear-cutting at the Rocky Mountain Fort site for one year would add $420 million to the project's tab "effectively illusionary" and based on "fundamentally flawed" analysis.) An affidavit from Robert McCullough, a US energy economist whose testimony before a Senate Committee had helped spark the criminal investigation into Enron for price fixing, also cast doubt on BC Hydro's arithmetic. McCullough showed that the net savings to BC ratepayers of a one-year delay in building Site C would amount to $268 million, that a two-year delay would save $519 million, and that a five-year delay would save $1.18 billion, largely because of rapidly falling energy prices, which were making Site C increasingly economically unviable.

Andrews acknowledged that the affidavits might contain more up-to-date information about electricity demand than the BC government's own projections. In fact, Andrews said, it was possible that electricity from Site C might not be needed in the time frame presented by BC Hydro, and the environmental impact would unquestionably be significant. But these issues were matters of public policy, he told the judge, asserting that "this is not the forum for debating these issues."

Sidestepping BC Hydro's questionable economic argument for Site C and its claim that a one-year construction delay would cost $1 billion, Andrews reminded the judge that elected officials establish public policy. The court's only role, he argued, was to rule on whether the law was being upheld. And legal permits and authorizations for Site C had all been granted, including thirty-six provincial authorizations for various Site C construction activities, as well as the fourteen federal permits from the Harper government. The campers, Andrews told the judge, had no legal right to stop permitted construction activities. (BC Hydro's lawyers also pointed out to the judge that the campers had failed to obtain a BC government permit to set up the shacks on Crown land and that they had breached BC's Heritage Conservation Act by not acquiring a permit to "damage, excavate, dig in or alter a heritage site.")

The provincial permits for Site C underscored the absurdity of having one arm of the government give permission to another arm to destroy heritage and archaeological resources and nature when provincial laws prohibited their destruction. For instance, for a permitting fee of $455, including taxes, which BC Hydro paid to the Ministry of Forests, Lands and Natural Resource Operations (FLNRO), BC Hydro was granted permission to remove or destroy an unlimited number of eagle nests over an eight-year period. Several conditions were attached. The Crown corporation, for instance, was obliged to record the location of the nests and the date and time each was destroyed or removed. It was also required to count the number of feathers it found in each ill-fated dwelling. All that information, including the feather tallies, was to be reported to the ministry once a year, for data collection. A second BC government permit, obtained for $880, including taxes, gave BC Hydro the legal right to destroy an unlimited number of beaver dams and muskrat houses and to hunt, trap, or kill the animals. Those incursions, too, had to be reported to the ministry, with detailed information about the date and time of destruction, the sex and age class of any animals killed, and a description of the dams and homes removed.

A third permit, also valid for eight years, granted permission under BC's Heritage Conservation Act to alter and then flood the heritage Rocky Mountain Fort site and 162 archeological sites. The sites were among 450 known archeological sites that Site C would destroy, including the Rocky Mountain Portage House fur trade fort founded by explorer Simon Fraser, across the river from Hudson's Hope. Other heritage sites that would be lost to the Site C reservoir included two unregistered cemeteries, pioneer homesteads, a historic ferry-landing site, and the Rocky Mountain Portage Trail, which had allowed First Nations, explorers, and settlers to bypass the fearsome Peace River rapids above Hudson's Hope.

The provincial authorization to meddle with archaeological sites was euphemistically called an "alteration permit." In the case of Rocky Mountain Fort and other sites, it seemed much more like a ruination permit. According to the sweeping licence granted by the BC government, BC Hydro's work on top of known archaeological sites like the fort could include, but was not limited to, invasive activities such as "clearing and grubbing; surface stripping and excavation; temporary placement of stockpiled materials and fill; construction of permanent

Ken Boon holds a section of spruce from the Rocky Mountain Fort camp area after it was clear-cut. The heritage site has been turned into a waste rock dump site for Site C | *Photo by Louis Bockner*

facilities and roads; and inundation of the reservoir." Indeed, it was hard to imagine there would be anything left to alter at the Rocky Mountain Fort and other archaeological sites following this type of work, especially once the sites were in the Site C reservoir.

Andrews and BC Hydro called the area designated for the waste rock dump "RSEN R5a," a moniker that conjured up images of a moonscape or a military manoeuvre, not the increasingly rare forest that it was. (RSEN stands for "relocated surplus excavated materials.") Besides holding great value for the local community as a designated heritage and archaeological site, the Rocky Mountain Fort area possessed notable ecological attributes. The site encompassed Crown land that had been set aside to become part of a new BC protected area known as the Peace-Boudreau. The area had been protected from most development since 1969 (when it was conserved as the South Peace Land Reserve) and had been included on tourist maps of the Peace, even though the BC government had never officially designated it a protected area, in large part because much of its land mass would be lost to Site C.

Part of the forest was also designated as critical winter habitat for moose, a staple in the local First Nations diet. Just before my arrival, the Rocky Mountain campers had spotted several moose bedding in the snow by the temporary Moberly River bridge, and they had seen stripped branches in the reddish willows where the animals had browsed. Site C, according to retired BC government wildlife biologist Rod Backmeyer, would destroy much of the Peace Valley's critical winter range for moose, whose populations were already diminishing so rapidly around the province that the Liberal government had appointed a special task force to ascertain the reasons for their demise. The area around the Rocky Mountain Fort site was particularly important to the ungulate's survival during snowstorms and cold snaps. Backmeyer, who wrote the government's management plan for the South Peace Land Reserve, warned that clear-cutting it could seriously impact the valley's moose population, which Aboriginal hunters warned was already in decline. He pointed out that "we're going to lose all of that lower slope and the big timber in the valley that's the thermal cover and the security cover during those big storm events."

The old-growth forest around the fort site was part of a vanishing ecosystem called the Peace Lowland, which enjoys a milder winter climate and warmer summer climate than the region surrounding it. BC had protected less than half of 1 percent of this ecosystem, underscoring a principal reason for its demise. The Peace Lowlands, among other things, were providing habitat for several mammal species vulnerable to extinction, such as the fisher, a cheeky mustelid that moves its young from nest to nest in old-growth tree cavities, and the elusive wolverine, whose tracks the sharp-eyed Ken had spotted in the snow near the camp.

The Rocky Mountain Fort site also lay within a designated Old Growth Management Area, established by the BC government to conserve most of the forest in its original ecological state. And last but certainly not least, the camp sat firmly on the territory of the Treaty 8 First Nations, whose members were using the land for registered trapping lines and traditional practices.

The Rocky Mountain Fort site would not be flooded by Site C for another nine years. However, Andrews and his legal team informed the judge that it was essential to clear-cut the forest without delay. The songbirds of the Peace Valley would return on the long journey from their southern wintering grounds as early as March 31, the lawyers said, and their nesting trees and bushes would need to be cut down before that date. Otherwise, Canada's obligations under the Migratory Birds Convention Act, and BC's similar obligations under the Wildlife Act, would force BC Hydro's logging contractors to wait for months before resuming clearing work.

BC Hydro's lawyers attempted one more strike at the campers' request for a one-year moratorium on construction. They informed the judge that any further delay to clearing the Rocky Mountain Fort site would boost the cost of Site C by another $8 million, and BC Hydro knew there was no reasonable prospect of recovering that much money from the campers. The original Site C construction schedule presented by defence lawyers had shown that the Rocky Mountain Fort site was not scheduled to be used as a waste rock dump that year, but BC Hydro introduced a new schedule to the court showing that the site was urgently required. According to a new BC Hydro affidavit, filed on the Friday afternoon before the court case was heard the following Monday, the additional $8 million would arise if acid-generating waste rock needed to be placed at a different site and then shipped across the river once RSEN R5a had been cleared.

The following week, the judge approved BC Hydro's request for an injunction. Justice G. Bruce Butler said it was not within his jurisdiction to inquire into whether it was the right time to proceed with Site C or if a construction delay might result in a net economic benefit to BC

Hydro. "Persuasive arguments can be advanced against proceeding with it at this time," Butler wrote in his judgment. However, the court was not the appropriate place to make those arguments, the judge determined. The Site C project had been approved, and permits and authorizations for construction had been granted. Given that hundreds of millions of dollars had been spent, that construction was rapidly proceeding, and that a delay would upset plans approved by the BC cabinet, Butler ruled that "it would run contrary to the public interest to allow protesters to continue their activities in an attempt to shut down the construction."

With tears and reminiscences, the Treaty 8 Stewards of the Land voluntarily dismantled the Rocky Mountain Fort camp the next day. Ken pointed out that they were law-abiding citizens. Privately, he said the campers knew the forest would be clear-cut regardless of whether they went to jail. They had other Site C battles to fight; the fort site was not their Waterloo. Despite a personal appeal that Ken and Arlene made five months later to BC Hydro's top executives, the Crown corporation refused to withdraw the civil suit. Over the following years, the suit stood as a sombre warning to anyone who might be thinking of setting up another protest camp or blockading a road to the dam's worksite.

In March, before the legal deadline to protect songbird nests, BC Hydro contractors fired up the backhoe and feller buncher and clear-cut the forest all around the Rocky Mountain Fort site. But they were not able to level all the trees. A pair of bald eagles, thought to be one of the pairs whose nests had already been destroyed for Site C, had built a new nest, high in a stately cottonwood tree near the Rocky Mountain Fort. BC Hydro contractors were legally obliged to leave a 300-metre fringe of trees and vegetation along the riverfront to protect the active nest.

Even before the legal window for the migratory birds' return forced a temporary stop to Site C logging, the female eagle was sitting on eggs.

4

The Birth of a Goliath

As the campers took stock of the demolished forest around Rocky Mountain Fort, BC Hydro awarded one of Site C's major contracts to the multinational corporation Voith, one of the world's leading suppliers of hydro equipment. Premier Clark described the $470 million contract, to supply turbines and generators, as a "major milestone" for completing Site C. Shortly after the announcement, I learned that Voith was a principal sponsor of what was billed as the biggest hydro convention in the world, and I made plans to travel to Minneapolis, Minnesota.

HydroVision International was held in the cavernous Minneapolis Convention Center in July 2016. The gathering drew almost three thousand people from more than three dozen countries ranging from Albania and Bhutan to Uganda and Zambia. In addition to the conference proceedings, tracked through an iTunes event app, HydroVision International featured a huge convention hall, with a small city of industry-sponsored booths offering all manner of free branded trinkets and draws for prizes (for example, a drone). Hydro Hall of Fame awards bestowed honours not on people but on operating dams that had reached their hundredth birthday. Hydro TV, an online newscast with daily reports about hydro projects around the world, Site C among them, broadcast the proceedings.

The Big DAM Street Party followed the Dam Good Networking Reception, the Women with Hydro Vision Awards, and the Turbine Runner 5K race. Some of the conference session titles revealed a similar wry sense of humour among the cerebral professionals who had organized the convention. There was the "Extreme Makeover" session: the engineering equivalent of facelifts and joint replacements for aging structures like the Bennett Dam. "Who Controls the Guest List for Fish Passage" seemed particularly relevant to BC Hydro's implausible plan to truck threatened bull trout past the dam for a hundred years. And how about the draft title for this workshop? "Extreme and Unusual Events: Ice Dams, Earthquakes and Downpours, Oh My."

Voith's booth in the convention hall resembled a glitzy room in a high-end car dealership, with a plush off-white carpet, track lighting, and stand-up tables with iPads. An artist's rendition of the Site C dam structure – in a valley that looked stark, uninhabited, and unappealing – covered one entire wall. "Site C: Advanced turbines and generators for Canada's largest energy infrastructure project," said the oversized caption below the picture, in a statement that might have given the wrong impression to those not already in the know. Site C might have been the biggest dam under construction in Canada at the time, but it was far from the country's largest energy infrastructure project. Eleven Canadian dams were already churning out more electricity than Site C would ever produce. They included BC's Bennett and Revelstoke dams, both of which dwarfed Site C in capacity. Site C would produce 1,100 megawatts of energy, less than one-third the combined output of the Bennett and Peace Canyon dams. But what German-based Voith lacked in clarity it more than made up for at the street party it threw outside the convention centre on the colloquium's final evening, where large blue-and-white helium balloons, emblazoned with VOITH in capital letters, were anchored down as flying centrepieces on tables decked out in red, white, and blue.

The late July evening in muggy Minneapolis, the birthplace of one of America's first hydroelectric dams, brought much to celebrate. Only two decades earlier, in the 1990s, it had appeared that Big Hydro had run its course in much of the world. The revelry was over, or so it had seemed. And what a party it had been. Large dams had driven the development of the American West, bringing water to the deserts and electricity and drinking water to homes. And they powered industrial development that brought jobs and relative prosperity to American communities. Dams like Hoover, Grand Coulee, and Glen Canyon were now household names. In Asia, large dams had made irrigation possible for previously parched and sometimes flooded land, boosting agricultural production and helping feed hungry populations. The burden of seasonal flooding was often alleviated once dams had tamed rivers, curbing their natural flow. The pent-up energy from restless waters could now be channelled through turbines to generate the electricity needed to attract industry and spur economic development.

Worldwide, for many decades, large dam construction had encountered few ideological or political barriers. The towering structures symbolized progress and national independence, embodying the prevalent world view that humankind could conquer nature.

The US Army Corps of Engineers dammed rivers across the United States; meanwhile, Vladimir Lenin famously declared, "Communism equals Soviet Power plus electrification of the entire country." In the early 1920s, the Soviet Union flexed its engineering muscles and set about building the mightiest dam in the world, the Dneprostroi Dam on the Dnieper River. It was completed in 1932 with much fanfare and the awarding of medals, flooding prime Ukraine farmland. If the communist brass was worried that fish populations might collapse in the Black Sea and Sea of Azov – which they did – they didn't show it. Five decades later, the Russian project found itself dwarfed by the Itaipú Dam on the Paraná River, a joint project of the Brazilian and Paraguayan military juntas. The Itaipú displaced ten thousand families and submerged the world's largest waterfall by volume, the Guaíra Falls, to provide three-quarters of Paraguay's electricity and almost one-fifth of Brazil's.

In Egypt, construction of the Aswan Dam on the Nile River generated electricity for industrialization and protected land from both floods and droughts. It also forced ninety thousand people to relocate, inundated Nubian archaeological sites, caused the Nile Delta to erode, and forced legions of farming families onto far less fertile land, where they could reap little more than parasitic diseases from the now stagnant waters.

Pakistan built the world's largest earth-filled dam, the Tarbela Dam on the Indus River. And Ghana boasted the imposing Aksombo Dam on the Volta River, erected mainly to power an emerging aluminum industry. The Aksombo created the world's largest reservoir, Lake Volta, flooding almost 4 percent of Ghana's land mass. The lake's waters became infested with Biomphalaria snails, which widely infected riverside villagers with schistosomiasis, a parasite that causes a range of illnesses ranging from mild fatigue to kidney failure and cancer.

The proliferation of Big Hydro projects was amazingly rapid, given that the world at the time was non-computerized and linked mainly by regular mail, the telegraph, and landline telephones. In 1950, there were five thousand large dams in the world; less than half a century later, forty thousand dams spanned the world's rivers. Among them were the Bennett Dam and Quebec's Robert-Bourassa Dam, one of eight generating stations in the James Bay Project that obstructed nine rivers, killed an estimated ten thousand caribou, and flooded an area the size of Belgium, all in the traditional homeland of the Cree. Phase 2 of the James Bay Project began in 1989, but before it could be completed, things began to falter for the global dam-building industry.

The first international rush to build major dams had taken place with little or no heed to their harmful impacts on the natural world, prime agricultural land in valley bottoms, and traditional communities. In many countries, dams were driving untold numbers of species towards extinction. From Africa to North America, they were disrupting migratory routes for large mammals such as elephants and caribou, with ruinous consequences for those species and others. The Bennett Dam, for instance, severed a caribou migration route, setting off a downward spiral from which the species – now highly endangered – has never recovered.

On the other side of the world, Tanzania's Kihansi Dam caused the extinction in the wild of the tiny, golden-skinned Kihansi spray toad, which lived in almost unvarying temperatures and 100 percent humidity at the base of the namesake Kihansi Falls, which the dam destroyed. An international toad rescue mission plucked populations of the rare amphibian from its 2-hectare habitat at the base of the falls, moving them to American zoos, where the spray toad now resides, its habitat now wet and humid cages.

As the reservoir of Zambia's Kariba Dam began to fill in 1959, game rangers risked snakebite and crocodile attacks to rescue drowning animals. Jacques Leslie writes that "the rangers found monkeys and baboons clinging to nearly submerged trees, bucks trapped on disappearing islands, and civet cats hissing as they hung onto floating logs." The *Rhodesian Sunday Mail*, on which Leslie based his account, referred to the rangers' efforts as the biggest animal rescue since Noah and his Ark.

Around the world, large dams helped push river dolphins to the brink of extinction. They also blocked access to spawning grounds for salmon and other migratory fish species, such as South Asia's commercially important hilsa. Dams on the west coast of the United States ruined salmon runs, with negative consequences for Indigenous peoples who relied on salmon for food and whose cultures revolved around their presence. And individual species were by no means the only ecological casualties. Dam reservoirs trapped sediments essential to the sculpting and preservation of deltas, river islands, floodplains, and wetlands. The Nile, blocked by four large dams, no longer even has a delta. Dams disrupted the ecological functions of freshwater ecosystems, which now are the world's most degraded major ecosystem.

Large dams had also forced thirty to sixty million people from their lands by the time the World Bank, a major funder of dams in developing countries, took stock in the mid-1990s and pressed the pause button. Under fierce attack from an increasingly impassioned grassroots anti-dam movement, backed by global human rights and environmental groups, the World Bank launched the World Commission on Dams, which revealed problems far more complex and intransigent than the bank had previously considered.

By 1996, flooding from large dams around the world had permanently inundated a total area the size of California. More than half the world's rivers were blocked by a dam at least four storeys high. As the commission noted in its 360-page report, "in some years our mightiest rivers – Africa's Nile, Asia's Yellow, America's Colorado, Australia's Murray – do not reach the sea." Having weighed all the evidence, the report concluded that large dams had not alleviated poverty in developing countries. Indeed, they had often made it worse. The Kariba Dam in Zambia, for instance, was the first large dam ever to receive funding from the World Bank, in the form of a US$80 million loan in the 1950s. The dam, built mainly to power a booming copper industry, displaced fifty-seven thousand Tonga people from their ancestral lands in the Gwembe Valley in what is now Zambia. The maize-growing Tonga were relocated from sediment-enriched soil along the Zambezi, where they had planted two crops a year, to infertile land with a brackish water supply. Some received no land at all. The relocation touched off what Leslie calls a "social catastrophe" – it sowed little more than poverty, hunger, disease, and death. In a similarly grim outcome, the tens of thousands of Nubians resettled to make room for the Aswan Dam on the Nile were moved from highly arable land to marginal areas prone to erosion and infested with the tsetse fly, a carrier of sleeping sickness, which exacerbated poverty and disease.

The World Bank faced not just social and environmental concerns but economic ones as well. In many developing countries, large dams had become synonymous with corruption. Lucrative construction contracts were becoming conduits for diverting money into the pockets of shady politicians and their business cronies. The Itaipú Dam on the Paraná River, showcased as an engineering triumph and a model of international cooperation, was a case in point. The dam's initial cost of $3.4 billion swelled to $20 billion, with untold sums skimmed off to flood the personal bank accounts of Brazil's and Paraguay's military rulers and their friends. In nearby Argentina, the cost of building the Yacyretá Dam ballooned from $2.5 billion in 1983 to $15 billion by the time it was completed a decade later, displacing forty thousand people. Argentine president Carlos Menem memorably called the concrete structure a "monument to corruption."

Based on the commission's report, the World Bank concluded that development assistance for power generation was a "sunset sector." It decided to bow out of financing large dams and handed that responsibility over to the private sector. This, however, left other entities that were far less financially flush to deal with the social catastrophes that dams had helped create. The bank also announced that it would focus on funding medium-sized dams and on helping rehabilitate existing major dams.

The global momentum behind large dam projects waned, except, notably, in China, a country that charted its own course with little regard for international opinion. Ignoring global criticism, Chinese authorities proceeded to build the Three Gorges Dam on the Yangtze River, a monolith so unimaginably huge that when it became operational in 2012, it slowed the rotation of the earth by displacing huge amounts of water. BC Hydro International, a wholly owned subsidiary of BC Hydro, was a member of the consortium that had conducted the $14 million, three-year feasibility study for Three Gorges, with financing from the Canadian International Development Agency (CIDA), which later withdrew from the controversial project. At the time, BC Hydro's international activities were viewed as a way of "priming B.C.'s economic pump," and the Crown corporation was also active in Malaysia, India, Pakistan, and other countries.

The Three Gorges reservoir submerged 13 cities, 140 towns, and more than 1,600 villages, displacing 1.3 million people, about the population of Calgary, Alberta. Among its profound environmental impacts, the dam flooded habitat for fifty-seven endangered plant species, including the Chinese Dove Tree, whose fluttering, petal-like bracts resemble doves sitting on branches, and the Dawn Redwood, the smallest of the redwoods. And it destroyed habitat for 177 unique fish species as well as the Baiji dolphin, also known as the Goddess of the Yangtze, now presumed extinct. Yet the Chinese government continued to describe Three Gorges as a "huge success in the development of green energy," in much the same way that Clark touted Site C as a green energy project even though its ecological impacts are severe.

Throughout the 1990s many countries cancelled plans for large dams as their social, ecological, and financial costs became more apparent. Hundreds of thousands of people on different continents took to the streets to protest Big Hydro. In Hungary, people risked reprisals from a repressive regime to try to prevent the damming of the Danube. They were motivated by the belief that proposed dams would "lead to the desiccation of the beautiful Szigetkoz (literally 'island region'), where the Danube meets the Hungarian plain and branches out to create a wildlife haven of countless streams, marshes, backwater lagoons, and forested islands." Similarly, a proposal to build the huge Belo Monte ("beautiful mountain") Dam in Brazil's Amazon generated a domestic public outcry, particularly from that country's Indigenous peoples. The project encountered so much worldwide condemnation that the Brazilian government eventually announced a halt to the project. The Indian government had planned a series of dams on the Narmada River that would submerge tens of thousands of small villages and displace millions of people. Faced with rising criticism, the World Bank withdrew its financial support, and that project, too, was scuttled.

In the Russian Federation, fierce opposition to the Katun Hydroelectric Station in the Altai Mountains persuaded the government to mothball the project. In Sweden, Switzerland, and Norway, public opposition halted all but the smallest of dam projects. Meanwhile, a growing anti-dam movement in the United States was demanding that several American dams be torn down. In Nepal, the Arun III Dam was scrapped in 1996 due to public opposition. In France, the proposed Serre de la Fare Dam on the Loire River was cancelled in 1994. Protracted protests by Thai communities that would be affected by proposed hydro dam projects persuaded Thailand's government to announce that no more large dams would be constructed for power generation. In Brazil, the Movement of People Affected by Dams (MAB) burst into existence, rapidly gained momentum, and began calling into question Big Hydro's future in the Amazon.

Even Canada, with its wealth of northern rivers, began to back away from building large dams. Pressured by the "environmental resistance of the Cree" and Quebec Hydro's mounting debt, in 1994 the Parti Qué-bécois government essentially ended three decades of hydro expansion in Canada when it cancelled a hugely expensive project planned for the Great Whale River – part of a plan to divert and dam every river emptying into James and Hudson Bays. Only the previous year, BC Hydro's board of directors had reconsidered plans to build Site C and discarded them.

Large dams had once been viewed as a way to bring electricity to the masses and to foster industrial growth and agricultural prosperity; now, they were seen as a preventable social and environmental plague. Indigenous and traditional peoples, whose ancestral lands were often in fertile river valleys, were hugely and disproportionately affected when dams flooded those valleys. And not least, large dams were very expensive to build. Their construction spanned many years, and nightmarish cost overruns were the norm.

The World Commission on Dams found that cost overruns for major dams averaged 50 percent. At about the time that Site C's construction was getting under way, researchers from Oxford University – a statistician and three management scholars – surveyed 245 large dams. Their conclusion: dam budgets were systematically biased below actual costs, and cost overruns averaged 90 percent. The same researchers found that the average construction time for a large dam was eight and a half years, prompting them to conclude that large dams were "ineffective in resolving urgent energy crises." They recommended that countries focus on what they called "agile energy alternatives" such as wind, solar, and mini-hydro. As Atif Ansar, one of the study's authors, pointed out, "We're stuck in a 1950s mode where everything was done in a very bespoke, manual way. We need things that are more easily standardized, things that fit inside a container and can be easily transported."

The dam-building industry, however, believed it had been given little chance to redeem itself. It now focused on how dams could be built to minimize environmental and social impacts. Compensation packages for some affected peoples were introduced. Environmental "mitigation" soon became a buzzword, and an entire industry sprang up to design, build, and monitor fish hatcheries, fish ladders, and "trap and haul" facilities to transport fish upstream past dams so that they could spawn. Mitigation measures did reduce some harmful impacts, but other pricey attempts to address the environmental impact of dams were deemed "worse than useless," in the words of Patrick McCully, author of an authoritative book about the global impacts of large dams.

Even with this new focus on mitigation, the pace of global dam-building slowed considerably heading into the 1990s. As McCully wrote in *Silenced Rivers*, instead of being revered as icons of progress, "big dams have instead become symbols of the destruction of the natural world and of the corruption and arrogance of over-powerful and se-cretive corporations, bureaucracies and governments." The large dam-building spree began to seem a thing of the past, much like steam engines and leaded gasoline.

Then a Big Hydro superhero made an unanticipated entrance.

The superhero arrived wearing the cape of heightened awareness and concern about global warming. In 1992 the United Nations organized the landmark Earth Summit in Rio de Janeiro. That summit was un-precedented in scope. It gathered representatives from 172 countries – including many heads of state – in one place to brainstorm new avenues to addressing the pollution and resource depletion threatening the planet. Almost ten thousand journalists observed the proceedings, transmitting its main messages and concerns to millions of people around the world.

A main topic of discussion was global climate change and alternative energy sources (alternative, that is, to fossil fuels). Out of the summit came a landmark convention to tackle climate change, one that committed the participating nations to control and cut greenhouse gas emissions and stabilize their own emissions. Climate change was now part of the global lexicon for the first time since scientists had first sounded the alarm about the dire consequences of a planet warmed by human behaviour.

For the weakened hydro dam industry, worldwide attention to global warming was manna from heaven. Not long after Big Hydro was rebuffed, it was welcomed as a "green renewable." "The Big Bad Dams of Past Decades Are Back in Style," announced one international headline. Previously viewed as an ecological scourge, Big Hydro now seemed so carbon-friendly that the Chicago Climate Exchange sanctioned hydro as a carbon credit source. Cities like Seattle met their Kyoto Accord goals to slash emissions by tapping into the Columbia River's hydroelectric grid. In the words of *Forbes* magazine: "As the world scrambles to embrace green energy, the hydroelectric industry is enjoying a massive resurgence. The high price of oil and surging demand for non-carbon fuels have energy executives dusting off old plans for major dams."

One project that was dusted off and polished with a climate-friendly cloth was Site C. It joined big hydro dams around the world, Brazil's Belo Monte Dam among them, as a phoenix rising from the ashes.

INTO THIS GLOBAL ARENA stepped BC premier Gordon Campbell, who had decided to make his political mark by tackling climate change. Campbell's commitment to taking action on global warming can be traced back to a series of events, although he insisted there was no single epiphany. In 2006, on a visit to China, the premier had endured a series of hazardous air days – days where particulate pollution exceeded 500 parts per million – in a country that at that time was generating most of its energy from coal-fired power plants, the dirtiest source of electricity when it comes to carbon emissions. Later, Campbell reportedly watched Al Gore's movie about climate change, *An Inconvenient Truth*.

Campbell also read Australian zoologist Tim Flannery's award-winning book about global warming, *The Weather Makers*, which

examines the history and future impact of climate change. The premier
appeared both alarmed and inspired by Flannery's account of where the
world was headed. He had found his Holy Grail. Global warming was
real, Campbell declared in his government's speech from the throne in
2007: "It leaves no room for procrastination."

Soon after, Campbell introduced policies aimed at slashing BC's
greenhouse gas emissions. But he was adamant that BC had to do more
to slow climate change than merely beat back its own emissions.
Campbell saw a future role for the province as a climate change big
brother, offering guidance and support to more carbon-troubled jurisdictions like California, where governor Arnold Schwarzenegger, another politician from the right side of the political spectrum, shared
Campbell's view that the need to reduce greenhouse gas emissions was
urgent. And so Site C was yanked from the embers of big bad hydro to
become the showcase project for Campbell's ambitious vision.

Campbell's vision dovetailed nicely with plans set in motion by W.A.C.
Bennett while he was premier. In the late 1950s, Bennett had dreamed
of throwing open the province's isolated north to resource development
and job creation. He envisioned pulp mills, gas wells, highways, and
railways. "We needed to develop power lines and generating stations
everywhere if we wanted to attract industry to British Columbia," he
later recalled. One day in 1957, Bennett travelled north to see the Peace
River. He described it as a "muddy little river," perhaps due to one of
the frequent landslides that had stained its waters brown. "I went to a
little town called Fort St. John, which was a very small place in those
days," he remembered. "Some RCMP men drove me along a dusty trail
to the shores of the river. I stood on the high banks looking down and
I saw something." What Bennett saw was the potential to build what he
soon dubbed the "greatest hydroelectric project in the world." As he was
aware, though, it was one thing to have a vision – financing it was something else entirely. A hydro dam on the Peace would not be cheap, and
Bennett knew he would need private investors with deep pockets to
realize his bold vision for the Peace.

As luck would have it, an international financier, the Swedish vacuum cleaner magnate Axel Wenner-Gren, had expressed a keen interest in investing some of his fortune in BC. Wenner-Gren had never travelled to Peace River Country, but the information he had gleaned about its vast untapped mineral and forestry resources piqued his entrepreneurial interest. A map of BC, painted on a piece of wood at the Pacific National Exhibition, proved sufficient orientation for the businessman, who was incredibly wealthy, suitably mysterious, and seemingly invincible.

In 1956, the year before Bennett visited the Peace, Wenner-Gren had given the BC government $500,000 in exchange for the right to develop the province's north – a region that amounted to one-tenth of the entire province. Bennett, ever the optimist, declared that the deal with Wenner-Gren would be the "greatest thing that ever happened in this province."

At Bennett's urging, the newly incorporated Wenner-Gren British Columbia Development Company organized an extensive waterpower survey of BC's north, deploying a fleet of floatplanes and helicopters to study every aspect of the Peace. The findings were even more promising than Bennett had dared hope, and he wasted no time in broadcasting that news. If BC dammed two rivers – the Peace and the more northerly Liard – Bennett said, the province could generate considerably more electricity than the largest hydro dam in the United States, the Grand Coulee Dam, which had become a popular tourist attraction as well as a generator of hydro power. The Liard River, however, couldn't be developed until the Peace River had been dammed and costly transmission corridors constructed.

The premier called a press conference in Vancouver, where he told reporters that the announcement they were about to hear would be his most momentous ever. It was feasible, he said, to build a dam along the Peace that would produce four million horsepower of electricity and create a lake 260 miles long – so huge that it could change northern BC's climate. The premier also revealed that his government had signed a second agreement with the Wenner-Gren company to develop a massive hydro project along the Peace. This second announcement was met with outrage and incredulity from the political opposition. Gordon Dowding, the leader of the NDP's precursor, the Co-operative Commonwealth Federation (CCF), called Bennett's plans to dam the Peace "tampering with the security and welfare of future generations," and demanded that Bennett call an election. CCF member Randolph Harding, who referred to Axel Wenner-Gren as Axel the First of Wenner-Grenland, warned that the Swedish industrialist had already generated more than $5 million in profits by selling shares in the development corporation. Some opposition MLAs took to calling BC "Swedish Columbia."

Bennett lambasted the opposition for its lack of vision and set out to overcome another obstacle along the road he was bent on taking. In those days, a private company called BC Electric supplied most of the province's electricity, servicing its two most populous areas: the Lower Mainland and southern Vancouver Island. Back then, municipalities outside of urban centres often had private utilities. For outlying regions not serviced by the private sector, the publicly owned BC Power Commission ensured connection to the grid.

To proceed with a hydro dam on the Peace, Bennett needed signed contracts from utilities agreeing to purchase the power it would generate. But BC Electric refused to buy power from the proposed Peace dam, saying – in terms that would be echoed decades later by Site C critics – that it was far too expensive and that cheaper alternatives existed. Bennett, a free enterpriser who eschewed anything that smacked of socialism, made a swift decision that contravened his political philosophy but was perfectly in keeping with his vision and his plans. If BC Electric would not do his bidding, he would nationalize the company. BC Electric "didn't have the vision for the kind of growth our province needed," he later recounted.

As Bennett placed his political and financial ducks in a row to dam the Peace, his government deliberated long and hard with Ottawa over the future of a second BC river with immense hydroelectric potential: the Columbia. Bennett sought to dam the BC portion of the transboundary Columbia as well as the Peace, and he shrewdly used the

Peace as leverage to get Washington and Ottawa to agree (after fifteen years of talks that Bennett likened to holding "pink teas") to damming the Columbia in BC. The ensuing Columbia River Treaty set terms for the United States to pay BC for power it would generate once dams were constructed on the Canadian stretch of the river. "The Peace is the only reason why, after all these years of talk, there has been some real action on the Columbia," Bennett commented.

Bennett's vision of harnessing the Columbia and the Peace for hydropower became known as his Two River Policy, and his government christened the vast Rocky Mountain area encompassing the Liard, Peace, and Columbia rivers the "Power Trench." The premier promised British Columbians he would deliver "the cheapest power in the world," and, for a while, electricity rates in BC were indeed cheap. (By 2017, before scheduled BC hydro rate increases unconnected to Site C's price tag, which was not yet on the books, Quebec and Manitoba had electricity rates lower than BC.) But Bennett was a fiscal pragmatist as much as he was a schemer and dreamer. He knew that the BC government could only afford to finance one major hydro project. Ideally, he wanted federal money to develop the Columbia. And he was not about to let anyone or anything, including the recalcitrant BC Electric, stand in the way of his plans to dam the mighty Peace.

On August 2, 1961, in a move that brought swift rebuke from the Canadian Chamber of Commerce, the Bennett government passed Bill 5 to nationalize BC Electric. This sent a jolt through the financial centres of the western world. Fidel Castro had recently seized power in Cuba, and the Cold War was reaching new heights. Bennett was compared to Castro and to less than savoury leaders of banana republics and dictatorships. The opposition parties went so far as to cry "Seig Heil" in the provincial legislature. But Bennett ignored all criticism. He went on to merge the newly nationalized BC Electric with the government's BC Power Commission. His government christened the new entity the British Columbia Power and Hydro Authority (BC Hydro for short).

The Wenner-Gren water power survey had identified eight potential dam sites upstream of Hudson's Hope. Site 3a, more than 100 kilometres upstream from where Bennett had first gazed out over the Peace River, was at Portage Mountain and was selected as the location for the first dam. When the structure – a triumph of engineering – was finally completed in September 1967, Bennett "hopped aboard a giant belly-dump Caterpillar to release the final eighty tons of earth fill on the dam," which stretched more than 2 kilometers across the river. Amid much fanfare, modesty not being one of his trademarks, the premier named the imposing structure after himself, and the dam became operational early the following year.

The Bennett Dam flooded an area fifteen times the size of the city of Vancouver, displacing nearly five hundred First Nations people and settlers. The dam's power fuelled pulp mills and sawmills, and electricity hummed through new transmission lines to Prince Rupert, Prince George, Squamish, and Vancouver. Yet some relocated farmers along the Peace River had to wait thirty more years for hydropower, and marginalized Sekani First Nations communities, moved from the flood zone, still lacked hydropower in 2017. They relied on diesel and gas for electricity during decades when most of the province enjoyed some of the lowest hydro rates in the country.

Today, the Bennett Dam is the fourth-largest dam in Canada. It is higher than the Great Pyramid of Giza and the Statue of Liberty and almost as tall as the Calgary Tower. As huge as it is by BC standards, it comes nowhere close to making the list of the ten biggest dams in the world (although its reservoir remains the seventh largest by sheer volume). It was the biggest dam in Canada for only a few years, until the Churchill Falls Dam in Labrador was finished, followed by two James Bay dams that were also larger in capacity.

The Bennett Dam's reservoir was named after one of Bennett's confidants, former cabinet minister Ray Williston. In area it is far larger than any natural lake in the province, and at its deepest point it would submerge all but the tallest Vancouver skyscraper. Ten rivers drain into the reservoir, including the Finlay and the Parsnip.

Site 1 became the Peace Canyon Dam, which blocked the treacherous canyon that had forced Mackenzie and his party to undertake the first

The Bennett Dam flooded an area fifteen times the size of the city of Vancouver, displacing hundreds of First Nations members and settlers | *Photo by Garth Lenz*

of many arduous portages on what they dubbed their "dubious journey." A little sister to the Bennett Dam, the Peace Canyon Dam inundated a much smaller area, less than one two-hundredth of the zone flooded by the Williston Reservoir. It flooded more than fifteen hundred dinosaur tracks, some of them one hundred million years old, including the earliest record of hadrosaurs, the duck-billed dinosaurs popularized by Disney. The dam also inundated more than two hundred delicate footprints, encased in siltstone, that turned out to be the world's earliest bird footprints. Scientists had time to investigate only 7 kilometres of the 27-kilometre-long canyon before it was submerged by what is now ironically called Dinosaur Lake, entombing all known (and undiscovered) Mesozoic trackways.

Bennett's master plan called for potentially five more Peace River dams downstream of Hudson's Hope, at sites labelled with the first five letters of the alphabet. Each new dam would capitalize on water storage from the previous site, generating electricity from the river's repeated capture and release. Site C sat almost 100 kilometres downstream from the Bennett dam, likely not far from the spot where Bennett had first gazed out over the Peace River.

Almost a decade after the BC Hydro board rejected Site C, Richard Neufeld, a Reform Party MLA for the provincial riding of Peace River North who later became energy minister for the BC Liberals, let slip that BC Hydro had kept plans for Site C "shelf-ready" all that time. The dam, Neufeld said in 2004, would cost $2.1 billion and displace twenty-five farming families.

Neufeld placed two clear caveats on Site C's future, caveats that successive Liberal governments would later sidestep, with apparent disregard for the future financial impacts for British Columbians. Site C, Neufeld said, would have to be reviewed by the BC Utilities Commission (BCUC) to make sure that new power could not be produced more cheaply in other ways. And the project would only go ahead, he promised, if the dam's surplus energy could be sold profitably. "You have to look at the markets and see if we can sell it."

The sleeping giant that the Boons and other Peace Valley residents had taken for dead was beginning to stir. Only one week before Neufeld's comments, BC Hydro had filed a blueprint document for meeting BC's electricity needs, and Site C had been included as an option. "It's still on the books ... still a viable resource option for us, we said that all along," commented BC Hydro spokesperson Dave Conway, who later became the main media spokesperson and community manager for Site C. In 2005, BC Hydro assigned two senior managers to prepare Site C, now billed as a $3.5 billion project, for final approval. The managers were instructed to set the direction for public and First Nations consultation, as well as for regulatory approvals and communications, according to a leaked internal BC Hydro memo that made the government's intentions abundantly transparent. Indeed, it referred to one of the appointments as providing "leadership to take the project through to the approval stage."

Publicly, BC Hydro said it did not want people "to think this is a done deal by any account." Privately, though, it was another story. Unbeknownst to most ratepayers, BC Hydro hired a rash of consulting firms to study every aspect of Site C, from lost and compromised heritage values to the impact the dam would have on nature and agricultural land. The Crown corporation also prepared a host of geotechnical studies, informed by the knowledge that, while the Site A and B dams rested firmly on bedrock, the Site C dam would require more engineering interventions to address the possibility of a geotechnical disaster. It also launched an extensive "consultation" program with Treaty 8 First Nations and twenty-three other First Nations, documenting every email it sent and every invitation to a meeting, which it later used against some of the same First Nations in court when they challenged dam construction.

While most British Columbians remained oblivious to the unfolding plans for Site C, residents of the Peace Valley readied themselves to fight the Goliath they had managed to keep at bay for almost three decades, long enough for an entire generation to grow up and have children of their own. "Prepare to gird your loins for an ambitious campaign," longtime valley resident Ruth Ann Darnall wrote in an email to the Boons, noting aptly that her research indicated that "the decision on Site C will be a political one and logic and facts will not win out. Facts are not enough."

This time around, the provincial government was unwilling to countenance rejection of Site C by the BC Utilities Commission. Included in the new Clean Energy Act, whose aim was to position BC as the North American leader in tackling climate change, was a clause that removed Site C from the BC Utilities Commission's purview. No longer would it be up to the watchdog commission to determine whether Site C was in the financial interest of British Columbians and to make sure that it was not merely a vanity project promoted for partisan political gain.

Campbell promoted the Clean Energy Act as a legal chisel that would enable BC to chip away at its greenhouse gas emissions by making unprecedented investments in renewable energy. As the premier explained on the day the act was introduced, "We want British Columbia to become a leading North American supplier of clean, reliable, low-carbon electricity."

BC Hydro would now do more than provide ample and reliable power for British Columbian homes, businesses, and industries. Its mandate would expand to allow BC to export more electricity. The Site C dam, Campbell proclaimed, would become a cornerstone of BC's new energy exports, even though there were no committed buyers. The premier chose not to delve into the project's acute and irreversible impacts on nature, farmland, the valley community, and First Nations.

Treaty Lands and
Corporate Plans

From the Boons' kitchen window, the couple could see across Cache Creek to the spot where a First Nations gravesite was etched high on the scrubby hillside. In the 1940s, back when Arlene's grandfather lived in the farmhouse, a simple wooden cross had marked the burial location. Nobody knew what happened to the cross, or even when it disappeared, and details about the burial it denoted were only slightly less foggy to valley settlers.

First Nations members knew there had been a burial during the 1918 Spanish influenza epidemic. That knowledge was corroborated by the historical record, according to which the surviving members of a stricken First Nations encampment at Bear Flat–Cache Creek had travelled to Fort St. John in search of help to bury their dead, and fort occupants had accompanied them back to Cache Creek for that purpose. Those victims, some said, included the wife of Chief Attachie, a skilled hunter who had himself succumbed to the galloping pandemic that killed more people worldwide than the bubonic plague. He had been buried close to the Halfway River, in the Site C reservoir zone.

For decades, the Cache Creek gravesite lay acknowledged but undisturbed. After an archaeologist visited the site in 1954, it was recorded as a pre-European contact site with an associated Christian burial place. (The Dunne-Za practice before the arrival of Europeans was to place their dead in trees.) Cultural materials were subsequently removed during archaeological investigations for Site C – lithic artifacts such as pieces of black chert, a sedimentary rock used to make stone tools in prehistoric times. One corner of the site had been bulldozed years earlier during construction work on the valley highway, but the burial depression remained, obscured by a green tangle of prickly rose, Saskatoon berry, snowberry, and wolf willow bushes, and later watched over by a garland of faded and wind-blown prayer flags placed in nearby trees.

In the summer of 2016, as Site C construction neared the one-year mark, First Nations identified a second depression, camouflaged by vegetation, on the Cache Creek hillside. They brought in an archeologist, who agreed with the elders that it had all the hallmarks of a Dunne-Za grave – a depression in the ground, high on a hill, at the confluence of two rivers where, as Chief Willson explained, "bodies are usually laid to rest, so that they have a view."

In keeping with Dunne-Za (Beaver) tradition, First Nations treated the area as a sacred spot that should never be disturbed. Chief Willson and Chief Lynette Tsakoza, from Prophet River First Nation, referred to the hillside with the burial places as a mass grave, meaning that it contained a cluster of burial sites known through oral history. The BC Archeology Branch called the boxy area with the first burial depression HbRh-2. The kite-shaped area near the second depression was a recorded archeological site called HbRh-16. Nomenclature aside, the sites came to symbolize far more than just another skirmish in the protracted battle over Site C.

Bear Flat had always held special significance for First Nations, who gathered there for many thousands of years before settlers farmed the land. Known as Tluuge sus, it is a place where ancient trails converge and the site of natural springs used by countless generations of ancestors. The nations continued to maintain a sweat lodge there, described by Chief Willson as "a spiritual connection to the land." Following a long-standing tradition, they also held annual cultural camps at the Boon family's private Bear Flat campground, across the broad Cache Creek Valley from Ken and Arlene's farm. The camps passed on ancestral knowledge, imparting skills to youngsters such as how to hunt, skin an ungulate, gather special herbs and medicinal plants like rosehip and yarrow, and play traditional guessing games. "The gatherings have changed somewhat," explained Chief Willson. "Now instead of coming in on horseback and carrying in all our supplies on horses we come in pickups ... We have an understanding with the Boons that own Bear Flats that this was a site. We have a relationship with them. They allow us to stay there. Just because it's private land doesn't mean we can't continue to use it."

Much to Chief Willson's consternation, the first gravesite would be submerged by the Site C reservoir. The campground and the rest of the First Nations cultural site, including the sweat lodge and the larger suspected burial depression, would be destroyed or rendered unusable when the provincial highway was relocated out of the flood zone. Highway 29 hugged the north side of the valley, sometimes dipping low, separated from the river by fields, wetlands, or forest, and sometimes rising high, offering the postcard views of the valley and the river islands featured in local tourism promotions. BC Hydro would need to move 30 kilometres of the highway – in six different sections that included four highway bridges – out of the flood zone, a project BC Hydro referred to as a highway "realignment." The cost of the Highway 29 relocation was originally pegged at $530 million in BC Hydro documents.

Two routes had been shortlisted for the new Cache Creek bridge and 8 kilometres of fresh blacktop near the Boons' farm. One option was to run the new highway lanes through the middle of the Boons' house and garden and to construct the new bridge across the widest part of Cache Creek, connecting to the family's bluff-top campground and First Nations cultural area. The highway would then continue through the farmhouse of Leslee Jardine and Colin Meek, vocal Site C opponents who were awaiting organic certification for a hemp heart crop on the family farm. The second shortlisted option was to place the new highway route several kilometres back from the planned reservoir, against the contoured hills that framed the valley, leaving some of the First Nations cultural area and campground intact.

In early March, the week after the Rocky Mountain Fort camp was dismantled, BC Hydro delivered some bad news to Cache Creek landowners and First Nations. The Crown corporation had chosen the highway route that would run through farmhouses and the First Nations cultural area. Over the next twelve months, West Moberly First Nations and Prophet River First Nation, along with the Peace Valley Landowners Association, requested repeatedly that BC Hydro use the other shortlisted route. The landowners' association also asked BC Hydro for a copy of the document (known as a multiple accounts evaluation) that compared the relative merits and costs of the two shortlisted routes. But BC Hydro refused to make that document public. Instead, BC Hydro produced a carefully worded information sheet that said the final route had been chosen because it was cheaper, cut through less agricultural land, and offered more passing opportunities for drivers.

For Chief Willson and other First Nations, BC Hydro's response to multiple requests to leave the gravesites and sweat lodge untouched, and to reroute the new highway, encapsulated everything egregious and unbalanced about the entire Site C process. It also underscored that the BC government, through BC Hydro, was in the driver's seat, while the valley's people were captive, seat-belted passengers speeding to a finish line they had no wish to reach.

As the chiefs soon discovered, the recommendations of Canada's landmark Truth and Reconciliation Commission meant little when it came to Site C. Prime Minister Justin Trudeau's election promise to forge a new relationship with Canada's First Peoples came to mean even less when the new federal government did not exercise its power to pause Site C construction, at least until First Nations court cases were resolved. Grand Chief Phillip, the long-standing president of the Union of BC Indian Chiefs, used the words "blatant hypocrisy" and "racist double standards" to describe the provincial government's treatment of the First Nations members who were fighting Site C. Perry Bellegarde, the national chief of the Assembly of First Nations, declared that proceeding with Site C contravened both Canadian and international law, for it trampled on the ability of Treaty 8 First Nations to exercise their inherent and treaty rights. Chief Willson, for his part, said the BC government was punishing his First Nation because they refused to be, in Willson's words, "good little Indians."

I met up with Chief Willson in the unpretentious restaurant of the Sportsman's Inn in Hudson's Hope, where he lived with his wife, son, and daughter, commuting to West Moberly First Nations reserve on the shores of Moberly Lake. Cogent and expressive, the chief has a strong presence and an infectious laugh. At the time of our meeting, he had been chief of West Moberly First Nations for fourteen years. Hardly a stranger to resource development, he sat on numerous boards and councils, including the BC First Nations Energy and Mining Council and the Pacific Trails Pipeline First Nations Limited Partnership. The amiable chief was a frequent presenter at forums and seminars across the country and in the United States, including in academic settings. He addressed issues of pressing importance to First Nations, including the disappearance of caribou from the landscape and his people's last-ditch efforts to resurrect the declining herds. He spoke passionately about Site C and the Peace River Valley, which he described as the only section of the riverscape left to First Nations for traditional practices guaranteed to them in the treaty their ancestors had signed.

Indeed, Willson said, there were few places remaining anywhere in Treaty 8's homeland where members could have "quiet, peaceful enjoyment of our treaty rights." Everywhere First Nations members looked, the landscape had been carved up by oil and gas development, mining, logging, agriculture, private land holdings, and the reservoirs from the previous two dams on the Peace River. Site C would flood the "last refuge" of river valley, and Willson was determined to protect it. In doing so, he often pointed out that his First Nation was not opposed to economic development. "What we're opposed to," he insisted, "are the unnecessary impacts of Site C. Site C is 100 percent unnecessary."

Just as coastal First Nations call the intertidal zone their dinner table, Indigenous peoples in Treaty 8 refer to the land as their grocery store. The valley bottoms slated for inundation by Site C are also their medicine cabinets and schools of traditional knowledge. Chokecherries,

Saskatoon berries, and blackberries, among many other traditional plants, grow in abundance at Bear Flat. The banks of the Halfway River, in the Site C flood zone, are important areas for harvesting wild mint and Labrador tea. On the southeast side of the confluence rests a forest of birch that has provided traditional materials and medicines, like chaga, for generations of Dunne-Za. Cache Creek and the Halfway River, along with Farrell Creek, also slated to be flooded, are prime moose-hunting areas.

Even though much has changed in just one century, the Dunne-Za are still part and parcel of the land. Losing the valley to Site C would be like losing an organ from your body, explained Chief Willson. "It's like cutting out a kidney. Our connection to the land is spiritual. We're people of the land. You take us off the land, and you destroy a piece of who we are."

BC Hydro had argued that Aboriginal traditional practices were adaptable and could readily be reproduced elsewhere. But the Joint Review Panel rejected BC Hydro's interpretation of First Nations practices, calling it "superficial." The dam's impacts on hunting, fishing, non-tenured trapping, and other traditional land uses would likely be adverse, significant, and impossible to mitigate, the panel concluded. According to BC Hydro's own documents, Site C would destroy forty-two sites of cultural and spiritual significance to First Nations: burial grounds, medicine collection areas, offering places for ceremonies and prayers, and locations associated with oral histories and place names such as Attachie and House before the Rocks. More than two dozen sites with First Nations transportation values, including portions of trails, horse crossings, boat and raft crossings, and canoe and boat routes along the Peace and its tributaries, would also be erased.

In the words of Blueberry River First Nations member Clarence Apsassin, "You're going to flood out a lot of traplines up that way, and our hunting territories, our old burial grounds. We don't want that to happen. How would you like me to go build in your cemetery and destroy all the cemeteries! That is just the same thing as our burial grounds; you are doing the same thing." Site C, said Blueberry member Malcolm

Apsassin, would "ruin our hunting, our trapping. We will just go down the drain. We will have no place to trap. I am still young, and I have a long ways to go, and I've got my family to raise, and if that dam comes up, it will just ruin our life."

Chief Willson worried about the deeply layered impacts of Site C. But he was especially perturbed that the dam's reservoir would destroy many known and presumed First Nations burial sites, including the Cache Creek sites. Even more galling was BC Hydro's own Site C Heritage Resources Management Plan, which stated that the preferred means of limiting the dam's effect on heritage sites such as burial grounds was to avoid them "by changing the design or placement of project components." One project component that could offer some level of avoidance of heritage sites, according to the plan, was the final route chosen for the highway relocation.

In the summer and fall of 2016, Chief Willson and Chief Tzakoza attended meetings and communicated with three different provincial cabinet ministers – Todd Stone (transportation), John Rustad (Aboriginal relations), and Steve Thomson (forests, lands, and natural resource operations) – in an attempt to resolve the highway issue. Why, the chiefs asked repeatedly, did the new highway have to cut through the heart of the First Nations cultural area, the burial grounds, and the Boon and Meek farmhouses when engineers had shortlisted a second route that would spare them?

When the meetings yielded no satisfactory answers, Chief Willson and Chief Tzakoza wrote letters to the ministers and BC Hydro, pleading for the gravesites to be spared. "Digging up graves is not acceptable in our customs," the letters stated. "Desecrating a Dunne-za grave is a serious assault on Indigenous peoples. BC Hydro does not have the right to do this at all."

But BC Hydro did have permission from the Clark government to destroy the graves, along with dozens of other sites of Indigenous significance. That right did not rest on firm moral ground, but BC Hydro had anchored itself to regulatory bedrock, unless a later constitutional challenge determined that Site C violated treaty rights, as legal scholars believed it would. More than a year before Chief Willson and Chief Tzakoza sent their letters to the cabinet ministers and BC Hydro, the Clark government had granted BC Hydro a permit to "alter" archaeological sites in the Site C project area, including known First Nations burial sites. That "alteration" permit included permission to put the smaller gravesite, on the skirts of the new highway, permanently under water.

BC Hydro had also obtained permits from the provincial government that gave it the regulatory right to destroy eighteen recorded archeological sites in the Bear Flat area. These sites included four designated Class 1 archaeological sites and ten Class 11 sites. Together, they comprised such a significant cluster of archaeological gems that the BC government referred to the Bear Flat area as an "archaeological site complex." Archaeology crews funded by the Site C project dug small pits at some of the sites to recover some of the artifacts, much to the dismay of Chief Willson and other Aboriginal leaders, who said that digging up their history was "not acceptable mitigation for Site C."

At the meetings with the provincial ministers, the chiefs had been told that the government would collaborate with them to find a solution. But after three months they hadn't heard back. The silence raised questions about the integrity of BC Hydro's much touted ten-point Statement of Aboriginal Principles. One principle committed the corporation to providing the clearest and most accessible and transparent information possible. Another declared that the utility company would seek advice on First Nations perspectives on how best to reduce or avoid impacts on the environment and cultural heritage. But if BC Hydro had accepted First Nations advice, it wasn't from Chief Willson or Chief Tsakoza, whose nations were fighting Site C in court.

THE FIRST NATIONS WERE forever scrambling to raise money to fight Site C, including through online appeals. The task of raising hundreds of thousands of dollars for court cases against a publicly funded corporation weighed heavily on Chief Willson and Chief Tsakoza; so too did rising tensions generated by Site C among the various Treaty 8 First

Nations. Those tensions stemmed from the considerable sums of money given to some First Nations by BC Hydro and the BC Liberal government (the total amount was a secret, but it possibly amounted to tens of millions of dollars), along with the promise of Site C contracts and resulting jobs for First Nations people and businesses, provided that their communities signed Site C economic impact agreements. As the old adage goes, money talks. And when it came to Site C, money flowed like a river of gold.

When Site C was first proposed in the 1970s, the First Nations of the Peace River Valley objected vocally. The spectre of a third dam on the Peace River (along with fast-creeping oil and gas development) helped fuel the creation of the Treaty 8 Tribal Association, founded to further educational opportunities and protect the interests of seven First Nations in light of large megaprojects. Members of the association were "gravely concerned" about Site C's environmental and socio-economic impacts. Flooding a large portion of what remained of BC's Peace River Valley, reported the chiefs, would interfere with traditional transportation routes that gave their people access to traditional hunting territories and "would directly impact their ability to maintain their traditional economy." According to testimony the tribal association presented at the BC Utilities Commission hearings on Site C in the early 1980s, that economy was essential to the well-being of Indigenous peoples, who had managed to maintain their adaptable hunting and trapping economic system over the centuries despite many incursions into their territory and the loss of significant tracts of traditional land.

When Campbell announced his decision to proceed with the environmental assessment process for Site C in April 2010, the nations that comprised the Treaty 8 Tribal Association shared an office on one of Fort St. John's main streets. The logos of each nation hung proudly on the wall and members from different communities gathered for events, discussions, and professional development workshops. That fall, elders, youth, and elected officials from the Treaty 8 First Nations travelled to Victoria to present Campbell with a declaration opposing Site C. The declaration was wrapped in a traditional birchbark container

made from trees growing in the Site C flood zone, and it was signed by
twenty-three First Nations from BC, Alberta, and the Northwest
Territories. It contended that Site C would, among its many impacts,
disrespect and destroy the graves of their ancestors, eliminate critical
warm lowlands where predators and prey survived harsh northern
winters, and disrupt migration routes for bull trout and other fish species (in addition to contaminating them with mercury). Treaty 8 Tribal
Chief Liz Logan told a crowd assembled in front of the BC Legislature
that Site C was "not green or clean." The Treaty 8 Nations, vowed Logan,
would use all legal means possible to fight the dam.

Six years later, the association's office was less active, and relations
among its members were somewhat strained. "The Tribal Council used
to be a united front," observed former Saulteau First Nations Chief Art
Napoleon. "Now the Tribal Council is only a shadow of its former self."
By early 2017, only two of the six nations who belonged to the association were still vocal in their opposition to Site C and fighting the project
through legal challenges. (The Blueberry River First Nations, also a
Treaty 8 signatory but not a member of the Treaty 8 Tribal Association,
had also launched its civil suit, claiming that rampant industrial development in the band's traditional territory, including Site C, prevented members from engaging in traditional practices guaranteed in the treaty.)

Members of the Treaty 8 Tribal Association continued to work together
on other pertinent issues, such as the BC government's legal challenge
to the boundaries of Treaty 8 – a little-known court case that the nations
ultimately won, retaining what they already had, though it cost them
greatly in time and legal fees. And First Nations collaborated on other
initiatives outside of the association. Saulteau First Nations joined with
West Moberly First Nations and Prophet River First Nation to hire a
hydrogeology expert, who then challenged BC Hydro's findings regarding Site C's effect on groundwater, pointing to gaps in data that could
compromise dam and water safety. West Moberly First Nations and
Saulteau First Nations continued to partner on an award-winning native plant nursery called the Twin Sisters. But on many issues related
to Site C, most of the treaty association's members gradually fell silent

in the public sphere. The not-for-profit Nun Wa Dee Stewardship Society (established by Prophet River First Nation and West Moberly First Nations) maintained a small office in a strip mall a few blocks from the Treaty 8 Tribal Association's headquarters. They published scientific studies detailing the deterioration of traditional lands and waterways. Chief Willson described Site C as an invasive and malignant growth: "It's like one of those nasty cancers that you just can't cut out."

TO UNDERSTAND SITE C'S true impact on First Nations, Chief Willson said, you first had to look at the distressing impacts of the two existing dams on the Peace River, especially the Bennett Dam, which had been built without any consultation whatsoever with First Nations. BC Hydro itself acknowledged many decades later that the dam's "social consequences were catastrophic as communities were cut off from each other, food sources disappeared, and traditional economies were wiped out."

By all accounts, the lattice of rivers, canyons, estuaries, and forests that the Williston Reservoir destroyed had been of a wild, dizzying beauty. Beyond their visual and spiritual appeal, rivers like the Finlay and the Parsnip were used by First Nations as highways linking seasonal camps and kin, whom in more modern times they would visit in rafts and flat-bottomed river boats. When the Bennett Dam opened without their consent and the waters of the Finlay, the Parsnip, and eight other rivers and creeks began to rise, Indigenous people were stripped of far more than their links to relatives and culturally important places upstream and down. Some had to flee so quickly that they lost not just their homes but also the tools they needed to live off the land – the very tools that gave them some measure of security in life, such as animal hide scrapers that had been passed down from grandmother to mother to daughter.

Emil McCook, the former chief of the Kwadacha First Nation, one of the Sekani nations whose Rocky Mountain Trench homeland included the area around the Bennett Dam, was one of many people whose lives were put at risk when the churning waters of the rising Williston Reservoir submerged First Nations riverboats. McCook, then a teenager employed to ferry supplies, plucked a young boy from the treacherous waters after his boat had overturned. He would recount the story decades later in a documentary video *Kwadacha by the River*. Georgina Chingee, an elder from McLeod Lake Indian Band, recalled "a really big noise," the sound of the waters rising. "It was coming quite fast, and we were packing up, and we were trying to move up to higher land." Members of Halfway River First Nation, children at the time, remembered seeing wooden boxes floating in the newly created reservoir. They were coffins from a flooded cemetery. "The loss of the land in and around what is now the Williston Reservoir means that my children and grandchildren will not be able to see the grave of my great-great-grandfather, because it is underneath that lake," explained former chief Gerry Hunter from Halfway River First Nation. "I cannot take my grandchildren to show them where their roots are. The dams destroyed my great-great-grandfather's resting place."

The Williston Reservoir also flooded the villages of 125 Ingenika Sekani families, who were collectively given $35,000 in a deal sanctioned by the federal government. The families were shipped off to two "model" reserves hundreds of kilometres away, north of the mill town of Mackenzie, from which they fled three years later. From tarpaper shacks at Finlay Forks, the Ingenika (now known as the Tsay Keh Dene) were moved to the Parsnip Reserve, where, according to former Tsay Keh Dene councillor Jean Chalifoux, "everybody turned to alcohol ... They may have given us these houses, but we have lost our culture, our spirituality."

After visiting one of the new communities in the mid-1980s, Stephen Rogers, a former Social Credit cabinet minister, described living conditions among the Tsay Keh Dene as "the most primitive I've seen." Terry Glavin, a *Vancouver Sun* reporter who travelled to the area not long after, found more than one hundred hunters and trappers living without telephones, electricity, or running water in "pinepole-and-plywood cabins scattered over three kilometres of a wooded promontory above the reservoir that had destroyed their former homes 20 years ago." At the time, McCook told Glavin, "we want something left for our children, whether it's in the new world or it's in our own culture and tradition. That's not asking much."

For more than four decades, until Site C was resurrected, the BC government largely ignored one of the country's most marginalized First Nations, living in a remote place most Canadians would never hear about, much less see.

Today, the Tsay Keh Dene live isolated at the northern tip of the Williston Reservoir, a ten-hour drive from Prince George. Children and adults alike endure rashes and respiratory problems from dust storms generated by the reservoir, whose banks continue to weaken and collapse with alarming frequency even after half a century. In 2016 Tsay Keh Dene paid exorbitant prices for food and depended heavily for their livelihoods on BC Hydro projects such as collecting and burning the logs that continued to float to the surface from the bottom of the reservoir, posing a hazard to barges and boats. The community disparagingly described these jobs as "almost like handouts."

When Tsay Keh Dene proposed building a biomass cogeneration system using logs from the reservoir and from pine beetle kill, BC Hydro blocked the initiative, even though it would have created more than a dozen long-term jobs and provided the village with inexpensive heat and power, as well as a greenhouse to grow food. The Crown corporation rejected the nation's energy demand forecast – a paradoxical outcome given that a later independent review found that BC Hydro's own energy forecasts were regularly inaccurate – and refused to enter into the power purchase agreement necessary for Tsay Keh Dene to secure debt financing.

As just one indicator of how much they have been relegated to obscurity, in 2017 neither the Tsay Keh Dene nor Kwadacha nations had hydropower. Instead, their electricity came from diesel generators. The Tsay Keh Dene had to endure brownouts and blackouts on a weekly basis. BC Hydro's commitment to improve the accessibility of clean, reliable, and affordable power to First Nations communities in remote areas of the province, outlined in its Statement of Aboriginal Principles that had garnered so many accolades, appeared to extend only so far.

In 1999 Tsay Keh Dene launched a lawsuit against BC Hydro and the provincial and federal governments for damages arising from the infringement on their Aboriginal rights and the construction of the Bennett Dam and Williston Reservoir. Two years later Kwadacha launched a similar suit. For years, both lawsuits crawled slowly through the legal system. Then, with Site C looming, the provincial government suddenly seemed eager to settle. In 2009, as the Campbell government geared up to announce publicly that it would seek regulatory approval for Site C, it reached a settlement with Tsay Keh Dene. The agreement provided the band with a one-time payment of $20.9 million and around $2 million a year thereafter. It also gave Tsay Keh Dene "direct award" BC Hydro contracting opportunities worth $6 million over a ten-year period and an annual $450,000 road maintenance contract to be shared with Kwadacha.

Kwadacha had inked an agreement in 2006, at a time when BC Hydro was commissioning the multitude of studies necessary to move Site C down the regulatory pipeline. The settlement awarded the nation financial compensation for what the government called "past injustices" related to the Bennett Dam and its reservoir: a one-time payment of $15 million and annual payments of around $1.6 million, with adjustments for inflation. The Kwadacha immediately began addressing a community housing shortage and improving living standards. The nation also planned to build a new arena and to found a guide-outfitting company with an ecotourism focus. Another provision in the agreement provided Kwadacha with opportunities for contract work related to the Williston Reservoir.

For Site C to proceed, BC Hydro needed to show that it had won over at least some Treaty 8 First Nations. The government knew that a First Nations blockade could slow down and perhaps even halt the construction of Site C. An image of First Nations elders who had been dispossessed by the Bennett Dam standing in front of Site C bulldozers and logging machinery was not one that Clark wanted seared on the minds of voters as the May 2017 provincial election approached. Nor did BC Hydro want to be viewed as unsympathetic to the difficulties

Rocky Mountain Fort camper Yvonne Tupper walks along the Peace River. Tupper is a member of Saulteau First Nations | *Photo by Lois Bockner*

facing Indigenous nations. So the Crown corporation set out to win over First Nations in a highly strategic manner that only a utility with deep pockets and concealed dealings could easily realize. Chief Willson, Art Napoleon, and other First Nations members bitterly referred to the strategy as "divide and conquer." BC Hydro's seemingly inexhaustible offerings of tens of millions of dollars, and of land and jobs – made with the full knowledge and support of the provincial government – split the First Nations apart.

THE SECURITY DETAIL at the Rocky Mountain Fort camp shed some light on BC Hydro's modus operandi. Yvonne Tupper and Rhoda Paquette were both from Saulteau First Nations, but they did not personally recognize the two security investigators, "Glen" and "Sten," who questioned them repeatedly at the camp. The men wore hefty black winter jackets emblazoned with the logo "Saulteau Safety and Security."

Tupper called this a "misrepresentation," given that the men were not from Saulteau First Nations. On court documents, Sten listed a Vancouver address, while Glen hailed from Calgary. According to the campers, most of the security guards and investigators wearing Saulteau Safety and Security jackets didn't appear to be from *any* First Nation. "People didn't know who they were," commented Art Napoleon, who visited the Rocky Mountain Fort camp. "They had never seen them before."

Glen and Sten could don winter garb with the Saulteau name because of a joint venture agreement that a new Saulteau First Nations chief and council had signed with a Vancouver security firm called Securiguard. The terms of the agreement were kept secret. Even Saulteau members like Tupper and Napoleon said they were not privy to the details. The business pact gave Securiguard, which described itself as western Canada's leading provider of corporate security, the right to use the Saulteau name. A company profile on the Work BC Employment Services Centre in Fort St. John described the joint venture agreement as "a significant opportunity to partner with the local first nations people and award them the right to protect their lands and represent their identity." Saulteau Safety and Security guard jobs, based in Fort St. John, were advertised as paying sixteen to nineteen dollars an hour. Duties included patrolling, crowd control, crime prevention, welcoming people to the Site C project area, and providing what the company called "excellent customer service."

BC Hydro awarded Securiguard two Site C contracts – one to furnish guard services and the other to provide security for Site C infrastructure. While BC Hydro was legally compelled to disclose the amount of money it allocated to specific Site C contracts (it did this only after the *Dawson Creek Mirror* made a freedom of information request), the Crown corporation declined to divulge how much public money had changed hands when contracts were awarded to firms, such as Securiguard, that had a joint venture agreement with a First Nation. It also withheld the total sums of money spent on contracts involving Aboriginal companies, including a contract for logging around the Rocky Mountain

Fort site and other Site C clearing work, which went to a private company owned by a Saulteau family.

BC Hydro disclosed only that $130 million had been allocated to what it described as "Aboriginal businesses" during the first year of Site C construction. But the fine print revealed that it had a broad definition of "Aboriginal business" – any business arrangement in which Aboriginal individuals or companies had an ownership or other interest or any company identified by an Aboriginal community as a business partner, including Securiguard. In exchange for Saulteau support for Site C, BC Hydro promised the nation an undisclosed lump sum payment, an annual payment stream, contract opportunities, Crown land transfers, and training opportunities, the values of which were not disclosed. Specific details about government-to-government negotiations are not generally made public, and BC's Freedom of Information Act protects information related to government-to-government transactions.

Saulteau First Nations had told the Joint Review Panel that the nation remained "gravely" concerned about Site C's potential effects on the community, its culture and traditions, and its treaty rights and interests, including the right to continue a traditional mode of life without interference. But following the council election in the summer of 2015, band members were asked by the council to participate in what turned out to be a controversial online vote about whether to sign the Site C agreement with BC Hydro. According to Art Napoleon, specific details about the proposed agreement were not made available to members, who were asked merely to vote yes or no. Out of 711 eligible voters, only 144 people cast ballots. In the end, it took 49 band members to vote yes in order for the Site C "impacts benefits agreement" with Saulteau to be announced by BC Hydro in a news release.

Shortly before BC Hydro's announcement that it had reached a Site C deal with Saulteau, another BC Treaty 8 First Nation that had vocally opposed Site C also changed its tack. McLeod Lake Indian Band, a small nation with one hundred members living on reserve and four hundred living elsewhere, pulled out of the BC Supreme Court lawsuit seeking to overturn provincial approval for the dam. The suit had been filed jointly with West Moberly First Nations and Prophet River First Nation. In a notice, the band said it had reached an agreement with BC Hydro to withdraw its claim.

In a later statement, in 2017, McLeod Lake Indian Band said the Site C impact benefit agreement it had signed with BC Hydro (along with a contracting agreement, a land transfer agreement, and a renewal agreement) sought to reset the historically fractious relationship between the band and BC Hydro by acknowledging and accommodating the "profound pain and hardship" the Williston Reservoir had caused. Chief Harley Chingee described some of those hardships:

> Members could not trap, hunt or fish like they used to. Members lost the ability to provide for themselves and the ability to pass those traditional skills onto their children. By the 1980s, almost all members had abandoned trapping. It was no longer viable as a way to feed yourself and your family or as a way to make money. Many families left McLeod Lake and moved to centres like Prince George. The displacement from their homes and their livelihoods meant that many MLIB members had to go on social assistance.

The agreement with McLeod Lake Indian Band included an undisclosed lump sum payment, a seventy-year payment stream, procurement opportunities for band companies, and the transfer of Crown lands to the nation.

As Site C construction progressed, and as the project appeared to be unstoppable, two other members of the Treaty 8 Tribal Association also inked Site C agreements. Halfway River First Nation signed an agreement that gave it, among other benefits, 1,800 hectares of Crown lands. Doig River First Nations signed agreements with BC Hydro that promised economic opportunities "and other benefits" related to the construction and operation of Site C. Those agreements, firmed up in March 2017, included an impact and benefits agreement, a contracting agreement, and a tripartite land agreement that would see the transfer of 1,200 hectares of Crown land. That summer, participants in the annual

Drummers at the annual Paddle for the Peace | *Photo courtesy of Reg Whiten*

Paddle for the Peace did not see Doig River First Nations drummers, who in previous years had stood on a grassy hill overlooking the Bear Flat canoe pullout, the sound of their drums echoing through the valley.

Bill Bennett, BC's energy and mines minister (no relation to Brad, Bill, or W.A.C. Bennett) sidestepped questions about whether payment awards to First Nations amounted to buying their support for Site C. If the impact of a project was purely negative, said Bennett, he himself might not support it. "All we're trying to do is put them in a position where because they're going to be impacted, they'll have an opportunity to derive benefits from the project."

Chief Willson, Chief Tsakoza, and others, however, saw the impact benefit agreements as one more way to divide First Nations and chip away at previously united opposition to Site C. Neither chief lacked empathy for First Nations that had signed economic benefits agreements, acknowledging that the pressures were great and that the project was racing forward. But Chief Willson said it was difficult for him to see members of his own nation left without comparable training and employment opportunities.

McLeod Lake Indian Band was not alone in its withdrawal from lawsuits against Site C. Downstream in Alberta, Mikisew Cree and Athabasca Chipewyan First Nations had launched two federal judicial reviews against Site C. They wanted the courts to overturn Ottawa's approval of the project on the grounds that they had not been properly consulted and that Site C would cause serious harm to the Peace Athabasca Delta in their traditional territory. The Peace Athabasca – North America's largest inland freshwater delta – lies in the heart of Wood Buffalo National Park, a UNESCO World Heritage Site that is the world's only known nesting spot for the endangered Whooping Crane and home to the planet's largest population of wild bison. Both judicial reviews had been discontinued in July 2015, just four days before the case was scheduled to begin, after agreements were reached with BC Hydro and the federal government, but not before the UN's World Heritage Committee leapt into the Site C fray. Petitioned by Mikisew Cree, the World Heritage Committee had asked Canada to ensure that no irreversible work on Site C would take place until it could send a mission to investigate the damage it would cause to Wood Buffalo National Park – a request ignored by both the federal and BC governments.

Mikisew Cree issued a public statement saying that they had brokered a deal with BC Hydro and the federal government because they faced "almost certain loss" in court and would be "exposed to paying more legal fees and costs." That deal, which did not include a cash settlement, gave the nation the opportunity to negotiate funding to participate in monitoring Site C's downstream impacts.

The following year, in July 2016, BC Hydro struck a deal with the Dene Tha' First Nation of northwestern Alberta. That nation, too, had expressed concerns about Site C's consequences for downstream First Nations who relied on the river for traditional practices such as fishing. BC Hydro awarded the nation a one-time payment and "on-going information" regarding contracts and employment related to Site C. Dene Tha' chief Joe Pastion called the agreement "a milestone in the relationship between BC Hydro and Dene Tha'," while BC Hydro CEO Jessica McDonald said in a statement that the utilities company was grateful for the opportunity to work with the Dene Tha'.

While West Moberly First Nations and Prophet River First Nation raised money for court cases against Site C one hundred dollars at a time, through online appeals, some Saulteau members benefitted from their nation's new approach to Site C. For example, the BC government contributed $91,000 to a construction craft worker training program for ten Saulteau youth, run by the Christian Labour Association of Canada, a union that donated to the BC Liberal Party and did not belong to the BC Federation of Labour. Upon completing the program, the youth were promised jobs on the Site C project as apprentices, hired by the Peace River Partnership, the consortium that held the $1.75 billion contract for Site C's civil works, including construction of the dam structure and river diversion tunnels.

Youth from First Nations fighting Site C received no direct sums from the BC government for apprenticeship training. Chief Willson worried that youth from his community would suffer from the decision to try to stop the project. It was a tough position for his people and for him personally, as a leader and a father, to take. BC Hydro had offered West Moberly First Nations a deal as well, one that the nation had rejected. Chief Willson said the terms of the deal were "ridiculous." "We're putting future generations kind of at risk by fighting this thing if we lose," the chief fretted. "But we think the impact outweighs the opportunity at this point."

For West Moberly First Nations, the economic repercussions of fighting Site C extended far beyond missing out on provincially funded direct award grants for youth training. Willson noted that his nation was not given the type of hydro maintenance contracts it had previously been awarded for work on the Bennett and Peace Canyon dams. "We're being spanked," he said.

Did BC Hydro's corporate commitment to respect and support the interests of Aboriginal people extend only to those sanctioning Site C? BC Hydro's Aboriginal contract and procurement policy hinted at the answer. It stated that direct procurement opportunities for Aboriginal communities would be in service of BC Hydro's relationship agreements, economic impact agreements, and other arrangements. The policy also noted that contract opportunities for Aboriginal businesses were available "outside of these arrangements" through BC Hydro's general procurement processes. This brought cold comfort for Willson and other members of West Moberly First Nations, who said they continued to be shut out from former contract opportunities. In Chief Willson's words, all his nation got were table scraps.

DESPITE THE ENDURING hardships that the Bennett Dam exacted on First Nations communities in the Peace River Valley, BC Hydro had never formally apologized to the affected nations and their members. In June 2016 it finally delivered that apology, at the official opening of the First Nations Impacts gallery at the Bennett Dam visitor centre. The corporation parachuted in its vice-president, Chris O'Riley, for the occasion. No press release or media advisory was issued, and the media were not officially invited, although the few that found out about it and registered for the event were not turned away. BC Hydro was ready to apologize quietly but clearly had little interest in making it too public.

And what a *mea culpa* it was. In the cold rain, standing on a stage in front of the mountainous Bennett Dam and the rippled waters of the Williston Reservoir, O'Riley told a sombre gathering that a popular photograph of the Bennett Dam reflected only part of the story. That photograph, looking downstream from the dam towards ribbons of transmission lines, had been made into a BC Hydro poster with this caption: "The Best Dam Operation in B.C." But the photograph didn't reveal what was on the land and in the rivers before the Williston Reservoir inundated them, O'Riley said, appealing to his largely First Nations audience:

And we know the photograph doesn't reveal the impacts of the dam on the people who lived here, on the First Nations and Metis people who lived on the land and drew sustenance from the land, the forest and the waters, and who travelled by boat up and down the river to connect with family and neighbours and communities. And it doesn't reveal the impacts on the people who had to move because their homes or villages were flooded and their travel routes were disrupted.

Fifty years earlier, O'Riley continued, the people who built the Bennett Dam simply did not see the impacts on Aboriginal communities. Neither did the government of the day or the larger society down south "who would benefit to such a large extent from the power of the dam." It took many years for BC Hydro employees to truly understand the impacts of the Bennett Dam, and they were still learning to be honest and blunt about it. BC Hydro, O'Riley declared, now recognized a need to acknowledge the parts of the picture of which it could not be proud, and to identify the adverse impacts of the dam on the environment and on the original people of the land. That acknowledgment, he said, was a very important part of reconciliation. "BC Hydro deeply regrets those impacts and we commit that we will not repeat the mistakes of the past."

Yet BC Hydro was poised to repeat some of those very same mistakes with Site C – an irony not lost on First Nations members who had gathered in the grey drizzle, eating a buffet lunch of sloppy joes, bannock bread, and soup under sheltering tents. Throughout the speeches and the ceremony, not one person publicly mentioned the Site C dam now being built 116 kilometres downstream. Nor did anyone mention the ongoing court cases against Site C championed by three of the First Nations represented at the gallery unveiling: West Moberly First Nations, Prophet River First Nation, and Blueberry River First Nations (indirectly).

Privately, First Nations members expressed their skepticism about O'Riley's message and fretted about the impact that Site C would have on their communities. "Buttering, they're just buttering," commented Della Owens, a member of BC Hydro's Peace Aboriginal Advisory Committee that had put together the First Nations Impacts gallery at the visitor centre, which was boldly titled "They Call It Progress, We Call It Destruction." Owens, who was from Saulteau First Nations, said that it looked as though BC Hydro would repeat the same mistakes it had made with the Bennett Dam. "They are just doing the same thing all over again." As Chief Willson had said on several occasions, "If you're really sorry, stop saying sorry. Stop doing it. [Sorry] doesn't mean anything if you just keep doing it."

Emil McCook, who had travelled along logging roads with a dozen other members of his community for the exhibit's official opening, said that the Bennett Dam and Williston Reservoir remained a painful reminder of what had been stripped from First Nations along the Peace. "We can't change that; we can't bring it back." But they could ensure that First Nations communities would benefit from hydropower and other resources moving forward, he added.

A poised and dignified man who had been the Kwadacha chief for thirty-eight years, McCook wore a cowboy hat and fringed leather vest over a brightly patterned shirt. In a low, husky voice that was almost a whisper, he cautioned that his participation in the gallery opening was by no means an indication of Kwadacha support for Site C. The project would not affect them directly because their reserve was now so far away. Rather, he said, his presence was a show of support for his neighbours who would bear the brunt of the dam's impacts. "We're not in support of Site C. We have to work with our First Nations brothers that live down the valley. Site C is going to be hurtful to our neighbours down here."

The new gallery featured stories from First Nations members, especially elders, about the Bennett Dam's largely undocumented impacts on Indigenous communities. As a committee member, Owens was proud that she had helped ensure that the stories were finally told. Snippets from the stories were posted on the gallery's carpeted walls. "We lost a way of life that used to provide us with so much and we got nothing in return." "It was a death trap for the animals." "Many of our gathering sites and the trails leading to them were destroyed." Chief Willson's mother, Betty, described the valley prior to the dam: "Oh, it was beautiful. A nice big, wide valley. Big, beautiful timber. Just sandbars and cut banks and nice. You [could] run for miles. Lots of animals. You could see all kinds of things. Big bald-headed eagle sitting out there. Now there's nothing left."

One indicator of the reverberating impact of the Bennett Dam on First Nations was the conspicuous absence of the Tsay Keh Dene from the gallery accounts. The nation had decided not to participate, said Chief Dennis Izony, in a statement posted on the impacts gallery wall, "due to the on-going trauma and lasting effects of the creation of the reservoir on our nation and its people that has yet to be resolved."

REGARDING SITE C, the Cache Creek highway relocation remained one of many unresolved issues for First Nations. Despite their efforts, Chief Willson and Tzakoza failed to obtain a satisfactory answer from BC Hydro about protecting the burial grounds, sweat lodge, and cultural area. BC Hydro said in an emailed statement that it was unaware of any burial sites at Cache Creek that would be disturbed by the new highway. The Crown corporation also said in the same statement that it had asked First Nations members to provide the precise locations of any graves in the Bear Flat–Cache Creek area, but they had not been able to do so. The nations said the statement was untrue: they had informed BC Hydro via written messages, maps, and photographs.

BC Hydro's statement, however, highlighted a related issue. As Indigenous peoples were edged out of the Peace River Valley by settlers and relocated to reserves, and as their children were forcibly removed to residential schools in an attempt to destroy their culture and connections to the land, generational ties and traditional knowledge, including about burial places, eroded. As a result, all First Nations members knew of multiple gravesites in the Site C flood zone. Bear Flat, for instance, was among the valley areas where ancestors had been buried. But where, precisely, most of those gravesites lay was difficult to determine when the landscape had been altered to such an extent by agricultural development and infrastructure. One West Moberly First Nations elder called the alterations topocide.

BC Hydro chose its words carefully. The Crown corporation said it viewed the matter of burial grounds as of the utmost importance, and there was no doubt that it did, especially given the recent media firestorm over plans to disturb an Indigenous burial ground on Grace Islet in the Gulf Islands, which resulted in the province paying $5.45 million to buy the disputed property to protect it. BC Hydro reassured the media that the new highway would not "directly affect" the newly discovered Cache Creek gravesite, but it neglected to offer details about how the highway would indirectly compromise it. Most notably, it omitted to say in its statement that Site C would flood the burial site originally marked by a cross, effectively washing away any undetected human remains.

In March 2017, five months after Chief Tzakoza and Chief Willson had sent letters about the Cache Creek burial site to three provincial cabinet ministers and BC Hydro, they finally received a response. Both chiefs were asked to fly to the coast for a meeting to discuss the highway relocation with BC Hydro, the transportation ministry, the BC Environmental Assessment Office (BCEAO), and the government's archaeology branch. Only Chief Willson could make the trip. While he sat in a Vancouver boardroom in late March, trying to broker an agreement that would spare the gravesites and sweat lodge, BC Hydro contractors finished clear-cutting most of the forest in Cache Creek. A few weeks later, only springy wood chip piles and pools of stagnant water remained. Although the known and suspected gravesites – marked off by flagging tape – were spared, many trees in the cultural area were mulched.

Chief Willson described the clear-cutting as "total disregard for our community and culture." He felt powerless to change anything. The only recourse left to the two nations was to file a complaint with the BC Environmental Assessment Office. In August 2017 the office ruled that BC Hydro could not proceed with the new highway bridge over Cache Creek until it had developed appropriate mitigation measures for the burial site and sweat lodge. The same ruling noted that BC Hydro was aware of the importance of the Cache Creek cultural area to local First Nations. Chief Willson and Chief Tzakoza were adamant that the only acceptable mitigation was to move the highway to the other short-listed route, and the issue reached an impasse. Like the Boons and other Peace Valley landowners, Chief Willson and Chief Tsakoza and their nations refused to surrender, no matter the consequences. In Chief Willson's words, the "cowboys and Indians," with their shared love of the land, had far too much to lose to give up now.

6

They Call It Progress,
We Call It Destruction

One small measure of what First Nations stood to lose was packed in two white coolers that Chief Willson and West Moberly elder George Desjarlais lugged to the lawn of the BC legislature on a cloudy day in May 2015. The coolers held a frozen token of the bounty found in Treaty 8 traditional territory: two hundred pounds of bull trout caught with lines and nets. The large fish were headless, tailless, gutted, and wrapped in plastic, but they were by no means ready to grill. Willson held up a silver Hershey's chocolate kiss. That tiny amount, he matter-of-factly told reporters, was the amount of the fish that women of child-bearing age could safely consume about every other day: one large mouthful every week, not even enough for a single meal once a month.

The bull trout had been hooked during a traditional spring fish camp on the Crooked River, a tributary of the Parsnip River, which had flowed into the Peace River before the Bennett Dam was built. The once robust bull trout populations that spawned upstream of the dam had migrated hundreds of kilometres downstream along the Peace River, into Alberta. After the dam blocked their annual passage, bull trout populations along the Peace greatly diminished, with the offspring of survivors continuing to spawn in rivers and streams like the Crooked, migrating only as far as the Williston Reservoir.

The fish in Willson's coolers were of varying sizes but shared one worrisome trait: they were so contaminated with mercury that a hazardous waste permit would have to be obtained before they could be disposed of in the local landfill after the press conference. Willson, a keen fisherman, had a message for any avid fishers who might be contemplating a trip to the Peace, a region promoted to tourists as a world-class fishing destination where there were buckets of rainbow trout, Arctic grayling, bull trout, northern pike, and walleye waiting to be caught. "Typically, you'd be proud of this fish. But we can't eat this."

Willson's family had been catching bull trout on the Crooked River, about 60 kilometres upstream from the Williston Reservoir, for almost a century, ever since the family had moved from north of the Finlay River to Summit Lake, at the head of the Crooked River. Each May, Willson and his brother Clarence joined other Willson-Miller family members at the spring camp to catch fish. They dried, smoked, canned, and froze the trout for their personal consumption, for other family and community members, or, in accordance with custom, for trade or sale. In 2012, two years after the BC government announced it would be seeking regulatory approval to build Site C, the brothers were sitting with their families around a campfire at the Crooked River fish camp when someone asked if the bull trout sizzling on the fire for dinner, wrapped in tinfoil with butter, onions, salt, and pepper, could be contaminated with mercury. The family had heard about Minimata disease, which was caused by eating fish tainted with mercury, so the question stirred alarm. Minimata had long ago been documented in Japan and at the Grassy Narrows Indian reserve in Northern Ontario.

Minimata disease is named after the Japanese seaport where its first outbreak, in 1957, was recorded. It is a neurological syndrome brought on by mercury poisoning. It leaves victims numb, weak, and crippled and reduces vision, hearing, and speech capabilities. In extreme cases it can cause paralysis and death. "Is that what's going to happen to us here?," Chief Willson asked. Everyone had seen a sign at the Hudson's Hope post office warning people to limit their consumption of fish caught in the Williston Reservoir. But what about fish that migrated from the reservoir to rivers like the Parsnip, which joined the Crooked? The Willson-Miller family was sufficiently concerned that, together with the neighbouring McLeod Lake Indian Band, they hired ERM Consultants Canada to test fifty-seven bull trout for mercury.

When forests and agricultural lands are flooded, naturally occurring bacteria called sulfate reducers feed on carbon in the sediment and soil. As the bacteria feed and decompose, they produce methylmercury, the type of mercury of greatest threat to human health. Fish, which are carnivorous and feed from multiple layers of the food web, ingest and accumulate more methylmercury than any other animal. High exposures are associated with changes to the piscine central nervous system, resulting in a wide range of ill effects on fish, including impairment of coordination and feeding ability. Wildlife that eat fish contaminated by mercury, including birds found in the Peace River Valley such as eagles, mergansers, and loons, also face potential neurotoxic effects, as do fish-eating mammals. The health impacts of methylmercury on mammals such as otter, mink, and fisher, which feed on fish in the Peace River, include reductions in immune function, reproduction, and growth, as well as various other ailments.

Most human exposure to mercury comes from eating fish. When methylmercury is ingested, almost the entire amount is absorbed by the human body. Even small amounts of methylmercury can cause such serious and permanent health problems – including impaired neurological development and kidney, lung, skin, and eye ailments – that the World Health Organization ranks it among the top ten chemicals of public health concern. Pregnant women, women of childbearing age, and children under twelve are particularly vulnerable.

When the results came back from ERM, Willson and his band members were stunned. Almost 40 percent of their frozen bull trout were so contaminated with mercury that they exceeded Health Canada's contaminant standard. Almost 98 percent of the samples had tissue mercury concentrations that exceeded the BC government's health guidelines for consumption, based on a 1 kilogram weekly serving – about the weight of a loaf and a half of bread. Participants in First Nations fish camps, which could last for several weeks, would sometimes eat bull trout two or three times a day. The larger fish, the ones most desirable for harvesting, contained the highest mercury concentrations. If you were a woman of childbearing years, each mouthful exceeded weekly guidelines. It was quite likely, then, that members of West Moberly First Nations had been unknowingly consuming levels of mercury that could cause adverse health impacts, especially among sensitive populations. "Everybody's shocked," said Chief Willson. "It shouldn't just be the First Nations who are shocked. This is an issue for everybody."

The chief's family wondered why their nation had never received a direct warning from BC Hydro or the BC government about potentially high levels of mercury in fish, which were a staple in their diet, providing essential nutrients such as protein, Vitamin D, and Omega 3 fatty acids. A mercury advisory for the Williston Reservoir had been in place since 1992, and if you went online to search for it, you would find that the BC government urged limited consumption of fish caught there. But no fish in the Williston Reservoir had been tested for fifteen years prior to the ERM study. Fish in tributary waters like the Crooked River had not been tested for a quarter-century. One independent consultant found that BC, unlike other provinces such as Ontario, Saskatchewan, and Quebec, simply had no strategy or communication protocols for tracking mercury contamination and issuing advisories.

Chief Willson was not impressed when BC Hydro, following widespread media coverage of the press conference on the lawn of the legislature, announced it would study the mercury issue. The damage was done, Willson said, but there was a simple solution to prevent bull trout and other fish species downstream of the two dams from becoming contaminated with mercury, a solution that would allow First Nations to preserve their cultural practices and safely fish for food – the government could halt plans to build Site C. "What we are trying to do now is to not make the problem worse," he explained. "BC and BC Hydro say there are already two dams on there, why not put three ... But because there are already two dams on the river it doesn't make what's left less important. It makes it more important."

BC Hydro's own reports showed that methylmercury contamination from the Site C reservoir would render fish unsafe to eat for twenty to thirty years – long enough to result in the permanent loss of Aboriginal knowledge of choice fishing sites, preferred species, and cultural attachment to specific sites, according to the Joint Review Panel. Furthermore, the enduring contamination of bull trout more than fifty years after the Bennett Dam was built raised the question of whether bull trout in the Site C reservoir would be safe to eat even after thirty years.

Site C's reservoir would also poison mountain whitefish and Arctic grayling, two other fish species important to First Nations. Almost thirty additional Peace River fish species, including rainbow trout, would be similarly affected. Mercury concentrations would peak three to eight years after the creation of the reservoir, but fish might not be safe to eat for more than twenty years after that, meaning that parents would lose the opportunity to bring their children and grandchildren to traditional fishing spots along the Peace River, to teach them family history and respect for the land as well as traditional fishing practices.

According to BC Hydro, First Nations fishing opportunities along the Peace were easily transferable to other locations. However, in its report the Joint Review Panel backed the disturbing conclusion of West Moberly and other First Nations: the tract of river they would lose to Site C was simply not replaceable. Site C, the panel stated, would have a "significant adverse effect" on fishing opportunities for First Nations along the Peace that simply could not be mitigated.

In May 2015, following the revelation that their spring catch was tainted with mercury, the Willson-Miller family did not return to the Crooked River to camp and fish. Nor did they return the following year. The loss of the fish camp, said Chief Willson, was a blow. He recalled how his grandmother had passed on traditional knowledge to his mother, teaching her how to pick wild onions and peavine and cook them with freshly caught fish. "Nowadays what I get to do is to teach my son how to throw contaminated fish back into the river."

THE PLIGHT OF PEACE region caribou was yet another indication of what First Nations had lost to the Bennett Dam. It served, as well, as a red flag for more than one hundred species vulnerable to extinction that would lose critical habitat to Site C. Willson was proud of his nation's extraordinary efforts to protect the region's caribou, and he extended an invitation to visit a model project that the West Moberly and Saulteau First Nations had developed high on a mountain in the Peace.

Little in the world is as cute, and as endangered, as a three-week-old mountain caribou calf. I spotted the mocha-coloured calf from a platform in the trees, in a secret location in an alpine meadow. It looked like a German Shepherd puppy on stilts, with dark eyes, a dark muzzle, and pointy ears too large for its face. The calf took a single, high-footed step, then another. A third step drew it closer to its scraggly mother, who turned her big brown eyes in my direction.

Four other caribou cows soon raised their necks and swivelled leaf-like ears. One had dark scars raked across her back where hair no longer grew. A second calf unbuckled long legs to stand, and then two more appeared like tiny phantoms rising from the thick June grass. The click-click of a camera seemed to attract the ragtag herd. Curious, they ambled closer, and Naomi Owens, land director for Saulteau First Nations, gave us a nod. It was time to leave. As I scooted down the platform ladder, my view panned to an enclosure the size of four football fields. Black geotextile fabric encircled the pen, to prevent wolves and other predators from seeing the prey inside. The compound was ringed by a solar-powered high-voltage fence. Two First Nations shepherds, Steve and Ryan, stood guard around the clock, rifles at hand, on a lonely hilltop isolated by a washed-out road.

For the fast-travelling reindeer species, which were known to migrate more than 50 kilometres in a single day, it had come down to this: an alpine corral with two daily feedings of domestic reindeer pellets. (Terrestrial lichens, hand-picked by volunteers, were fed to the caribou when they arrived and before they were set free.) Just as passenger pigeons had once been so plentiful that their flocks blocked out the sun, so had the caribou roamed the Peace in such profusion that First Nations elders remembered a sea of caribou like "bugs on the landscape." They had once been a food staple for the Dunne-Za, providing sweet dried meat for winter and tasty marrow to spread on bannock, like butter or jam. They had also yielded hide for tents, moccasins, gloves, and leggings, babiche for lacing snowshoes, and antlers for tools such as ice chisels.

In the 1970s, after the Williston Reservoir severed the migration route for the southern mountain population of woodland caribou, their numbers fell so swiftly that elders from West Moberly First Nations issued an edict: no caribou could be hunted until their numbers rose. But the rebound never happened, and caribou numbers continued to plunge at an astonishing pace.

By 2016, according to the BC government, five of the six caribou herds in the south Peace region were imperilled. A seventh, the Burnt Pine group, had died out three years earlier. Another herd, the Klinse-Za (or Moberly) herd, had fallen precipitously from two hundred animals to just sixteen. The penning project represented a last-gasp attempt at survival for this herd – a costly life-support system that just might save it from extinction. The prognosis became morbidly clear when Owens, a biologist, explained that the eleven caribou cows and five newborn calves in the enclosure were not just from the Klinse-Za grouping. They were among the lone survivors of two herds: the Klinse-Za and the Scott. Only thirty-two caribou remained in one amalgamated herd, its members so precious that surviving animals were counted one by one.

Five of the caribou in the combined herd were yearlings from the first crop produced by the penning project, in 2014. Another five calves born in the pen that year died. One became entangled in the wire fence. A second, crossing a highway after it was released, was struck by a vehicle. Wolves killed the other three. The year 2015, when I visited, had not begun much more auspiciously. Two newborns had already perished, one a stillborn, the other arriving on a wet and cold May night and found by the shepherds lying dead in a puddle. Owens, who wore hiking boots and a black sweatshirt that said "Keepers of the Natural Law," quickly put those deaths into perspective. "It's almost zero percent survival rate in the wild."

After the Bennett Dam opened, industrial activity had invaded the caribou habitat, paring down the remaining populations. Logging, mining, oil and gas activity, and, to a lesser extent, wind farms carved up the caribou terrain with roads, seismic lines, wells, pits, and platforms. Eighty percent of the Klinse-za herd's range was disturbed by oil and gas activities between 2003 and 2012; other local herds saw up to 99 percent of their ranges impacted by the industry.

The West Moberly and Saulteau First Nations pleaded with the provincial and federal governments to take action, to no avail. Banking on the future restoration of caribou habitat, they devised their own plan to rescue caribou herds. They would capture pregnant caribou, airlift them to the pen, and hold them there until the calves were strong enough to have a chance of surviving in the wild. Chief Willson said they had no other option. "It's important to our people that we try and do something. We didn't cause this situation, but we can't stand by and watch what's happening."

In 2014, the first year of the penning project, each calf that lived cost $106,000 to save, a figure the two nations hoped to slash significantly in succeeding years. To pay for the project's first year of operations, the First Nations partnered with some of the same resource extraction companies that were logging, mining, and fracking on caribou habitat, or building pipelines through it – including Canfor, Spectra Energy, Walter Energy, Anglo American, TransCanada, and Teck (sponsorship varied from year to year). They also persuaded the BC government, whose promotion of resource development over biodiversity values had facilitated the caribou's demise, to chip in a significant amount of money for the penning enterprise. But core funding shrank as the project's second year approached. So the nations embraced a new form of fundraising to try to save the local caribou herds from extinction: crowdsourcing.

FOLLOWING THE DESTRUCTION of the bison herds during the fur-trading era, and the near eradication of caribou following construction of the Bennett dam, moose took on heightened importance for the local First Nations diet and culture. At one time they were hunted with spear, club, snare, or bow and arrow; today, they are pursued mainly with rifles, on foot or horseback. Just one of the hefty ungulates can provide up to six hundred pounds of meat. A single tanned hide can be turned into almost a dozen pairs of hand-stitched and beaded moccasins to sell. Meat is made into sausages, moose burgers, and steaks or sliced into fillets and smoked over a poplar fire. For special occasions, moose nostrils are cleaned to make a tasty soup with the consistency of clam chowder. Moose "horns" and hooves are used to make lamps and for decorative purposes.

As oil and gas development accelerated, hunters like Marvin Yahey, chief of Blueberry River First Nations, noticed disturbing details about the moose they killed for food and that they were increasingly hard to find. "Twenty years ago, moose were all over the place," Chief Yahey told me in 2016 when I visited a Blueberry River cultural camp. "Nowadays you have to go to the extreme to find one. You hunt for days, on foot, on horseback. The province claims that there's a healthy population. Tell me where it is. I haven't seen it. My elders haven't." When Chief Yahey and other hunters did find a moose, it was rarely edible. "When we gut open those animals, there's huge cysts and lumps on the kidneys and livers and cases where the animals have to be thrown away. The meat is all yellow and tarnished and smells like natural gas. How do you eat that?"

In Beaver, Chief Yahey's language, moose is called *hutaaa*. And from the chief's point of view, what had happened to the hutaaa symbolized everything that was wrong with the industrial development that now mantled his people's traditional territory. Even the Blueberry's reserves had been deeply impacted by development. After surrendering their original reserve near Fort St. John in 1945, when the land was granted to war veterans, the nation was forced off their second reserve in 1979 by a sour gas leak. Sour gas, or hydrogen sulphide, is sometimes released during gas drilling and fracking operations or when gas pipelines break. The colourless, odourless gas is so poisonous that even a small amount can kill people and animals. The leak was so dangerous that Blueberry members fled with only the clothes on their backs, and they were never able to return to their homes. Everything they left behind was destroyed, including their animals, pets, and personal belongings.

The government found a home for the nation at its current location, a reserve 80 kilometres northwest of Fort St. John. There, flares from nearby natural gas operations light up the sky at night, giving the reserve its nickname of "Little Kuwait." The 250 community members who live on the reserve (an equal number live off-reserve) have purchased sour gas monitors to ensure they will have time to evacuate if there is another gas leak. They haul in drinking water because they do not trust their water supply, which they suspect might have become contaminated with harmful chemicals from the unconventional method of gas extraction known as fracking.

Under Chief Yahey's leadership, the Blueberry commissioned a study to determine just how much of their homeland had been impacted by industrial development. Community members could see for themselves that just about every valley, waterway, and mountain in their territory had been carved up for roads, pipelines, industrial logging, oil extraction, or fracking. As Chief Yahey pointed out in a letter to the corporate proponents of yet another liquefied natural gas (LNG) project on Blueberry territory, "wellpads, pipelines, gas plants, seismic lines, dams, transmission lines, cutblocks, access roads, gravel pits, mines, farms, and other developments authorized by the Crown have driven our members away from core parts of our territory towards areas that are harder to access and, in many cases, less productive and unable to support the meaningful exercise of our treaty rights."

But what did the science say? The findings of the Blueberry's eighty-six-page study, based on BC government data, were deeply troubling to the nation. The study indicated that up to 84 percent of the Blueberry River's traditional territory had been negatively impacted by industrial activity. More than three-quarters of the territory lay within a short stroll – 250 metres – from an industrial disturbance such as a fracking well pad.

The Blueberry repeatedly asked the BC government to slow the rate of approvals for new industrial development and to declare some wildlife-rich areas off-limits to new development. But instead of making changes to address the nation's concerns, the Liberal administration accelerated the rate and scale of development. Over a four-year period starting in 2012, Clark's government authorized the construction of more than 2,600 oil and gas wells, 740 kilometres of petroleum development roads, 1,500 kilometres of new pipelines, and almost 10,000 kilometres of seismic lines on the nation's traditional territory. Within the same time frame, almost three hundred forestry cutblocks were harvested. And there was even more. The study documented that even though the Peace region had experienced a disproportionate share of the province's industrial activity, it lacked protected areas compared to other parts of BC. Less than 1 percent of Blueberry River traditional territory was conserved in parks and protected areas, compared to 14 percent province-wide.

"Our very life, our way of existence, is being wiped out," Chief Yahey told a Vancouver press conference when the Blueberry released the report. "It's devastating. It's really impacted my people, culturally but socially also. It puts a lot of stress on a community."

The nation published a time-release map to accompany the report's release. Each industrial activity, including forestry, fracking, and gas wells, along with all waste disposal sites, water extraction sites, and pipelines, had a different coloured dot or symbol. The time release, starting before 1950 and finishing in 2015, showed the accumulation of industrial activity by year, with ever increasing dots and symbols and, as the years went on, a solid blur of colour. By 2015, almost the entire map was coloured in.

Prior to the study, Blueberry River First Nations had launched what Chief Yahey called a "last hope" lawsuit against the provincial government. The lawsuit claimed that the cumulative impacts from extensive industrial development, including Site C, were a violation of Treaty 8.

It also asserted that instead of protecting the Blueberry River First. Nations' interests, the Crown had chosen to undertake or allow land alienation, resource extraction, and industrial activities in traditional territories that were integral to the nation's cultural, economic, and treaty rights. Those activities, the suit claimed, had damaged forests, lands, waters, fish, and wildlife. Hunting, eating moose, harvesting berries and medicinal plants, and teaching children their language while on the land were cited as patterns that, because of the government's actions, could not be sustained. While oil and gas corporations came and went, the people of Blueberry River First Nations had to live with the accumulating consequences of their activities, which the government had sanctioned. "Our backs are against the wall," explained Chief Yahey, the youngest grandson of Charlie Yahey, one of the last Dunne-Za prophets and dreamers. "This was our only way to get them to the table to protect our way of life." Like Chief Willson, the Blueberry chief was quick to point out that his nation was not opposed to development and was only seeking a balance to protect a traditional way of life, with some zones off-limits to industry in order to protect wildlife habitat.

In a costly effort to preserve one of the last areas in their territory where they could still hunt moose, the Blueberry purchased a lodge in a spectacularly biodiverse area called Pink Mountain, in the Rocky Mountain foothills, where they could gather for seasonal cultural camps. The camps, Chief Yahey explained, focused on bridging the gap between youth and elders. Youth were taught moccasin making, beading, drumming, and how to hunt. But even Pink Mountain, a haven for rare and endangered species, especially plants, was under siege despite the Blueberry's best efforts to preserve it. It was the site of intense fracking operations by Progress Energy, a subsidiary of Malaysian-owned Petronas, one of the leading LNG proponents in BC. Expansion of fracking operations in and around Pink Mountain, leading to further landscape fragmentation and habitat loss, would proceed apace if, as planned, a privately built transmission line bisected Blueberry River traditional territory to link fracking projects with hydro facilities on the Peace River, including Site C.

THE RESOURCE DEVELOPMENT blanketing Treaty 8 traditional territory was taking a disproportionate toll on women and girls. Like many other women, Helen Knott, the social worker at the Rocky Mountain Fort camp, had first-hand knowledge of how women's lives had been scarred by unchecked resource development and the myriad changes it was bringing to communities. When Knott was in her early twenties, transient workers from outside the Fort St. John community sexually abused her. "My body, my choices, my rights, my voice, taken that night," Knott wrote in a personal essay about the violent assault, which sent her spiralling into an abyss of alcoholism, cocaine use, and self-loathing so deep that she contemplated suicide.

Knott eventually fled to Edmonton, where she hit rock bottom in a pool of grief. With the help of a treatment program, and comforted by a barrage of supportive messages from friends and family, she swam slowly to the surface and found not just sobriety but her voice. In her job as a social worker, Knott saw first-hand how a resource-based, up-and-down economy harmed women and girls. One day while she was at work, with a client in her car, she tried to help a young, barefoot, Indigenous woman who had been dumped outside Fort St. John's city limits, half-clothed. Knott called the police, but the woman stumbled off before they arrived. The distressing encounter only bolstered her resolve to become an effective advocate for her people, despite her abiding shyness when facing an audience.

No matter how many times Knott spoke publicly, she always felt nervous. She felt it as butterflies in her belly, a tightening of her hands, an awkwardness that belied her poised and confident demeanour. The Amnesty International speaking tour on Site C in early 2016 and the same organization's press conference that Knott joined at the end of the same year were no exceptions. At the press conference, she squeezed a nickel in her hand, willing it to absorb her nervous energy, and reminded herself, as she always did before a talk, that "there is power in speaking the truth."

Amnesty International had been watching Site C with growing apprehension. In November 2015, the international secretary-general, Salil

Shetty, wrote a seven-page letter to Clark and Trudeau that outlined nine reasons why Site C violated basic human rights, including UN guidelines protecting the right to housing. Site C, according to Shetty, did not even come close to meeting UN standards for resource projects on traditional Indigenous lands. Those standards had been codified in the 2007 Declaration on the Rights of Indigenous Peoples, which Canada had signed only in 2016. They included the requirement for free, prior, and informed consent from the affected First Nations and for a thorough exploration of alternative projects. Governments that sought to limit or restrict the rights of Indigenous peoples had to meet a very high standard of justification that included a compelling rationale, the exploration of alternatives for achieving the project's objectives, the minimization of harmful impacts, and the taking of steps to ensure that the benefits to some people would not be outweighed by harm to others. "In Amnesty International's view, the Site C project does not meet any part of this test," the organization wrote.

Amnesty launched an international letter-writing campaign to try to stop Site C that featured Knott, Chief Willson, and others from the Peace. The organization produced a report, "Out of Sight, Out of Mind," and released it at the press conference where Knott spoke. The report documented how northern BC's boom-and-bust economy, including the construction of Site C, was increasing the risk that Indigenous women and girls would experience violence. The rising prices for food and housing that accompanied such development were trapping women in abusive relationships, and the influx of men working long hours at hard jobs and with few roots in the community exacerbated the risks.

Amnesty chose Site C for one of its Canadian human rights campaigns, along with the Northern Gateway pipeline project and the Lubicon Cree's ongoing struggle to prevent further destruction of their traditional territory in northern Alberta. Together, the three resource issue–based campaigns gave Canada the dubious distinction of becoming one of Amnesty's priority countries, along with Mexico, Colombia, Ukraine, and Syria.

WEST MOBERLY FIRST NATIONS and Prophet River First Nation, armed with ample evidence of Site C's negative impacts on the traditional activities guaranteed in Treaty 8, invested substantial amounts of time and money in court cases against the project. A single win in court might have brought the entire project to its knees. But the court cases did not provide the legal returns that they had hoped for. Chiefs Willson and Tsakoza found the verdicts deeply disappointing and even nonsensical, because they left little avenue open to challenging approval for Site C in the legal system before the project was likely too far advanced to halt.

In January 2017 the Federal Court of Appeal determined that treaty rights – protected by the Canadian Constitution – fell outside the scope of the environmental assessment process for Site C and the federal cabinet's decision to issue an environmental certificate for the project. The court had been asked to determine if the cabinet should have ascertained whether Site C's impacts would infringe treaty rights prior to green-lighting the project. It ruled that the cabinet did not have the expertise to make that determination, and it dismissed the case with costs. Five months later, in June 2017, the Supreme Court of Canada declined to hear an appeal. At the same time, it also declined to hear an appeal of the nations' case seeking to overturn Site C's provincial environmental certificate on the grounds that it, too, violated treaty rights. As was customary, the court gave no reason for its decisions. Did Site C infringe on treaty rights? At the start of 2018, the question remained unanswered in the legal realm.

If West Moberly and Prophet River First Nations had followed Blueberry River First Nations' lead and launched a civil suit in federal court, claiming that Site C infringed on their constitutionally enshrined treaty rights, they would have had to wait several years for a court date for a full trial, a trial that could have lasted hundreds of days, with all the expense that entailed. Any favourable civil suit verdict would come far too late to stop the project. The only possible legal means to halt dam construction in the early stages was the path they had taken: challenging federal and provincial environmental certificates and permits for Site C on the grounds that adequate consultation had not occurred

A sign at the Rocky Mountain Fort camp | *Photo by Don Bain, Union of BC Indian Chiefs*

and that treaty rights had been violated. But the Supreme Court ruling had now slammed that door shut. Echoing the landowners' association's similar concern, Chief Willson and Chief Tsakoza questioned the merits of investing in an expensive and time-consuming environmental assessment process if neither the provincial nor the federal government was legally bound to consider its findings and recommendations, much less treaty rights, when approving Site C.

In February 2017 the BC Court of Appeal had also dismissed the nations' court case seeking to overturn provincial permits for Site C (permits such as the authorization to clear the forest around the Rocky Mountain Fort site) on the grounds that they violated treaty rights and that there had been no adequate consultation. The court had been asked

to consider two questions: Was the provincial cabinet required to determine whether Site C infringed upon treaty rights? And were BC
Hydro's consultation and accommodation efforts with the First Nations
adequate? The court determined that provincial ministers were not
legally bound to consider infringement of treaty rights before issuing
the certificate allowing Site C to proceed. It also found that the consultation process for Site C was adequate "in the sense of being reasonable
in all the circumstances."

BC Hydro's frequent use of the word "consultation" embittered Chief
Willson and other First Nations. Battalions of lawyers and consultants
working for the Crown corporation had meticulously documented every
single piece of Site C correspondence sent to the West Moberly and
other First Nations over many years, along with details from each workshop and meeting to discuss the project. By the time the Joint Review
Panel hearings took place, BC Hydro had documented 430 meetings
with twenty-eight Aboriginal groups. That, according to the Crown
corporation, constituted consultation. Consultation did not mean that
dissenting First Nations viewpoints were incorporated into project
planning or that BC Hydro needed to consider alternative clean energy
options, such as geothermal, to Site C, as was repeatedly requested by
Chief Willson's nation. It also didn't matter if some First Nations and
provincial and national groups representing Canada's First Peoples
remained staunchly opposed to Site C on grounds that included the
project's violation of Canada's commitment to the UN Declaration on
the Rights of Indigenous Peoples.

What did consultation mean if you were staring down the throat of a
monster project like Site C? When Liz Logan, then Treaty 8 tribal chief,
appeared before the Site C Joint Review Panel during hearings in Fort
St. John, she recounted how local First Nations were buried under an
avalanche of Site C technical reports prepared by BC Hydro and its consultants. They struggled, with limited time and resources, to respond.
"Consultation is not coming to our office with the volumes of info they
have and say, 'Here, have a look at this and let us know what you think,'
and then leave," Chief Logan told the panel. "We need to be informed

fully and meaningfully, and we need to have the capacity and the expertise to help us make our decisions, and we don't have that."

Chief Willson explained to the panel that "a consultation process with a determined outcome is not consultation – that's an informative session." Later, he called BC Hydro's consultation process a farce. "Their definition of consultation and ours are completely different," Willson pointed out. "We believe consultation is a dialogue, where they listen and we listen. They take into consideration, and make accommodations, for our rights."

Chief Willson said that during Site C consultations, BC Hydro "let us blow off steam and then went and made their decision. Actually, they had already made their decision and then they came to talk to us and told us what their decision was. We asked them to amend it and they said 'No' ... We offered them reasonable accommodation measures. We told them we would work with them with a geothermal plant; we would work with them on a gas-fired power plant. Anything to save the valley, but they refused."

Subdivide and Conquer

The Boons' farm can be described as a treasure trove of human and natural history. Plough the fields or scrape the sandstone banks of Cache Creek and sooner or later you will uncover a fragment from the past: a glistening arrowhead, or perhaps the fossilized remains of an extinct sea creature. If you walk to the Peace River along the rutted tractor path that skirts the Boons' bottom fields, as I did one summer evening when the light was golden and birds trilled from every bush, you will find yourself stepping on another piece of ancient history: some of the world's finest topsoil, 3 metres deep.

In the Cretaceous period, beginning 145 million years ago, marine sediments settled over eons into a large inland sea that covered most of North America's interior. The muddy, silty, sandy sediments hardened into layered rock formations through tectonic processes. Over time, they eroded, and glaciers pounded and ground the rock formations further, creating new sediments and leaving behind an immense amount of unsecured debris. Some of the debris – stretched hundreds of metres high – trapped meltwater into a massive glacial lake called Lake Peace, which included much of what we today call the Peace River Valley. As Lake Peace drained, the newly formed Peace River carried grains of silt and sand and specks of clay from the ancient soil, little by little shaping the broad river flats and fertile benches of the valley we now know.

The loamy soil along the fabled Peace River drew farmers from across Canada. In those days, the Peace was advertised to settlers as Canada's great agricultural "Mecca of the North." One of those settlers was Arlene's grandfather, Lloyd Bentley, who arrived in the Peace in 1914 on horseback, after leapfrogging his way west from Ontario. Bentley rode into the Peace on a black western saddle that Arlene later displayed, faded and tattered, in the family's log museum. At first, Bentley homesteaded near Dawson Creek. Then, in the 1940s and 1950s, he purchased farmland at Bear Flat, where he raised sheep and cattle and planted wheat that grew thick and tall.

The value of the Peace River farmland was once undisputed but is now a matter of debate. One view, held by BC Hydro and the BC government, holds that the agricultural land Site C would destroy – well over 12,000 hectares when land behind the reservoir's stability impact line is included, which is more than double all the farmland in Richmond – is not particularly important either to the Peace region or to the province. A contrasting view – voiced by scientists, food security advocates, and farmers like the Boons – holds that the Site C dam would flood some of the best soil in the country, ideal for growing vegetables because of its unique topsoil composition. At the core of the debate is a critical question: As climate change brings about widespread drought, and parched California almond groves and vegetable farms find a profitable new harvest in the form of solar farms, how will British Columbia feed itself, not just today but in ten years, fifty years, and eighty years?

Harold Steves, the father of BC's visionary Agricultural Land Reserve, asked these questions all the time. Steves was almost eighty when I met him but seemed far younger. He was sprightly and blue-eyed and preferred Twitter to email as a communication tool. He also had an illimitable memory for anything to do with farming in BC. I caught up with him on the century-old Richmond farm his grandparents had established during the First World War to supply the young city of Vancouver with milk. On my way to visit him, on an uncommonly hot and sunny October day, I had a first-hand look at some of the issues that had sent

Ken Boon climbs on his haystacks | *Photo by Garth Lenz*

Steves on a lifelong quest to protect BC's farmland. As I travelled along the Steveston Highway, once a rural road, it became increasingly apparent that agriculture was struggling to keep its place against a far more forceful opponent. The congested highway, named after the Steves family, was lined with shopping malls, crammed parking lots, and new housing developments, with the occasional field of black soil squeezed in between. Even more out of place among the brand name stores were hand-painted signs announcing pumpkins, potatoes, and corn for sale at a scattering of roadside stands.

At the highway's terminus, beside the Richmond dike, which had been built to hold back the Pacific Ocean during storm surges, stood the farm where Steves lived with his wife, Kathy, a former science teacher he had met fifty years earlier while studying agriculture at UBC. Their tall, grey stucco farmhouse, built in 1917, was almost all that was left of what had been a thriving farming community. One of the first houses ever constructed in that area, it now seemed strangely dislocated. The Steves' farm had become an 11-hectare island of fields and heritage buildings, surrounded not by an encroaching Pacific Ocean but by a sea of residential and commercial developments. "Fifty thousand houses," is how Steves matter-of-factly described his contemporary surroundings.

The Steves raised grass-fed Belted Galloway cattle, a hardy breed originally transported to Scotland by the Vikings that looked like a bovine version of a giant panda: black and white with fluffy hair, big eyes, and endearing faces. The couple also sold eggs from their flock of chickens, and heritage seeds from their garden, including Alpha tomatoes, a rare and prolific red tomato plant that creeps along the ground like a zucchini. But their property was no longer a dairy farm, and the untimely loss of the family's business is what had galvanized Steves, as a young university student, to lobby for the creation of the Agricultural Land Reserve.

One morning in 1958, after milking the cows before classes, Steves had sat down to breakfast and some life-changing news. His father, Harold Steves Sr., had applied to the municipality of Richmond for a permit to build a new dairy barn that would meet modern standards as the industry shifted from milk cans to milk tanks. Unexpectedly, his application had been turned down. Unbeknownst to the senior Steves and other Richmond farmers, twelve thousand acres of farmland had been silently rezoned from agricultural to residential. Farmers like the Steves could no longer get permits to invest in farm buildings on their land. And anyone who did not wish to sell their farmland to developers suddenly found their fields of grains and vegetables, and their dairy barns and chicken coops, taxed at far higher residential rates. "Nobody knew how to fight city hall in those days," recalled Steves. "Taxes went up. Farmers sold and left." But Steves' father hung on, even though he was eventually compelled to sell big chunks of his farmland to pay his rocketing tax bill.

The young Steves was so incensed at the turn of events that, at the urging of a friend, he joined the Co-operative Commonwealth Federation, the prairie-spawned, farm-friendly precursor to the New Democratic Party (NDP). Inspired by an initiative in the Netherlands to protect vanishing farmland, Steves soon set about persuading the BC NDP to adopt a policy to create a land reserve. It took him several years, but the unrelenting Steves succeeded. Inspired, he ran for office himself and was elected as Richmond's MLA in the 1972 NDP sweep that saw Dave Barrett become BC's first socialist premier. At that time, the province's top-quality farmland was fast disappearing. As Geoff Meggs and Rod Mickleburgh describe in their book about the Barrett government, *The Art of the Impossible*, BC's best valley-bottom farmland was being gobbled up by subdivisions, "flooded for hydroelectric power, held by speculators, or lost to hobby farms, and more was disappearing at the rate of 4,000 to 6,000 hectares a year." Despite some post-election dithering at the highest levels of the NDP, an outcry from land developers, and a filibuster by the opposition Social Credit Party, the NDP passed landmark legislation in 1973 to create the Agricultural Land Reserve (ALR).

The ALR would "save farmland and the family farm," declared Premier Barrett. But the visionary reserve did far more than protect working farms in the 1970s. The ALR also functioned as insurance against the uncertainties of food imports from places like California, where rivers were being diverted to carry water to industrial farms in desert regions. Some ALR land with rich, deep soils lay fallow, waiting for the day when unforeseen global and ecological events would oblige BC to produce more of its own food. As cities like Vancouver, Kelowna, and Victoria swallowed up surrounding land under the unrelenting pressure of residential and commercial development, the ALR helped ensure that farms remained around their perimeters to help feed the expanding populations, and that the province's most arable soils would be preserved for growing food.

When the newly minted Agricultural Land Commission identified BC's best soils to protect them for future food production, four regions stood out from the rest of the province: the lower Fraser Valley, the Okanagan Valley, the Creston Valley, and the Peace River Valley. The regions enjoy a rare triple advantage: ample available land, alluvial soil that can grow a wide variety of crops, and a favourable climate. Most people do not think of the Peace as prime agricultural land or of the Peace River Valley as the best of that land. But even though the Peace is in BC's north, the valley's protected elevation means that winters are milder than in the surrounding region. The valley's east-west orientation, protection from north winds, and southerly exposure afford it a climate advantage like that of the Okanagan and Creston valleys. In the summer, the Peace River Valley's northerly location brings daylight at four in the morning. And the sky is still dimly lit at midnight, adding enough extra hours of light-fed growth to plants, as though they were on sun steroids, to help compensate for the Fraser Valley's longer growing season.

Eveline Wolterson, a Vancouver soil scientist and physical chemist, describes the Peace Valley's enviable conditions for agriculture as "counterintuitive," adding that the growing climate is "equal, if not slightly better, than in the lower Fraser." According to Wolterson, the Peace River Valley's soil is among the best in Canada, "incredibly, incredibly rich and productive." As the Peace River altered its course over millennia, sometimes flooding, it acted as a giant sifter, leaving behind extremely fine soil in the valley bottom that is part clay, part sand, and part silt – a natural garden bed several metres deep that retains sufficient water to nourish plants yet drains fast enough to prevent roots from becoming waterlogged.

With Wendy Holm, the former president of the BC Institute of Agrologists, Wolterson examined the soil, climate, and economy of the Peace for the Peace Valley Environment Association and the BC Women's Institute. The duo concluded, using a 1980 BC Hydro consultants' report that evaluated Site C's potential impact on agriculture and food production, that the Peace River Valley has the capacity to produce high-yielding fresh fruit and vegetables to meet the nutritional requirements of more than one million people. "That's a conservative estimate," Holm told me. "We have this breadbasket sitting right there, and it's closer to Vancouver than [California's] Central Valley. As California dries up, as fossil fuel and transportation costs go up, we are beyond vulnerable in importing [such a] high percentage of our fruits and vegetables. What are we thinking?"

The Peace is one of the agricultural areas in Canada expected to benefit, not suffer, because of global warming. Modelling by scientists at the

University of Victoria indicates that climate change will result in a
noteworthy increase in the number of frost-free periods and growing-
degree days in the Peace. Also, prolonged drought will likely hit other
areas hard, but not the Peace, which will receive more precipitation
with climate change. In BC Hydro's own words, global warming is predicted to bring about "a significant improvement in climatic capability
for agriculture" in the Peace River Valley. According to BC Hydro, those
improvements could be so pronounced that Class 2 and Class 3 farmland in the valley will become Class 1, further enhancing future agricultural worth.

TEN DAYS AFTER THE Rocky Mountain Fort camp was dismantled, BC
Hydro summoned the Boons and about a dozen other Cache Creek
landowners to a meeting in Fort St. John. The meeting confirmed what
the Boons and their closest neighbours already suspected: the Crown
corporation had chosen the highway route that would cut right through
some of their best fields, their homes, the First Nations cultural area,
and the family's Bear Flat campground.

While the news was one more worry for Ken and Arlene, they and
other Cache Creek property owners assumed they would be able to
remain in their homes for at least several more years. Preliminary construction work for Site C had been under way for less than eight months
and was slated to continue for at least eight more years. Court cases
against the project were still waiting to be heard, and a scheduled provincial election was drawing near. Anything could happen over the next
few years, and the Boons and many others believed the dam could still
be stopped.

Two weeks after the Fort St. John meeting, the Boons and other
Cache Creek landowners received an email from their shared lawyer,
informing them that BC Hydro "required" Cache Creek landowners
to sign over their properties for the highway realignment by the end
of that year, just nine months distant. If landowners refused to negotiate a price with BC Hydro, the utilities company would set the price
for them. Either way, they would soon be expropriated; it was just a

question of the terms. "It was a shocker," remembered Ken. "We didn't know they wanted us out by Christmas."

The landowners' association had hired an expropriation lawyer, who advised its members to seek a framework agreement with BC Hydro. That way, BC Hydro could not pay two landowners different amounts for land of equal value or for equivalent disturbances. But BC Hydro had adamantly refused to discuss any sort of framework agreement, and that backed the Boons and other Cache Creek landowners into a corner. They would be unable to negotiate collectively.

BC Hydro justified the surprise timeline by saying it was "moving up the valley" and that Cache Creek was "one of the first areas affected by the highway realignment." But Arthur Hadland, the local farmer and former Peace River Regional District director who had been arrested for blocking a road to the Site C construction site, believed there was another motive for compelling the Boons to leave their property many years earlier than they had anticipated. Hadland pointed out that if the outspoken president of the Peace Valley Landowner Association were forced from his land, others would feel demoralized and be less inclined to fight long and hard to stay on their own properties, which landowners knew BC Hydro would expropriate if they did not voluntarily approach the Crown corporation and offer to sell. "It's divide and conquer," Hadland explained. "The landowners have been a pretty solid group. But just like any organization if you cut the head off you will lose the power. They just want to diminish the power of the landowners."

Based on legal advice, that spring the Boons and the other Cache Creek residents reluctantly signed the access agreements that BC Hydro demanded, allowing the Crown corporation to access their land for geotechnical, wildlife, and heritage studies, in exchange for modest financial compensation. Ken and Arlene said they didn't have a choice in signing because Hydro had the legal right to access their land, with or without their agreement.

The couple subsequently saw a map of their farmland with seventy-three drilling sites marked on it. They then had to put up with noisy and intrusive drill rigs right outside their kitchen window, along with excavators, pumps, compressors, water tanks, and support vehicles, as drill holes were bored around their house and into the banks of Cache Creek to test the land for geotechnical stability. They also had to deal with BC Hydro contractors that Ken said "should be required to take a course in Sensitivity 101," a fluid leak on one of their planted fields, and two security investigators parked in a truck at their end of their driveway without the Boons' prior consent. One of the investigators was the same man – Sten – who had compiled evidence against the Boons and four other Peace Valley residents for BC Hydro's ongoing lawsuit against some of the people involved in the winter camp at the Rocky Mountain Fort site. Ken and Arlene felt that they were being monitored in their own home.

A letter the Boons received from BC Hydro pointed to the haste with which drilling work was being conducted on their land in anticipation of the highway work. "To complete the work on your property as quickly as possible, it is anticipated that investigations would occur up to 10 to 12 hours a day, and up to 5 to 7 days a week, with flexibility to accommodate residents and businesses," the letter stated. Not long after, Arlene chased away a crew on a Sunday when they arrived to work while the family was celebrating her mother's eighty-first birthday.

When Site C was first planned in the mid-1970s – when Arlene was barely a teenager – the Bentleys were one of fifty-five families, many of them multi-generational, who were living in the flood reserve. At the time, Arlene's grandfather and eight other valley landowners owned the largest parcels of land that would be affected by the dam. Many of them, including Bentley, refused to talk to BC Hydro, which needed to access Bentley's farm or a neighbouring farm to conduct a study on Bear Flat's microclimate.

The archives at the North Peace Museum in Fort St. John offer a glimpse into BC Hydro's long-standing strategy for dealing with valley landowners. The evidence resides in a binder of BC Hydro inter-office memos that sits, incongruously, in a box of materials from the BCUC investigation into Site C in the early 1980s. It is clear from the memos, written in the 1970s, that the task of selling Site C to the local community and proceeding with studies on private land had bogged down to the point that little progress was made, despite great effort.

In one memo, a senior properties official for BC Hydro posits that by buying out landowners willing to sell, including those who might not be prepared to say so publicly, BC Hydro "will remove much of the anxiety and fear of the unknown from the realm of the rancher and transfer it to the broad shoulders of the Corporation." The memos show that BC Hydro subsequently developed a land acquisition policy for Site C, announcing that it would purchase properties in the Site C flood and erosion zone (what it called the "safe line" at the time) at fair market value. Sellers would have an option to lease back their lands indefinitely. To reassure anyone who might be contemplating a sale, landowners were given the right of first refusal to buy their land back later at the original purchase price should the Site C project be terminated. Some memos voice concerns from senior BC Hydro officials that the strategy might be viewed publicly as "divide and conquer"; but ironically, other memos posit that if just three of the larger acreages could be purchased, the remaining landowners might be prompted to follow suit.

In contrast to BC Hydro's later land acquisition modus operandi, which the Boons and other valley landowners found heavy-handed and inconsiderate (the word "bullying" was often used to describe it when I spoke with different landowners), BC Hydro in the 1970s appeared to sympathize with the uncertain future faced by valley ranchers and farmers. "It is important that Hydro consider the position of the ranchers and farmers in the Peace Valley who view the prospect of Hydro taking the heart of their operations (the cultivated bottom lands), leaving them with a nonviable remainder," one senior Hydro employee pointed out in 1976. Accordingly, Hydro agreed to buy entire properties that would be affected by Site C instead of purchasing only the acreage that would be destroyed or affected by the dam's reservoir. This was in notable contrast to the Crown corporation's approach after Site C was approved, which entailed expropriations that left ranchers and farmers like the Boons with small and sometimes separated pieces of their former properties, along with many questions about whether it would still be economical to farm their remaining holdings.

The land acquisition policy of the 1970s worked like a charm. By the spring of 1977, five of the valley's largest ranchers had indicated their willingness to be bought out by BC Hydro. Together, these ranchers owned 40 percent of the private land that would be affected by Site C. As BC Hydro had hoped, other ranchers and landowners soon followed their lead and sold all or part of their properties. Even the hostile Bentley was swayed. On August 2, 1978, Bentley signed a deal with BC Hydro, selling one piece of his land for $48,000 and a second piece for almost $36,000. The uncultivated range and bush land had not been utilized by his farm operation, and he figured he might as well get some money for it. Decades later, Ken and Arlene leased some of the land back from BC Hydro.

Those two sections of the Bentley homestead were among the $4.5 million worth of land purchases for Site C that BC Hydro made during the 1970s, when the total cost of all necessary Site C land purchases was estimated at $15 million (about $66 million in 2017 dollars). That was followed, in the 1980s, when the utilities commission first reviewed Site C, by another $3 million worth of land purchases for the project. Throughout the 1990s, when it appeared that Site C was indeed "dead," the Crown corporation spent only $16,000 buying land for Site C. But after the election of the Liberal government to a second term in office in 2005, land purchases accelerated.

In the four years before Site C received final approval in December 2014, BC Hydro had spent more than $20 million quietly buying up valley property for the dam – an indication of the Crown corporation's high rate of confidence that the project would proceed. To put that price tag into perspective, in 2017 the cost of an average three-bedroom de-tached single-family home in Hudson's Hope – the district most affected by the dam – was about $220,000.

By 2012, even before BC Hydro began to expropriate some of the dozens of additional properties it still required for Site C, the public utilities company owned almost 1,000 hectares of Peace Valley farm-land. Notably, the landholdings included more top-class farmland within Site C's "Project Activity Zone" than the farmland owned by the Boons and all the valley's other farming families combined.

IN JULY 2015, as four hundred people gathered in the Boons' bottom field for the tenth annual Paddle for the Peace, an unobtrusive man with wavy grey hair stepped up to the microphone. He spoke emotionally about his boat trip down the river, past the leafy islands that shelter moose, deer, and elk each spring when they gave birth, islands that would disappear, he later pointed out, as the Site C flood waters rose. "This land can grow anything," the man said. "This valley is too import-ant for us to be filling it with water. This river has given enough. This valley does not need to give another inch. Let's not cover it with bloody water. That's a sin against humanity – and I will not have it."

The statement might not have been so powerful, especially given the nature of the gathering, had it not been for the identity of the speaker. Only two months earlier, Richard Bullock had been the government-appointed chair of BC's Agricultural Land Commission, a post he had held for five years. As chair of the supposedly independent commission, Bullock, an Okanagan farmer, was tasked with preserving agricultural land and enabling farming in BC. But that May, with only five months remaining in his contract, Bullock had been fired by the government in a thirty-second phone call.

Several weeks before his summary dismissal, BC's cabinet had removed the largest tract of land from the Agricultural Land Reserve that had ever been deleted. It happened on a Friday afternoon in April with no fanfare, no press release, and no public announcement. Almost 4,000 hectares of protected Peace River Valley farmland, an area the size of ten Stanley Parks, suddenly vanished from the ALR. That land included some of the province's most productive soils and the best farmland in all of northern BC. The Boons were certain that it included their river-side fields at Bear Flat, where Bullock stood that day, but nobody knew that for sure because a map of land deleted from the reserve was being withheld from the public. Two years after the deletion, when the provincial government expropriated their property, the Boons still had not received any notice from the government that their working farmland had been excluded from the ALR.

If you are Ken and Arlene Boon or some other ordinary BC farmer and you want to remove some or all your land from the ALR, there is a strict, time-consuming procedure you are obligated to follow. As noted by the Joint Review Panel, the procedure includes but is not limited to "a lengthy formal application, posting of signs, advertisements, a public information meeting, possibly a hearing and a decision by the [Agricultural Land] Commission. The proposal might also require local government approval."

If you are BC Hydro, you do not have to do any of this: the laws and rules established to promote food security and a thriving agricultural sector in BC simply do not apply. A clause in the Agricultural Land Reserve Act allows cabinet to remove land from the ALR without consultation, scientific justification, or a public hearing, if it deems the removal to be in the public interest. In the end, all it took was a letter to BC Hydro from BC energy minister Bill Bennett assuring the Crown corporation that it would not have to apply to the Agricultural Land Commission (ALC) to have farmland it needed for Site C withdrawn from the reserve. Bullock and his commission were not even informed. The ALC chair read about Bennett's letter to BC Hydro in the *Globe and Mail*.

I met up with Bullock five months after he had been fired, over tea at his friend's house in a seaside neighbourhood in Victoria. His friend, it turned out, was a retired BC Hydro executive who had spent most of his career building large dams, including in the Peace. Bullock, in contrast, was born into an Okanagan farming family and had dedicated his entire life to agriculture. In his seventies, Bullock still owned and operated his family's Okanagan plum and cherry orchard along with a cattle ranch. He was a former director of the Canadian Federation of Agriculture and chair of the BC Farm Industry Review Board: hardly a novice farmer who had just stepped into the political muck. He was also the former president of the BC Fruit Growers' Association, BC Tree Fruits Ltd., and SunRype Products Ltd., appointments that carried him to far-flung corners of the globe to promote BC fruit sales. "Am I pissed off?" Bullock said about his dismissal. "No. Am I disappointed? Yes. I was determined that we were going to make good decisions. We weren't going to make quick decisions, and that goes against this government's philosophy."

Bullock said that several cabinet members had spoken to him informally and asked what he would do if the proposal to delete ALR land for Site C was referred to the commission. Bullock stressed that due procedure would be followed. Public hearings would likely take place throughout the province. All British Columbians would be able to comment on the proposed removal of the Peace Valley's prime soils from the ALR, because it was an issue that could affect everyone in the province. "I was very frank that we would go to public hearing on something of that scale. And that was the end of the discussion. They no more wanted that than they wanted to fly to the moon."

The month before Bullock lost his job, the Liberal government had taken another hatchet to the ALR. In a move condemned by scientists, food security organizations, and the National Farmers Union, the government split the province's ALR land into two different zones, each with different rules. Zone 1 held ALR land in the south of the province, while Zone 2 held ALR land in the north. The rules for removing ALR land in Zone 1 remained strong, but new, weaker rules for Zone 2 made it far easier to splinter off farmland in BC's interior and northern regions, including in the Peace. Agricultural land in Zone 2, for instance, could now be used to support the oil and gas industry or for different kinds of uses such as RV parks and rodeos.

Bullock opposed the decision. Farmland in the north of the province had the capacity to produce just as much food as farmland in the south, he explained in a letter to the government. In terms of sheer land mass, the large majority of BC's best agricultural lands were in the north, Kootenay, and Interior regions, including in the Peace River Valley. The new system, the ALC chair said, was unfair. Bullock's letter followed

another that he had sent to the government, this one noting his dis-
pleasure at the Liberals' decision to allow foreign investors to buy up
BC farmland and plant trees in the ALR. Their new harvest was not
apples or hazelnuts; instead, with the government's blessing, quality
farmland was now being used to plant fast-growing pine trees to silo
corporate carbon credits.

The Site C land reserve deletions, the new two-zone farmland policy,
and the conversion of farmland to tree farms sharply undercut the ALR's
capacity to protect farmland. When it was established in 1973, the ALR
had been the envy of other North American jurisdictions. But the land
reserve was now being sliced and diced by a selection of sharp policy
knives. No longer guided by sound science, the ALR was now piloted
by political expediency.

WHEN I MET CLAY and Katy Peck in the late fall of 2015, they struck me as
just the type of young farmers that BC's Liberal government said it
wanted to support to ensure "a reliable food source for years to come."
They were highly educated, industrious, and passionate about the upcoming launch of their organic fruit and vegetable business to serve the
area around Fort St. John. They had a big leg-up in the business world.
They owned their Peace Valley farm (a wedding present from Clay's
family) outright, and they had also been gifted a stud stallion to kick-
start one of their other ventures – a horse-breeding business.

The enterprising Pecks were eager to discuss what they were doing
to prepare for the certification of their organic market garden. They
also wanted to talk about their plans to investigate and experiment
with permaculture, community-supported agriculture, and the idea
of a food forest. Their first few summers of planting had gone far better
than expected. "There was basically nothing we put in the ground that
we couldn't grow," said Katy, a blogger with a marketing degree and
an MBA in green business, who was expecting the couple's first child.
"We grew corn, melons, field tomatoes ... I planted everything from
hazelnuts to goji berries. We have a microclimate here because we get
so much sun."

The Pecks' modular home and 65-hectare farm were high enough and far enough from the Peace River that they were not included in BC Hydro's 2012 list of thirty-four farms that would be impacted by Site C. But the couple, along with dozens of other Peace Valley farmers, stood to lose sizable tracts of their farmland to Site C in various other ways, along with crops and income. The reservoir would contain so much water that its weight would cause groundwater levels to rise for 2 kilometres around its perimeter. Rising groundwater, the Pecks learned, would result in decreased crop yields and restrictions on the range of viable crops they could grow. As the reservoir filled, it would displace wildlife like deer and elk, and the ungulates would move uphill onto farmland like theirs in search of food, potentially adding to crop loss. Higher groundwater levels could also contaminate well water, a resource on which many valley families, including families not directly affected by Site C, depended. BC Hydro was obligated to test hundreds of existing wells throughout the dam's lifespan and find alternative sources of potable water if necessary.

The Pecks and other valley residents also feared local climate change. The reservoir's sheer size would create conditions for a mini global-warming experiment. The new water body would boost the annual average temperature by up to one degree Celsius in every direction within a 1 kilometre radius. It would generate higher winter temperatures and lower summer ones. At Bear Flat, where the Boons lived, average summer temperatures would likely dip by more than three degrees. Precipitation and winds in the valley would increase, and fog would shroud parts of the valley, including the Fort St. John airport, for up to 118 extra hours each year.

The increase in precipitation would be most noticeable in the late summer and fall, just as any remaining valley farmers would be drying crops for market. "If there's fog, the crops could spoil, and it might be a total loss," explained Clay, an environmental scientist and articling agrologist who worked for the oil and gas industry in addition to farming. (His wife affectionately described him as a "tall dark cowboy.") And to top it off, about one-quarter of the Peck's productive land fell within

Farmer and long-time valley resident Ross Peck fishes in the Peace River |
Photo by Garth Lenz

the dam's stability impact zone, the area likely to be eroded by the reservoir over time. Almost 6,000 hectares of valley farmland was in that
zone, in addition to the 6,500 hectares of agricultural land that BC Hydro
stated would be permanently lost to Site C.

Clay's uncle, Ross Peck, faced a similar dilemma. His grandparents,
Ross and Margaret Darnall, had been dispossessed of their land at the
mouth of the Carbon River, a tributary of the Peace, when the Bennett
Dam was built. After a lifetime of hard work, farming and trucking in
the Peace, the Darnalls had purchased the Carbon River property in the
late 1940s, and it had become a summer retreat for friends who fished
and played bridge. BC Hydro's final offer was about $6,000 for a quarter
section of land and for buildings with river frontage on both sides.
Darnall claimed that the timber on his land alone was worth more than
that. The land was expropriated and, following an extensive court battle,
Darnall was awarded a $20,000 settlement, a good portion of which
went to pay his legal bill.

Ross Peck and his wife, Deborah, now stood to lose their best agricultural land – and possibly their home – to Site C. The Pecks owned 130 hectares of agricultural land just below Clay and Katy's, snuggled between the Tea and Wilder creeks, just upstream from the Rocky Mountain Fort site. For more than fifty years, Ross and Deborah had run a grain and livestock operation in the area, and they grew wheat and canola on their river bench holdings. Some of their farmland was in Site C's flood zone, some was in the stability impact zone, and some would have a new BC Hydro statutory right-of-way placed over it. "With flooding, slumping, and erosion we question if there would be anything left on our lower Wilder property that is suitable for grain crops," Ross Peck told me. "Is it really worth it if we've only got five or ten hectares of field left?"

The Pecks lived in a custom-built log house near Farrell Creek, an hour's drive up the valley from the bulk of their family's agricultural landholdings. They too faced an uncertain future in their sunny home, high on a Peace River cliff. Looking at BC Hydro maps, the Pecks had discovered that their house would eventually come to roost near the edge of the eroded cliff overlooking the reservoir and what little would remain of their tremendous view of the forest on the river's far bank. Even though their house would still be habitable after the valley was flooded, how could they ever be compensated for the other losses? Peck, an affable man in his sixties with a weathered face, showed me the thin line that he and Deborah would be walking between safety and disaster. "They told us the house will be fine but our cabin will fall in," he explained, pointing to a guest cabin about 20 metres from the house. "Yes, we sleep in our house, but we live on our land."

Of concern to Ross was the wave impact line, marking the distance to which waves caused by landslides would reach, waves generated by the heavy hand of the reservoir scraping away at the river's finely textured banks of silt, sand, clay, and, in places, shale bedrock. Landslides were a familiar sight along the Peace River and its tributaries. Most were small and inconsequential, but Peck remembered others that were not. The May 1973 Attachie slide had hurled 14.7 million cubic metres of debris a distance of almost 1 kilometre, damming the Peace River for twelve hours and generating a wave so large it snapped trees more than 20 metres above the river's water level. And on August 20, 1989, a slide at the Halfway River had sent 3.6 million cubic metres of debris into the Peace, blocking it for six hours and sending the river north across a vegetated floodplain. More recently, in 2016, it had been revealed that a series of landslides at Lynx Creek, upstream from the Pecks, had sent a plume of toxic metals, including arsenic, barium, cadmium, lithium, and lead, into the Peace River. The destruction had gone unchecked for two years, depleting insect and fish life downstream. Reservoir clearing and the reservoir itself would further undermine the unstable valley soils, and Peck was certain that landslide frequency would accelerate in a post-Site C environment.

Not even geologists studying the valley understood exactly what the damage would be. One measure of their uncertainty concerned the new highway bridge scheduled to be constructed over the Halfway River to replace the existing bridge, which was in the flood zone. The chances that a landslide-induced wave would seriously damage the new bridge and its support structure are so great that BC Hydro factored the cost of "mitigating the effects from the impact" into its original half-billion dollar estimate for the highway relocation budget.

The Pecks' precarious future mirrored that of dozens of other valley residents, including the Ardills, a family who raised premium grass-fed beef. The family had lived in the Peace ever since Renee Ardill's Irish-born grandfather had received a soldier's land grant after fighting for Canada in the First World War. He and his wife, Betty, had cleared the land for cattle and grain crops, turning up arrowheads and spear points that spoke of the people who had lived on the land before them. The Ardill ranch, which included more than a half dozen homes, sat atop a Peace River bluff. "I expect BC Hydro will think we should relocate, but they haven't flat out said so," said Ardill. "Their idea of consultation is 'This is what we're going to do. We don't really care what you think about it.' In my mind, consultation is a two-way process ... If Site C is such a good deal, it should be right out in the public eye, and everybody should know what's going on. They shouldn't have to hide things."

Like the Boons and many other farmers, the Ardills grew a variety of vegetables and fruits (corn, tomatoes, cucumbers, cantaloupes) but only for their own consumption. It had simply not been economical for Peace Valley farmers to invest in vegetable and fruit production. According to Bullock, the former ALR head, rather than sinking money into long-term ventures like growing vegetables for commercial sale, farmers living in the shadow of the Site C flood reserve had chosen to grow yearly crops like hay or canola, or to raise cattle, focusing on farming endeavours that required far fewer inputs and investments. "Why would you make that commitment if the end result in a short period of time is that you're going to be under water?" he asked. "You can pick the cattle up and move them. You can't pick up a vegetable farm and move it willy-nilly someplace else." Ardill said it pained her to see so much valley farm-land, including parcels owned by BC Hydro, so under-utilized: "It's disgraceful the way the land has been allowed to just sit there. The potential is enormous."

Bullock and Steves, along with other food security advocates and scientists, warn that the day will come – sooner than we might care to think – when the price of imported food spikes so high it will become far more economical for Canadians to sow their own underutilized agricultural land instead of importing food from California and even farther-flung locales, especially given that state's susceptibility to drought. Three-quarters of all the lettuce sold in BC comes from California, along with 95 percent of the broccoli. It takes 20 litres of water to grow a single head of broccoli, and lettuce is also a heavy slurper, with a single head swallowing 13 litres of water as it matures. One study predicts that British Columbians will pay 34 percent more for fruits and vegetables if drought continues in California – broccoli alone could jump to seven dollars a pound by 2019. Extrapolate from that, and the average BC household's monthly food bill will rise by $720 a year. If you live in the province's north, where a weekly basket of fresh produce costs three times as much as it does in Vancouver, the bite out of your bank account will be even bigger.

Steves, too, predicts that food prices will likely double and quadruple. "So many agricultural regions around the world are getting hit by floods, drought. We can't depend on them. Instead of trucking food all the way from California and Mexico, we need to grow it here." As we try to slash carbon emissions to slow climate change, that harbinger of drought, growing more food locally will help. A Granny Smith apple picked in New Zealand and eaten in Victoria, for instance, travels more than 11,000 kilometres, with a correspondingly heavy carbon footprint.

As the mighty pythons of development and climate change tighten their squeeze, the world's arable land continues to shrink at an accelerating rate. At the Paris climate talks in December 2015, scientists released a report showing that the earth had lost one-third of its arable land in just forty years, and Canada is no exception. Over the past four decades, it lost an area of agricultural land the size of Vancouver Island, the equivalent of almost 4 million hectares. In BC, despite the ALR, which includes only a portion of potential farmland, around 95,000 hectares of farmland has vanished since Steves won his quest for farmland preservation. That includes more than 5,000 hectares of Fraser Valley's once protected farmland (an area the size of Bowen Island) that was paved over and filled in between 1974 and 2013.

David Montgomery, a geomorphology professor at the University of Washington, has documented how the loss of agricultural soils has contributed to the decline and fall of ancient societies such as the Greeks and Romans. His conclusion: "We are running down our stock of fertile topsoil, the one thing we absolutely need to support civilization in the long run." In *Dirt: The Erosion of Civilizations,* Montgomery shows how the lifespan of civilizations has largely been determined by the health and abundance of their soil, what Charles Darwin called the "skin of the earth." "Oil is what most of us think of as a strategic material," Montgomery writes. "Yet soil is every bit as important in a longer time frame."

According to Montgomery, most civilizations before ours lasted eight hundred to two thousand years, about the amount of time it took them to exhaust one to three feet of topsoil. Societies fared slightly better in fecund river valleys like the Peace. Civilizations prospered only as long as their soil remained productive or there was new land to cultivate. Only civilizations that learned how to conserve their soil, or that were blessed with a natural environment that rejuvenated soil, survived longer than thirty to seventy generations. The world can't afford to lose any more farmland, says Montgomery: "Fifty years from now every hectare of agricultural land will be crucial."

INSTEAD OF ASCRIBING monetary value to the potential for large-scale, diversified agriculture in the Site C flood and erosion zone, BC Hydro focused on the dollar value of crops, mainly canola and hay, grown in the flood zone, including on its own land. That amount was small by any standards, a mere $220,000 a year. BC Hydro did not include crops from fields that farmers like the Pecks feared would no longer be viable for farming once their land was carved up and BC Hydro's planned right-of-ways were instituted. Based on that figure, BC Hydro calculated a $2.2 billion loss to agriculture over the 100-year lifespan of the Site C dam. When it came time for the Joint Review Panel to examine Site C's impact on agriculture, the panel concluded that Site C's impact on farming in BC would be "negligible," a statement that scientists and food security advocates like Holm and Steves continue to challenge.

To "mitigate" the loss of agricultural land for Site C, BC Hydro customers will shoulder the cost of a $20 million Peace agricultural compensation fund established by the Crown corporation. The fund will be available to the wider Peace region for everything from 4H projects to irrigation schemes that have nothing to do with the valley itself. It is not earmarked to assist long-time family farming operations like those of the Boons or the Pecks, or for valley areas that will be directly affected by Site C.

For the Boons and other farmers and ranchers in the Site C flood and sloughing zones, no amount of money will ever begin to make up for the loss of some of Canada's richest farmland. They tell us that while their crops may not be worth much right now in terms of actual dollar value, the valley's fertile, sun-soaked farmland should be anything but disposable for our throwaway society. As prize-winning valley farmer Colin Meek explained in a letter to Trudeau, asking him to stop construction of Site C: "I came back to work on the family farm from the oil patch because I realized that I'll never be able to eat oil, drink liquefied natural gas, or breath electricity but that I can help feed the world and clean the air with the food I grow."

The Nature of the Peace

On her last day in the Peace River Valley, botanist Erica Wheeler finally spotted the elusive species she had sought. There it was, in full flower, on the Boons' farm. The brittle prickly pear cactus, *Opuntia fragilis*. It looked as though someone had stuck a frilly yellow rose on a stubby cactus spiked with needles. With a nod from Arlene Boon, who had led Wheeler through native grassland to this concealed spot along Cache Creek, the botanist scrambled down the sandy embankment to survey her find.

The flower's outside petals were almost sheer, its centre deep yellow like a yolk. Wheeler, the botany collections manager at the Royal BC Museum in Victoria, needed only a second's prompting from Arlene to pull out her sampling knife. Carefully, she sliced the cactus near its base, leaving roots to grow other stems, fruit, and flowers. Then she tucked the sample into her plastic collections bag. It would be dried in a press for several days and shipped back to the museum by Greyhound bus, in the company of hundreds of other plant specimens that Wheeler and other museum botanists had collected during five memorable days of sampling in the Site C flood and erosion zone.

It reassured Arlene to know that somewhere in a metal cabinet in the Royal BC Museum 1,300 kilometres away, a small token of her family's land would remain for future scientists to study. She asked Wheeler to record that the cactus had come from Cache Creek, whose lower reaches – a full 9 kilometres – would be swallowed by the Site C reservoir. The area around the creek had yielded natural gems many times already: a sliver of woolly mammoth tusk, the fossilized bark and cast of a cycad tree trunk, fossil shells of ancient gastropods and clams, the tracks of an ancient three-toed reptile. Some had been found in the nine hundred areas of "paleontological sensitivity" that would be lost to Site C, three hundred of which were classified in BC Hydro documents as highly or extremely sensitive.

Almost a decade earlier, in a natural gully on the Boon farm, one of Wheeler's colleagues, Richard Hebda, the Royal BC Museum's curator of botany and earth history, had stumbled upon the eleven-thousand-year-old fossilized bones of a dozen taiga voles, a species unknown in BC in historic times. The hamster-sized vole, with brightly coloured cheeks and a delicately pointed snout, is plentiful in the Far North, where it burrows in boreal forests. But on only one other occasion had taiga vole fossils been discovered so far south in Canada, suggesting that the furry species was at the fringe of its range in the Peace River Valley even in the Late Pleistocene epoch. In this regard, the taiga vole shared a curious affinity with the cluster of cacti that Wheeler, the prickly-pear sample now safe in her collections satchel, stooped carefully to view.

Wheeler was not interested in the brittle prickly pear cacti on the Boons' farm because the species is rare or endangered. Indeed, it is common in western North America and has a generous range that extends from Washington State to Wisconsin and from Texas to BC. First Nations in the Peace Valley boil its inner stem for soups and mix it with berries for baking. They also use the cactus to concoct a cough medicine. What piqued Wheeler's scientific interest was its remarkable location: on the dry skirt of a Peace River tributary, at a latitude of 56.17°N, farther north than Moscow.

The prickly-pear populations on the threatened slopes of the Peace River and its tributaries are part of the northernmost occurrence of this species. They also represent the northernmost of any of the planet's 1,800 species of cactus (*Cactaceae*).

According to Wheeler, the fragile prickly pear populations in the Peace River Valley are "a unique slice of global *Cactaceae* biodiversity." She wrote about her find in a national newsletter for Canadian scientists, highlighting that "this is a good reminder that it's not only the rare and the beautiful that deserve our attention but also the tenacious outliers that have a story to tell about life on the edge."

Scientists are discovering that the Peace River Valley is home to a surprising number of tenacious outliers. Some, like the prickly pear cactus – and the carnivorous purple pitcher plant also known as "turtle socks" and wild chives with their distinguishing purple flower spheres – are recognized far outside the scientific community. Other botanical outliers, including rare mosses and lichens with endearing names like snow-white dimple, are known mainly in botany circles. But however famous or obscure they are, these plants share a common bond: they represent important range extensions for the species or the family.

In addition to gems long known, the Site C flood zone constantly reveals new biological treasures. Since 2014, scientists have discovered outlier bee, insect, spider, and snail species, including a species of spider previously known only from records in Florida and New York State. Studies that BC Hydro was obliged to conduct in preparation for Site C found a green-eyed dragonfly named Whitehouse's Emerald that had never been spotted east of the Rocky Mountains before it was encountered in the Site C flood zone. A second dragonfly species, the Crimson-ringed Whiteface, documented at four sites in the future reservoir area, had been recorded east of the Rockies only once before.

According to scientists like Wheeler and Hebda, outliers are the flashing beacons of specimen collection. Studying outliers can lead to exciting discoveries as scientists probe what, exactly, enables them to live at the edge of their range and adapt to different climates. Outliers may even offer a snapshot of evolution at work. They are found in extreme locations like the Peace River Valley for one of two reasons: they are either extending the range of their species or they are remnants of past populations. Just as the brittle prickly pear cactus populations in the Peace push the limits of a largely southern species north, the carnivorous pitcher plants help shift their species' boundary a little farther to the west. Out-liers provide raw material for future expanding populations and offer a glimpse of future biodiversity in a warming world. They help answer questions that intrigue scientists. How does a species like the fragile prickly pear cactus evolve to adapt to a changing climate? Which species are likely to survive global warming, and how?

Everybody knows a cactus, but the smaller outlier species that we don't commonly recognize often reveal the most to science. The surpris-ing bugs and spiders that were discovered in the Site C flood zone in the summer of 2015, only weeks before clearing for Site C began, piqued the interest of scientists across the country. As Hebda explained, "They're a reflection of the things we don't see, where a lot of the action can be, in the insects and spiders, in the fungi and other soil organisms." That action is evolution, or changes in the genetic traits of species that are passed down over multitudes of generations.

When I met Hebda in his museum office, he was about to embark on a trip to the Peace to launch the museum's newest undertaking, a two-year pilot project called Peace Region Expedition and Community Engagement, or PEACE for short. Its aim was to celebrate the Peace region's biodiversity and encourage its two-legged vertebrates to discuss how they interact with the land in a place Hebda described as "one of the most magnificent places on Earth." He talked about the great river valley at the heart of the Peace region, calling it an exceptional place with a unique microclimate, full of natural treasures, both living and long dead, like the taiga vole skeletons he had unearthed on the Boon family's land.

If the true sign of a creative mind is a cluttered desk, then Hebda was likely to win a prize for ingenuity, on top of the Queen's Diamond Jubilee Medal and other awards he had amassed for his exceptional work in botany, ethnobotany, and paleontology. An astonishing array of magazines, topographical maps, papers in asymmetrical heaps, poster tubes, and bubble wrap were piled high on his barely visible desk. Ad-joining tables were weighed down with test tubes, a large microscope, plants pressed between pieces of cardboard, an eclectic collection of precariously stacked papers, cardboard file boxes, and various scientific flotsam and jetsam. "Too much to do," commented Hebda, who was also the province's science adviser in paleontology and expert adviser on the globally unique ecosystem of Burns Bog in the Lower Mainland.

Hebda is among a growing number of scientists who posited that the Peace region's uniqueness also stems from the fact that parts of it might not have been glaciated during the last major ice age, more than ten thousand years ago. As new evidence of an ice-free corridor in the Peace emerges, it offers answers to some perplexing questions about species distribution. Why, for example, does the Peace River Valley host so many plant species that are rare in BC and lie at the outer edge of their distribution range? It also lends scientific credence to the understanding of the Beaver and Sekani First Nations, that their ancestors inhabited the valley well before the last of the glaciers slipped across North America. Indeed, one theory holds that the continent's First Peoples populated the Peace region before the last glaciation, moving south and subsequently following large game back north as the climate slowly warmed.

The Peace River Valley lies in Canada's boreal region, a pastiche of forests and wetlands dotted with tufa seeps, muskeg, bogs, and fens and crossed by creeks, streams, and rivers. For Hebda and other scientists, the Peace Valley's magnificence stems, in part, from an unusual convergence. It's a place where four biomes meet. The boreal, eastern plains, montane, and alpine ecosystems bump up against one another in the valley, creating a profuse and colourful mix of species and fostering rich biodiversity. In this great meeting place, each ecosystem contains elements of the others. The valley, Hebda pointed out, cannot be excised from the connected landscape of which it's part. "That reductionist approach is actually not ecologically or biologically true because it's not as if it's an island, it's not as though it's a planet. It's part of a continuum. It's not as though you can cut it out and talk about it as if it's not related to anything else."

If Site C and other industrial projects in the region destroy enough habitat in the comparatively narrow Peace region that forms part of the

Yellowstone to Yukon mountain corridor, it will sever the longest remaining wildlife passageway on the continent, fragmenting habitat and
populations for wide-ranging species already vulnerable to extinction,
such as the grizzly bear and wolverine. In the words of Clayton Apps, a
biologist who studied the impact of industrial development on wide-
ranging species in the Peace, "In the near future, the Peace region landscape is likely to be reduced to about one-half of its potential to support
certain wide-ranging species, like wolverine. Site C will exacerbate this
loss and will further erode our ability to conserve and recover some
species. This in turn would fracture wildlife populations that are otherwise mostly continuous along the Rockies."

The Peace Valley's zonal confluence stitches together a vibrant quilt
of habitats. Native prairie grasses grow cheek by jowl with aspen and
poplar forests and their dense and edible understories of Saskatoon
berry, chokecherry, highbush cranberry, and red raspberry. Riparian
woodlands, including the area around the Rocky Mountain Fort site,
anchor centuries-old black-and-white spruce. Old-growth trees shelter
at-risk species like the fisher, a species with low reproductive output
that, in BC, whelp only in declining black cottonwoods and uncommon balsam poplars.

The venerable forest in the Peace River Valley is no less ecologically
important than the mist-shrouded cedars and Douglas firs of the coastal
Great Bear Rainforest. Some scientists say it is even more important
because far less of it remains. Rod Backmeyer, the wildlife biologist who
wrote the management plan for the protected area around the Rocky
Mountain Fort site and who subsequently managed major projects for
BC's Ministry of Forests, Lands and Natural Resource Operations, describes the old-growth forest ecosystem that would be flooded by Site C
as even more ecologically significant than the Great Bear Rainforest. "It's
more important from a biodiversity point of view because there's far less
of it," Backmeyer explained. "You don't get those classic giant trees with
moss-covered ground and logs under them that are so picturesque. It's
different here. It doesn't mean that it has less value. It just doesn't have
that romantic flavour that some of the coastal old-growth has."

Despite its trove of intriguing species and diverse habitats, the Peace River Valley remains poorly known biologically compared to other regions of the province. In 2015, for instance, the Peace region accounted for less than 1 percent of the Royal BC Museum's natural history collection. That unflattering statistic perturbed scientists affiliated with the Biological Survey of Canada, a not-for-profit organization that helps coordinate scientific research among Canadian biota specialists. David Langor, an Edmonton-based entomologist and president of the survey, pointed out that areas like the Peace Valley "that are poorly understood have the potential for great biological excitement."

Calling the Peace "one of the most biologically fascinating areas of British Columbia" in a bulletin for scientists, the Biological Survey described scientific surveys in the Site C project area undertaken by BC Hydro consultants as "incomplete." It noted that most of the surveys did not include the deposition of specimens into museums for future study, meaning that they had been forever lost to science. After all the surveys BC Hydro had commissioned as a requirement for Site C, only a portion of the surveyed plants were deposited at the UBC Herbarium. The Royal BC Museum, for its part, received nothing but dragonfly collections. Claudia Copley, the museum's senior collections manager for entomology, said that the dearth of Site C collections would create a knowledge gap for further scientific research. "An actual specimen allows scientists to look at morphological variation, genetic variation, and even potentially discover cryptic species – in perpetuity," she explained. "We cannot know what sort of questions we will even be asking in the future and how we may be using the specimens to answer them." Scientists are still trying to discover and catalogue all the species in BC, the most biodiverse of all of Canada's provinces and territories. Copley put it starkly: "We haven't catalogued the province's diversity and we're destroying it."

Scientists were not willing to be caught out by a third dam on the Peace River that would erase barely studied habitat and species, and the Biological Survey of Canada put out a call to scientists to gather for a Peace BioBlitz in June 2015. The bulletin circulated to scientists to

promote the BioBlitz highlighted the Site C stakes: "Assuming development proceeds, this project would forever change the natural landscapes
– not just in the area of the flood zone, but also in the surrounding
and downstream areas ... Sites A and B were built without detailed study
and without comprehensive collections of specimens." This time, said
the survey, scientists had been warned of Site C's impending impact and
"should use this time wisely to systematically document the biota for
posterity and public benefit."

BioBlitzes, a relatively new phenomenon, are growing in popularity.
Susan Redy, US National Park Service naturalist, coined the term in the
late 1990s after she joined a species biodiversity count in Washington,
DC. Around the same time, the famous Harvard biologist E.O. Wilson
and wildlife expert Peter Alden launched a program called Biodiversity Days. Their objective was to catalogue all the organisms around
Walden Pond, a kettle lake in Massachusetts where Henry David Thoreau
had spent two years and written his classic work, *Walden; or, Life in the
Woods*. The idea of documenting species in one location, in a limited
period, quickly captured the imagination of both scientists and the general public. BioBlitzes were soon under way all over the world, including
in BC, near Whistler and in the wildlife-rich and unprotected Flathead
River Valley in the province's southeast corner.

The survey's first BioBlitz took place in 2001. But the BioBlitz that
drew the greatest number of scientists over the following fifteen years
was the one organized in the Peace River Valley during the sun-soaked
week of summer solstice, four weeks before the Clark government authorized the start of clear-cutting, bulldozing, and road building for Site
C. The valley, Langor explained, is "home to a lot of interesting things
we don't commonly find at those latitudes." For five days, two dozen
scientists from Canada's western provinces fanned out across the valley
on foot and in boats. Most of them focused on the Site C flood zone,
sampling insects, plants, spiders, molluscs, and other aquatic inverte-
brates from the first beam of dawn until late-night dark. Copley and her
husband, Darren, also an entomologist with the Royal BC Museum, set
up tent-like Malaise traps and scattered soapy dishes of water to collect

Entomologists Claudia Copley and Darren Copley gather specimens at the Peace Valley BioBlitz | *Tristan Brand, Y2Y*

insects at strategic locations throughout the valley, converting their hotel room in Hudson's Hope into a temporary laboratory for pinning and preserving specimens. Insects were pinned shortly after they were collected, and soft-bellied spiders were preserved in vials of alcohol.

While flipping over stones near the Hudson's Hope boat launch in the Site C flood zone, Claudia Copley spotted an unfamiliar, yellowish-brown insect in a tiny burrow that appeared to be of its own construction. She knew it was a "true bug" from the insect order *Hemiptera*, comprising an estimated 80,000 species worldwide and more than 4,200 in Canada, including cicadas and stinkbugs. But this bug struck her as "weird," so she scooped it up and later sent it to an expert in *Hemiptera*, Dr. Geoff Scudder, for identification. The insect turned out to be *Boreostolus americanus*, the first species of the bug family *Enicocephalidae* ever to be found in Canada. Only one other species in the genus, from the Ussuri region of Russia, has been named. "It's the only place we've ever found it in Canada, and its habitat along the river's edge is going to be lost due to the flooding," said Copley.

When I visited Copley in her museum office, the true bug was on loan to another institution, but she was eager to show me other novel findings from the Peace Valley. The entomology section of the museum was strangely devoid of life, considering that the people who worked there were so connected to nature. There were no plants, no terrariums, and no pet spiders or other eight-legged, horned, or flying creatures. Not even a stray orange or apple sat on anyone's desk, much less a vase of flowers. Scientists were forbidden to bring their lunch, snacks, plants, insects, or animals of any sort into the building, Copley explained, lest they attract or harbour insects that could destroy collections that had taken decades to amass.

Copley's office space, along with an adjoining room, contained floor-to-ceiling metal lockers, labelled in alphabetical order with the Latin names of insects. Copley, who talks rapidly and has a knack for making science fascinating in her frequent public talks, strode to the aisle with the bees and pulled out a drawer of pinned bumblebees. One tray held about two dozen specimens of *Bombus terricola* Kirby, the Yellow-banded Bumble Bee. One of the specimens had been found in the Site C flood zone, and a second specimen had been collected just above it.

Fuzzy black, with bright yellow on its thorax and abdomen, the plump queen dwarfed the workers and males. To me, *Bombus terricola* Kirby looked pretty much like any bumblebee collecting pollen from the flowers in my yard, but for Copley and other entomologists it was something special. Historically, the species is common in the eastern and upper midwestern United States and throughout much of southern Canada. But it is not common in BC. "For British Columbia this is a rare species," Copley enthused. "We don't have a lot of suitable habitat for this bee."

The Yellow-banded Bumble Bee, which pollinates wildflowers, potatoes, alfalfa, raspberry, and cranberry, has suffered the same plight as thirty-four other bumble bee species found in BC and forty-four species throughout Canada. Its numbers have declined significantly since the mid-1990s. In 2016 it was listed as a species of special concern.

Bees play a vital role in pollinating food crops and other plants (indeed, they pollinate about one-third of the world's food crops), yet they were not included in BC Hydro's Site C environmental assessment. Nor were spiders or gastropods, a class of molluscs that includes snails and slugs. In the Site C flood zone, BioBlitz scientists discovered a snail species, *Galba parva*, a small freshwater snail that breathes air and is vulnerable to extinction, that had previously been known only in southern BC. They also found two other snail species previously known only in southern BC, including *Zonitoides nitidus*, also called the shiny glass snail, a small, air-breathing land snail with a reddish-brown shell that was classified as vulnerable to extinction until it was delisted provincially in 2016.

Langor described the finds as "quite a significant range extension." "There are a few species in there that are surprises to us," he said. "Undoubtedly, there are more. Perhaps this is just the tip of the iceberg ... If we were to have a more intensive sampling I'm quite sure that we would come up with quite a pile of other things that are interesting, unique, and outside of normal ranges, and perhaps even species that are new to science."

He highlighted the BioBlitz spider findings to illustrate his point. Almost five hundred spider specimens had been collected. Ranging from a few centimetres to less than 3 millimetres long, they represented eighteen families, sixty-three genera, and ninety-three species.

After the BioBlitz, arachnologists Robb Bennett and Darren Copley spent hundreds of hours peering through microscopes to identify the eight-legged creatures. Fully one-third of the species collected during the Peace BioBlitz were notable records. Five of those species represented the southernmost populations in their known range. Nine had never been documented so far north, underscoring the Peace River Valley's significance as a biological mixing zone. For twelve species, it was only the second time they had ever been collected anywhere in BC. And four spider species had never been reported in BC prior to the BioBlitz. One tiny sheetweb spider, *Poeciloneta bihamata*, had never been reported west of Quebec.

Even more exciting was the discovery of a brand-new species for Canada. Prior to its collection in the valley, the teeny dark spider, *Ceratinops obscurus*, had only been found in New York and Florida. To date, only the male of the species has been found anywhere. The elusive female remains undescribed. These entomological finds highlight the important role the Peace River Valley could play in helping species adapt to climate change, said Copley: "It's often populations at the extremes of their distribution that are best able to adapt to the impacts of changing conditions."

On an island in the Peace River where the Copley duo collected spider specimens, Wheeler spotted a flowering chive she had never seen in the wild, even after ten years studying the genus *Allium*, commonly known as the flowering onion, which is her specialty. To an untrained eye, the wild chive looks much like the chives you would grow in your garden, with small purple flowers packed tightly into a circle. The wild chive, or *Allium schoenoprasm*, is unique because it is the only allium that is both a New World and an Old World plant, meaning that it is found in the Americas as well as in Europe and Asia.

The chive was an alpine plant, and Wheeler was stunned to see it growing on a low-elevation island in the middle of the Peace River, one of the islands that would be inundated by Site C. "What a find!" she wrote to fellow scientists. Her museum colleague was left to finish collecting sedge species in a nearby wetland while Wheeler observed and collected the wild chives. She had done her PhD thesis on chives and felt she was back among old friends. But the flowers on these specimens looked unusual. Closer inspection revealed that the purple flowers had been replaced by bulbils – asexual propagules that resembled tiny bulbs. Propagules often sprout leaves while growing on the mother plant. The scientific term for this phenomenon, uncommon in flowering plants, is pseudovivipary.

Wheeler was intrigued. Was the chive deviation a genetic mutation that could unlock information about how the species was evolving? Or was it caused by an environmental factor? She dug out a chive sample and popped it into her collections sack to press and ship back to the museum for further study.

SEVERAL KILOMETRES UPSTREAM from the Boons' farm lies Watson Slough, a marshy area separated from the Peace River by a swatch of fields. A sign beside a highway pull-off describes the slough as a wetland conservation project: a partnership among not-for-profit groups, local scouts, and the BC and federal governments. BC Hydro is listed as a Cooperating Partner in protection. (Hinting at the unfolding drama in the valley, someone has added the word "Kills" in black marker after BC Hydro's name.)

The slough, a 20-hectare complex of different kinds of wetlands, including two rare types, provides habitat for dozens of bird and plant species vulnerable to extinction. It is also home to the at-risk Western Toad, the only true toad found in BC, commonly recognized for its white or cream dorsal stripe and the peeping sound it makes when handled. BC Hydro claims that Site C's impacts on the Western Toad will be insignificant, but the Joint Review Panel disagrees, noting that the amphibian's habitat will be difficult to re-create. (Ironically, as the BC government is preparing to destroy the toad's habitat at Watson Slough, it has spent almost $200,000 of taxpayers' money trying to preserve the same species in the Kootenay region by building a toad tunnel under a highway.) Rare plant species recorded in the slough include Hall's willowherb, northern bog bedstraw, and an unusual water hemlock that, according to one BC Hydro report, may be one of five previously undescribed plant species found in the flood zone. Rare plants in the slough are among three dozen vascular plants vulnerable to extinction that will lose habitat to Site C.

The slough, however, is best known as a globally significant birding area. Tourism BC promotes the slough as one of the finest places in the province for birdwatching. Ebird, an online birding checklist program launched by the National Audubon Society and the Cornell Laboratory of Ornithology, calls the slough one of the world's birding "hotspots," while the BC Naturalists Association points out that it is one of Canada's "best habitats for rare breeding birds." Rare bird species found at Watson Slough include the Common Nighthawk, a federally listed at-risk species, and two species vulnerable to extinction in BC, Le Conte's Sparrow and the Surf Scoter, a large sea duck whose males have a distinctive orange, white, and black bill. They are among thirty avian species vulnerable to extinction whose habitat will be erased by Site C.

One evening in June 2017, as the sun finally began to set, eleven men and women tumbled out of vehicles at the Watson Slough parking area, just upstream from the Boons' farm. Weighed down by binoculars, tripods, scopes, and telephoto lenses as wide as teakettles, they wore safari-like hats, baseball caps, and hiking shoes. They had travelled from as far away as Australia and Martinique and were in Watson Slough on a guided holiday – the "Ultimate British Columbia" fifteen-day tour – in search of a close encounter with the Yellow Rail, a secretive and endangered marsh bird.

Their guide, Steve Ogle, a trim, tanned ornithologist from Nelson, explained that Watson Slough is "the primo spot" in BC for observing the rail, one of the least understood birds in North America. The tiny Yellow Rail resembles a week-old chicken, with a yellow belly, mottled brown plumage, and spindly yellowish-green legs. It comes to life in the gathering twilight to feed on beetles, spiders, and snails. Its call is heard mainly after dusk. In BC, the Yellow Rail is found mainly in a few wetlands in and around the Peace River Valley, where it nests on the damp ground in a clutch of woven grass and leaves, sheltered by a miniature umbrella of dead plants.

For twenty minutes the birders stood, trying to ignore the amassing squadrons of mosquitoes, while Ogle and his assistant guide took turns playing the Yellow Rail's call on their smart phones. It sounded like someone pecking with two fingers on an old Remington typewriter. *Tic-tic, tic-tic-tic. Tic-tic, tic-tic-tic.* Every once in a while, the typewriter sound was augmented by a squeak. The Yellow Rail, it is fair to say, is not one of your more melodious birds.

The group strained to listen over the whine of blood-seeking insects, the trill of Red-winged Blackbirds, the *hu-hu-hu* of a Wilson's Snipe in flight, and the *reeeek reeeek* of countless boreal chorus frogs, a brown amphibian the size of your thumbnail whose powerful vocalization belies its tiny stature. Nothing. After a few tries, Ogle announced he was going to find some rocks. He returned with two round stones cupped in his hands and banged them together. *Clack-clack, clack-clack-clack. Clack-clack, clack-clack-clack.* Ogle clacked the rocks again, and then his assistant followed suit. The birders had almost given up when, suddenly, from the other side of the cattails, they heard a faint echo. *Tic-tic, tic-tic-tic. Tic-tic, tic-tic-tic.* A Yellow Rail hid in the bone-dry cattails. And then another Yellow Rail made its presence known. Together, the rails sounded like two people pecking out letters on Remingtons.

"Everybody happy?" asked Ogle.

He already knew the answer.

Early on another June day, as the morning mist in the valley magically lifted to reveal blue sky and a softly glowing sun, I met a local birder, Chris McDonald, at the slough. I hoped to catch a glimpse of the Horned Grebe, a water bird known for its approachable nature and dazzling courtship displays. The "horns" are really yellowish tufted feathers behind its eyes that it can lower and raise at will.

The previous week, in late June 2016, the Horned Grebe had been listed under Canada's Species at Risk Act as a species of special concern, in part because of widespread degradation of its wetland breeding habitat, habitat like Watson Slough. Once a species is listed under the act, it is illegal to kill, harm, or harass individuals or to damage or destroy their nests. But the act's provisions for protecting species vulnerable to extinction apply only to federal land, which is a scant 1 percent of BC, including national parks. Watson Slough is owned by BC Hydro – the Crown corporation had purchased the slough and surrounding land for Site C some years earlier – so the federal act does not apply. Furthermore, at-risk species in the slough do not merit any protection under provincial law, as BC does not have a stand-alone law to protect endangered species. (In 2017, it was one of only three provinces without such a law.)

McDonald had spotted the rust-and-grey-coloured grebe at the slough in each of the preceding two years. He played its call for me on his iPhone app. It sounded like a muted cross between a loon and a rooster. Only moments before I arrived, McDonald had heard a Nelson's Sparrow, a marsh-loving bird with an orange face endangered in BC, and a Baltimore Oriole, another bird species at the limit of its range in the slough.

McDonald, a middle school math, science, and physical education teacher, looked every bit the gym teacher in black sweatpants and Nikes. A Canon camera and binoculars hung around his neck. We strolled along the overgrown path that fringes the slough, pausing every few steps to listen intently to the melodious concert of bird song. McDonald called out the names of the birds he could distinguish in the mix, a fraction of the 130 bird species documented at the slough. American Kestrel. Olive-sided Flycatcher. Least Flycatcher. Red-Winged Blackbird. Northern Flicker. Yellow-Bellied Sapsucker. Swamp Sparrow. Marsh Wren. Sora. Song Sparrow. Chipping Sparrow. American Coot. We didn't hear the Horned Grebe, but we did spot a Trumpeter Swan with three clay-coloured babies, peeking out from a watery maze of cattails.

The wetlands that comprise Watson Slough include a marl fen, the rarest type of wetland in North America. Botanist Curtis Björk tried to capture the significance of such a find: "Any well-seasoned botanist would do a 'woo-hoo' when they first come across a marl fen." Noteworthy for their rich plant diversity, marl fens host unusual (and sometimes rare and endangered) orchids, primroses, carnivorous plants, and gentians. Five bands of different types of vegetation – including peat mosses and tussocks of sedges and spike rushes – grow on the margins of the fen.

Björk explained that the fen had formed over thousands of years as water percolated through underground strata and bubbled to the surface of flat benches above the Peace River, where it became trapped on the surface. Little spheres of calcium carbonate deposits then formed in pools, giving them a greyish-white hue. When the water evaporated, the pool bottom had the texture of tapioca, and it could suck you in like quicksand if you were unwise or unlucky enough to step in it.

I had phoned Björk to ask about his discovery of a new plant species in the Peace River Valley that bears his name: *Erigeron pacalis C. Björk.* The endangered Peace daisy – distinguished from others of its ilk by traits that include its leathery leaves and very short stature (it is about as long as a pinky finger) – is now preserved on white cotton paper and tucked into a red file folder in a fireproof cabinet at the UBC Herbarium. The red folder tells scientists that the species is a type (the specimen on which the description of a new species is based), the cotton will outlive any other paper source, and the locked metal cabinet guards 591 other type specimens.

The daisy's wispy pressed leaves have a purplish tint, and filaments of white rays spread around a yellow centre like a teeny cloudburst. The formal description in the daisy's file folder records that Björk found the specimen in the Peace Lowlands, 18 kilometres west of Fort St. John, at an altitude of 460 metres. What the folder doesn't say is that Björk discovered the new species in the Site C flood zone and that the Peace daisy will face extinction if Site C proceeds, along with another plant called persistent sepal yellowcress, which is likely to become locally extinct.

Björk suggested we also talk about something called a tufa seep – another rare and endangered wetland in the Peace River Valley. As with the marl fen, the unfamiliar name seemed better suited to a starter dish on a Japanese restaurant menu than to the unlikely fusion of water and minerals that hosts extraordinary plant species, which Björk went on to describe in enthusiastic detail. He prefaced his account by confessing that he had been somewhat reluctant to accept a Peace River Valley assignment because there are generally fewer plant species in northern locales, and he did not believe his stint up north would be particularly interesting. But it had turned out to be an enlightening experience personally and professionally, one that was still very much on his mind eight years later. "When I got up there my eyes were popping out of my head. The biodiversity was through the roof."

For several weeks, Björk and his colleagues tromped through the designated flood zone, documenting rare and endangered plants that would lose valuable habitat to Site C. When BC Hydro later published a list of rare plants "potentially occurring" in the Site C project area, it was three pages long, single-spaced, and worth reading for the evocative names alone: the purple rattlesnake root, marsh fleabane, hairy butter-wort (a carnivorous purple-flowered plant that traps and feeds on in-sects), and moonworts (a rare fern with fronds that have crescent-shaped leaflets). There was also a list of forty-one rare and at-risk lichens that would be flooded by the dam, with equally enchanting names such as the electrified millipede lichen, the cryptic centipede lichen, and the vagabond rockfrog lichen. Additionally, BC Hydro had documented seventeen ecological communities in the Site C project area that were vulnerable to extinction even before dam construction got under way. These included an endangered wet alkaline grassland called Arctic rush–Nuttall's alkaligrass–Seablite, first identified in 1975 at Bear Flat near the Boons' farm.

But one of the most striking finds made by Björk and his colleagues was the tufa seeps. "To use a very non-scientific term, they're magical," Björk said. Long known to valley residents as moss-covered hillsides with arresting limestone formations and pools of crystal-clear water, the seeps had not been studied by scientists in any systematic way. Cold tufa seeps, as opposed to those at hot springs, are found in only a few places in BC, including in the Rockies, Wells Gray Park, and the Marble Range north of Lillooet. However, the cold tufa seeps Björk had seen elsewhere in the province were small compared to the grand seeps he and other scientists documented in the Peace River Valley. The stretch of the Peace River that Site C was slated to flood was home to a dense concentration of tufa seeps unlike anything Björk had ever seen. The botanist and his colleagues enthusiastically documented a record seven seeps in the flood zone, including one right across the river from the Boons' farm.

Over thousands of years, tufa seeps can grow to the size of a small room in a house. Björk recalled that "we found tufa seeps that were so large that they had waterfalls and little pools enclosed in calcium car-bonate rims. The pools are like these tiers that you can step up like a staircase, and the water will spill from one pool to the next to the next to the next." Near Hudson's Hope, the scientists encountered one tufa seep so big it had a chamber they could enter, a discovery still memorable for Björk years later: "The ceiling was coated in mosses and liverworts, and the walls were just dripping with this carbonate-rich water."

The *seep* part of the name reflects the slow movement of water (some travelling from the distant Rocky Mountains) as it moves through layers of underground plateau and sheet-like aquifers until it reaches the precipitous banks of the Peace River. Some of the sediment layers in the riverbanks are soft and have not compressed into hard rock. But other layers are harder, and water has a tough time seeping through. Instead of continuing its gravitational movement downward, the water begins to flow horizontally, very, very slowly, almost drop by drop. By the time the water pops out on the steep slopes above the Peace River, it carries a high mineral content, most notably calcium carbonate, a different form of the same mineral taken as nutritional supplements to build bone density. Over thousands of years, deposits of calcium carbonate, a substance similar to limestone, have built up in essentially the same process that creates special features inside limestone caves, such as stalactites and stalagmites.

Specialized mosses grow on the calcium carbonate deposits. In a race for survival, they are compelled to grow faster than the carbonate deposits themselves. The mosses' lower leaves become encased in the carbonate, essentially becoming rock. The older portions of the mosses die away or are eaten by bacteria, leaving spongy pores in the calcium deposits. The resultant porous rock is the tufa.

The mosses Björk and his colleagues collected at the tufa seeps were among the most diverse he had seen in almost two decades of fieldwork in western North America as a botanical consultant and research associate with the UBC Herbarium. One curious species flummoxed the scientists, so they sent it to a bryologist, a moss expert. It turned out to be a rare find called *Didymodon glaucus*, a moss that had been identified only in Russia and a few other locales.

As BC Hydro prepared to destroy the tufa seeps and Watson Slough for Site C – some of the 800 hectares of wetlands that would be lost to the dam, a total area four times the size of Vancouver's West End – the BC environment ministry website expressed concern about the escalating rate of wetland loss in the province, calling wetlands "one of the most important life support systems on Earth." BC Hydro itself has noted that tufa seeps in the Site C inundation zone have high conservation values and should be conservation priorities. Yet five out of the seven recorded tufa seeps in the Site C project area face certain destruction from the dam's reservoir. The future of the other two is highly uncertain. In the sobering words of the Joint Review Panel, Site C's impact on the valley's grand tufa seeps will be "permanent and irreversible."

SITE C'S ADVERSE ENVIRONMENTAL effects and impact on First Nations will be so pronounced that the Royal Society of Canada – the country's senior academy of distinguished scholars, artists, and scientists – has broken with convention and called on the federal government to halt the project, saying it is deeply concerned about how the dam was approved. In a May 2016 open letter to Justin Trudeau, society president Maryse Lassonde notes that Joint Review Panel members had identified a number of environmental issues that, as she diplomatically puts it, "beg further consideration under the federal Environmental Assessment Act and Clean Energy Act."

Simultaneously, more than two hundred of Canada's leading scholars signed what they referred to as a Statement of Concern about Site C, which was supported by a separate statement issued by the Royal Society of Canada. A group of researchers led by the Program on Water Governance at UBC found that the project will have more significant adverse environmental effects than those of any project ever assessed in the history of Canada's Environmental Assessment Act. In their words, "the number and scope of significant adverse environment effects arising from the Site C Project are unprecedented in the history of environmental assessment in Canada." Karen Bakker, a UBC geography professor who is also a Canada Research Chair and director of UBC's Program on Water Governance, was surprised when she and others sifted through the tomes of scientific research. "We checked this many times," she said, "because it was hard to believe at first."

The projects against which these scholars compare Site C include the unpopular proposal by the multinational corporation Enbridge to build a pipeline from Alberta's Oil Sands to Kitimat, BC. The pipeline would have transported bitumen through the Great Bear Rainforest archipelago – a prospect that galvanized many residents along the BC coast. Ironically, given its stand on Site C, the Trudeau government scuttled the project on the grounds that its impact on First Nations and the environment would be too severe. The scholars found that Site C would have twenty adverse environmental effects, while the Enbridge Northern Gateway project would have one.

Even the claim from the BC government and federal government that Site C's ecological impacts can be justified on the grounds that the project will deliver electricity with lower carbon emissions than other sources has been debunked. Using BC Hydro's own numbers, the authors of a 2016 UBC report found that Site C will not deliver energy and capacity with significantly lower greenhouse gas emissions than BC Hydro's alternative energy portfolio, which includes wind. "The federal and provincial governments stated that the unprecedented level of significant adverse environmental effects from Site C are justifiable, in part, because the project delivers energy and capacity and substantially lower GHG emission than the available alternatives," notes the report. "Our analysis indicates this is not the case."

US scientists, working with colleagues from around the world, published a study that same year that showed that reservoirs are producing considerably more carbon emissions than anticipated. About 80 percent of those emissions are in the form of methane, a greenhouse gas thirty-four times more potent than carbon dioxide. Methane, whose production is enhanced by fluctuating water levels in reservoirs, is generated when microbes eat rotting material in sediment buildup behind dams. Washington State University researcher Bridget Deemer, the study's first author, said scientists found that estimates of methane emissions from reservoirs are about 25 percent higher than previously thought, pointing out that the finding "is significant given the global boom in dam construction."

WHEN THE BENNETT DAM flooded a vast area of the Peace Valley before it could be studied, valuable information about the region's biological diversity was forever lost to science. Back then, neither BC nor Canada had an environment ministry or department. By the time plans to build the Peace Canyon Dam were set in motion a decade later, environmental impact studies were becoming more commonplace. Even so, the amount of time that consultants were allotted to assess the dam's potential impacts (not just on fish and wildlife and on the behaviour of the shoreline but also on aesthetic values, recreational resource use, archaeological sites, and the value of forest lands) totalled a scant four weeks. Notwithstanding the constricted time frame, the authors of the Peace Canyon Dam environmental assessment report reached a provocative conclusion. They note that "there are no reliable and economical means by which the losses of fish and wildlife species or habitats may be avoided or mitigated." They go on to make a curious suggestion, more in keeping with the public relations focus of successive governments than with careful scientific work. Priority for future fieldwork, they suggest, should be given to species with the greatest public appeal, such as fish.

BC Hydro, as a condition for receiving an environmental certificate for Site C, was compelled to develop environmental mitigation plans. However, it is highly unlikely that Site C's reverberating impact on wildlife and wetlands can be much alleviated, no matter how much money ratepayers invest in mitigation. For instance, to compensate for the extensive loss of valley wetlands to Site C, BC Hydro said it would enhance existing wetlands and create new wetlands with similar functions. That strategy left Björk and other scientists incredulous. "How could they re-create tufa seeps?" asked Björk. "I'd like to see such a mitigation plan." BC Hydro's wetland mitigation plan (notably, one that does not include any special provisions for Watson Slough) goes so far as to suggest that a new wetland could be created on top of a piece of land

The 2017 Paddle for the Peace launch at the Halfway River, a Peace River
tributary that is spawning grounds for bull trout vulnerable to extinction |
Photo by Louis Bockner

near Watson Slough. The wetland would poke up from the top of the
Site C reservoir.

Site C's mitigation strategy, while prioritizing the creation and en-
hancement of wetlands in the Peace, allows substitute wetlands to be
located anywhere in the province. The strategy obscured the total cost
to ratepayers of enhancing existing wetlands and creating new ones. Yet
there was no doubt that Site C was good business for organizations such
as Ducks Unlimited, the recipient of $600,000 for consulting work on
wetland assessment, mitigation, and compensation related to Site C.

In keeping with the conclusion of the Peace Canyon environmental
report, which suggested focusing on species with the most popular appeal, like fish, BC Hydro's mitigation strategy for bull trout was outlined

in eyebrow-raising detail. Three-quarters of the Peace River's bull trout population, estimated at about eight thousand fish, are found upstream of the dam site, which will block their way to spawning grounds. In a plan that sounds like a scenario out of a Dr. Suess book, in which fish hop on land and drive cars, BC Hydro plans to siphon threatened bull trout from the Peace River and transport them past the Site C dam in refrigerated trucks for the lifespan of the project.

According to the plan, sanctioned by both the BC and federal governments, bull trout stymied by the dam will be lured to a fishway entrance. They will then be enticed to jump up 10 vertical metres, through a series of pools known as a fish ladder, to a trapping pool. On leaving the trapping pool, the trout will enter an adjacent pool where they will be anesthetized. Next, the fish will travel in a mechanical fish lift to a sorting area, where they will be organized by species, counted, and then placed in aerated tanks for truck transport to waiting watercraft, which will take them 30 kilometres upstream to the Halfway River.

While designed for bull trout, the trap-and-haul facility will also accommodate Arctic grayling, mountain whitefish, rainbow trout, and other large fish seeking to swim past the dam. Arctic grayling will be transported to the Moberly River several kilometres upstream from the dam; other fish species will be released right into the reservoir. Any fish that manage to ascend the ladder but that do not meet BC Hydro's unstated criteria for upstream transport will be fed back downstream through a return pipe, perhaps to ascend the ladder once again.

Then comes the truly disconcerting part of the Site C mitigation strategy for bull trout. On their way back downstream, up to 40 percent of the trout – including the same fish BC Hydro customers have spent many millions of dollars to transport safely upstream – will die trying to swim past the dam. In an industrial game of fish roulette, bull trout and other fish will be left to take their chances in the dam's whirling turbines. While less than 10 percent of smaller fish are expected to die, as many as two out of five of the larger fish will perish.

The trap-and-haul facility for the bull trout – the cheaper of two shortlisted mitigation options – will cost British Columbians more than $25 million to install and another $1.5 million a year to maintain, according to one BC Hydro report. Stretched over the hundred-year lifespan of Site C, the total cost to transport fish past the Site C dam will be a conservative $175 million, not accounting for inflation. To put that tab into perspective, it would cost about the same amount to build nine new elementary schools in Vancouver, the most expensive city in BC and one of the most expensive in the world.

The scheme is a high-risk gamble with ratepayers' money. Fish ladders are a common dam mitigation strategy for salmon, but by 2016 a bull trout ladder had only been attempted on one other river in North America, the Clark Fork River in Idaho and Montana, where it had proven to be an expensive and rather embarrassing failure. Ryan Kriener, a fisheries biologist with Montana's Fish and Wildlife Service, explained that "bull trout seem more reluctant to enter these non-natural traps than some other fish." Out of twenty-five thousand fish that used a ladder at one of the river's three dams after it was built in 2011, only twelve were bull trout. During 2015, only seven bull trout attempted to ascend the ladder. Two made it to the top, Kriener reported, and five turned back en route. He said that stunning bull trout one by one and hauling them upstream by hand has been a more effective mitigation strategy.

According to the Joint Review Panel, Site C will result in a net loss of fish habitat and "a profound change in the type and character of the remaining habitat." The changes will start with construction and continue for the lifespan of the project. The panel describes these changes as "probable, negative, large, irreversible and permanent."

The nonsensical nature of mitigation strategies for bull trout and other species that will lose habitat to Site C (BC Hydro has proposed, for example, to trap and move western toads and other amphibians to new habitat and to translocate rare plants but has not said to where) is even more apparent in a leaflet on bull trout produced by the BC environment ministry. The leaflet points out that BC contains the core area of the bull trout's multi-jurisdictional range, emphasizing that the province has a global responsibility to conserve this species. Dam construction, logging, road-building, pipelines, and the removal of stream-side vegetation are all cited as reasons for the bull trout's demise. In this regard, the pamphlet notes that bull trout are particularly sensitive to habitat change.

A different government publication singles out the two existing dams and reservoirs on the Peace River as having already dealt a blow to the local bull trout population by eliminating "significant amounts of stream habitat through inundation" and by creating barriers that have altered historical migration patterns. In a final burst of irony, the pamphlet on bull trout counsels sports fishers to conserve trout populations by increasing their awareness of conservation issues and protecting trout habitat and aquatic ecosystems. It even lists a phone number for reporting violations.

Other species already vulnerable to extinction that will lose valuable habitat to Site C include two species of bat – the Northern Myotis and the Eastern Red Bat – that are threatened outside of BC by a fast-spreading fungal disease called white-nose syndrome. Fourteen at-risk butterfly species will also be impacted by the project, including the Old World swallowtail and Aphrodite fritillary. The red-listed coral hairstreak, a light brown butterfly with a line of coral spots on its wingtips, and the great spangled fritillary, with its intricately symmetrical silver, tan, and orange markings, will lose so much habitat they may become extinct locally. Site C will also have significant adverse effects on dragonflies and damselflies once the reservoir eradicates 500 hectares of dragonfly and butterfly habitat and construction activities eat away more. Impacted species include the blue-listed Prairie Bluet damselfly, which is a vivid blue with dark markings and half-green elfin eyes. It was found at Watson Slough and Bear Flat.

Birds, too, will lose such a huge chunk of varied habitat to Site C that some species will become imperilled in the valley and beyond. Other species already vulnerable to extinction will see their status elevated. Two bird species that were not considered to be species of concern in 2017, the Sharp-tailed Grouse and Baltimore Oriole, may become blue-listed species, or species vulnerable to extinction. And two blue-listed birds, the Eastern Phoebe and Le Conte's Sparrow, could become red-listed (i.e., endangered) species, the BC government admitted when questioned by the Joint Review Panel.

Site C's assault on biodiversity in the Peace River Valley comes at a time when species are winking out all over the world, as the planet's sixth mass extinction gathers grim momentum. Species are going extinct at rates not seen since the Cretaceous mass extinction, when three-quarters of all species on the planet disappeared, including the non-avian dinosaurs that once thundered and prowled through the Peace. More than one hundred species of amphibians, the world's most endangered class of animals, have already become extinct. One-fourth of the world's mammals are headed towards extinction, along with one-fifth of all reptiles and one-sixth of the globe's bird species. Almost 40 percent of North America's fish species are now imperilled. Habitat destruction, including from projects like Site C, is a leading cause of the extinction crisis.

Yet both the federal and BC governments justified Site C's unprecedented environmental destruction on the grounds that the project was needed for the "greater good." To drive home that point, the BC government and BC Hydro pumped up the need for Site C, while a national hydropower association representing BC Hydro and other Canadian utilities set about to change federal laws that protected fish and species at risk.

9

Harnessing Political Power

As the Boons and others at the Rocky Mountain Fort site steeled themselves for a second month of winter camping, Clark attended a memorial service for former BC premier Bill Bennett. Standing behind a podium flanked by floral arrangements, Clark delivered a memorable, if unconventional, tribute to the recently deceased premier and his unrealized plans to build Site C in the 1980s. "Well, Premier Bennett, you got it started, and I will get it finished," promised an emboldened Clark. "I will get it past the point of no return."

Clark's statement underscored the government's fixation on the short-term appeal of a "photo op" megaproject at the expense of generations of hydro customers. The government would stop at nothing in its determined quest to propel Site C forward, letting neither facts nor protocol hinder its objective. From inaccurate messaging in media statements to brokering an increasingly cozy relationship with BC Hydro – a relationship that Crown corporation experts cautioned had inched far too close for comfort and good governance – the Clark government endlessly replayed the message that BC's appetite for electricity was growing. All the while, it pandered to people's fears of not having enough electricity to power up their smart phones, coffee makers, computers, and flat screen TVs. If there's one thing British Columbians don't like, it's a power outage.

BC Hydro, for its part, blatantly seized opportunities to advertise higher electricity use, no matter how fleeting. The Crown corporation stated repeatedly, and without merit, that demand for electricity was expected to rise 40 percent over two decades. "Cold snap drives electricity demand to all time high," pronounced one BC Hydro news bulletin headline in early 2017. A new record had been set for electricity use in the province, BC Hydro announced, and demand was expected to remain high as coastal residents shovelled snow and the thermometer continued a chilling freefall in the province's interior. But not to fear, the bulletin informed hydro customers, because BC Hydro's ample system meant "the power will be there on the coldest, darkest days of the year – without brownouts or without having to import expensive power from other jurisdictions." Investments like Site C, the bulletin went on to say, would meet the growing demand for electricity and ensure reliable power in the future.

As the government and BC Hydro peddled their Site C message like travelling salesman selling snake oil, BC Hydro made substantial cuts to its successful energy-conservation programs and paid independent power producers across the province millions of dollars a year *not* to produce electricity because of oversupply. The egregious situation stemmed from the Campbell administration's directive to BC Hydro to sign contracts with independent power producers (some of them notable donors to the Liberal Party) to supply electricity to the grid from operations such as run-of-the-river, biomass-connected to pulp-and-paper operations, and natural gas.

The contracts committed BC Hydro to buying power for a set number of years, even when it wasn't needed. In April 2016, for instance, one state-of-the-art natural-gas thermal plant in Campbell River sat idle 90 percent of the time while BC Hydro paid the company an estimated $55 million a year to ensure that emergency power would be available if needed. One former plant employee who could not be named because of an agreement with the company, Island Generation, pointed to another quirk in the deal: "The strangest thing is [the company] is making more money than if they had it running."

The combination of flat energy demand in BC and contracts with independent power producers (not all of which could easily turn off electricity generation at the source like Island Generation) meant that BC's excess power was dumped on the export market for far less than it cost to produce it. Adrian Dix, then the Opposition energy critic, pegged BC Hydro's loss from independent power commitments at $1.4 billion.

That loss, and BC Hydro's swiftly accelerating expenditures across the board, would normally be reflected in hydro rate increases. But the Clark government, in a dubious practice Swain referred to as the "miracle of loaves and fishes," found a way to postpone the bulk of rate increases leading up to the 2013 and the 2017 elections. Known also as Enron-style accounting, the trick allowed BC Hydro to claim record profits and pay a handsome dividend to the government even though expenditures exceeded revenues.

The trick was based in deferral accounting, a standard practice among utility companies to smooth out high and lumpy expenditures over several years and avoid rate hikes. Regulators closely scrutinize deferral accounts. But the Liberal government exempted BC Hydro from having to follow generally accepted Canadian accounting procedures (GAAP), instead imposing an American standard. The government then exempted BC Hydro from the standard's requirement of independent regulatory scrutiny. Faced with demands for rate hikes from BC Hydro, which were on the point of being approved by the utilities commission, the government again creatively devised a method to avoid pre-election rate shocks. It simply changed the rules, allowing predicated future revenues to count as current cash and thus a significant contributor to profits. Those profits allowed BC Hydro to pay a huge dividend to the provincial government, which in turn helped balance the books to show a surplus. Site C exacerbated the government's accounting tricks because it incurred expenses (more than $2 billion by December 2017) that were mostly placed in deferral accounts. "Everything is being massaged so that in May 2017, the province's finances will look good," Swain wrote in an opinion piece co-authored by Richard McCandless, a former assistant deputy minister and chief financial officer for the BC government.

I chatted with Swain in his Victoria home in March 2017, the month before the provincial election campaign officially commenced. A tall, affable man in his mid-seventies, Swain was no newcomer to energy issues. Nor was he a stranger to industrial projects that affected Canada's First Nations, having worked for the federal government for more than two decades in positions that included deputy minister of Indian and northern affairs and director general for electricity, coal, uranium, and nuclear energy. Swain had also been Canada's first senior adviser for renewable energy such as hydropower. He had chaired the Research Advisory Panel for the Walkerton Inquiry into the tainted water scandal that had killed seven people and sickened thousands more in Ontario. He had also chaired the subsequent Ontario Expert Panel on Water and Wastewater, as well as the federal Expert Panel on Safe Drinking Water for First Nations. Swain had a generous smile and an even larger sense of humour. He had given up hope, he said with a chuckle, of ever receiving a Christmas card from Clark.

Swain knew that the Site C Joint Review Panel's recommendations would not be binding, in the sense that neither Ottawa nor Victoria would be legally obliged to follow them. But he did expect – quite wrongly, he was later to discover – that the panel's evidence-based report would provide "strong guidance" for the ultimate decision-makers on Site C and that these decision-makers would be "strongly disposed to listen carefully to the results." In the case of the Walkerton Inquiry, Swain observed, the Ontario government had accepted every single recommendation made by the judicial inquiry.

But far from paying heed to the Joint Review Panel's most important recommendations and conclusions, BC's Liberal government cherry-picked the ones to highlight, said Swain, while ignoring other consequential recommendations that did not suit its agenda. He was so perturbed by distortions in the government's messaging about the panel's report that he decided to break convention and go public, calling the government's refusal to allow independent scrutiny of Site C by the utilities commission a "dereliction of duty." The Clark administration, Swain said, had taken some of the panel's conclusions out of context in a "story that kept changing." "They were trumpeting our conclusions," he explained. "I felt that the story being told by BC Hydro and the BC government was seriously incomplete."

The panel's conclusions, Swain pointed out, had been based on the $7.9 billion price tag for Site C they were given at the start of their deliberations. Among other findings, the panel had determined that there was no need for Site C's power in the time frame provided by BC Hydro. Swain and his colleagues had concluded that if indeed energy demand in BC should start to climb, for reasons unforeseen by the panel at the time, Site C would be the most cost-effective means of meeting the new energy demand. They also noted that "justification must rest on an unambiguous need for the power and analyses showing its financial costs being sufficiently attractive as to make tolerable the bearing of substantial environmental, social and other costs." The Clark government wasted no time in disseminating only the conclusion that Site C would be the most cost-effective means of meeting new demand. And even that statement was repeated without the panel's qualifications, said Swain.

The panel's statement had been based on BC Hydro's cost projections for different forms of renewable energy, projections that the panel had neither the time nor the resources to scrutinize. Moreover, after the panel submitted its final report, the cost of Site C soared by almost $1 billion to $8.8 billion. Swain said that the $8.8 billion price tag immediately negated the panel's conclusion that Site C would be the most cost-effective means of meeting any new demand. The project, he said, "was simply going to be an economic burden for future generations with no environmental benefit." He was also quick to point out that the panel had been given neither the time nor the mandate to scrutinize BC Hydro's Site C cost projections for accuracy, which was why it had strongly recommended that the whole kit and caboodle be dispatched to the BC Utilities Commission – Swain called it "the public guardian" – for prompt review.

Other missing components in the government's messaging to the media and the public included the pivotal fact – Swain called it the "dark heart of the matter" – that energy demand in BC had been stagnant for almost a decade, since 2005. He pointed out that BC had an energy surplus, that BC Hydro's load forecasts were not credible, and that there was no prospect of load growth for years and possibly decades. Contrary to Clark's repeated assertions that Site C needed to be constructed as quickly as possible ("to literally keep the lights on," she said during the 2017 campaign), the panel did not find any objective need to build the project for at least twenty years.

Clark, who was facing an election in May 2017, spoke endlessly about the jobs Site C would create. Despite the premier's much-touted BC Jobs Plan and her failed promise to deliver one hundred thousand jobs in the LNG industry, most new jobs under Clark's watch had been generated in the most populated areas of the province. Rural BC had lost jobs while the Liberals were in power, and Clark was fixated on showing improvements. Site C, a project over which the premier wielded full control, was the fastest way to guarantee new jobs announcements leading up to the election. But, as critics pointed out, if BC were going to dish out many billions of dollars from the public purse for a job-creation program, why not create long-term jobs instead of the twenty-five permanent jobs that Site C would deliver upon completion?

Crown corporation experts questioned the snug relationship between the Premier's Office and BC Hydro, suggesting that BC Hydro had become too politicized. Instead of serving BC Hydro customers, a Crown corporation that should have been arm's length from the government was now helping to demonstrate job-creation gains promised by the Liberal administration and providing ample opportunities for the premier to pose wearing a hard hat, repeating her jobs mantra over and over for the television cameras.

Several aspects of the increasingly cozy relationship between BC Hydro and the BC Cabinet troubled Luc Bernier, the former head of the Institute of Public Administration of Canada, but he zeroed in on Premier Clark's decision to push Site C "past the point of no return" before the May 2017 provincial election. "If you don't need the electricity you're going to have a bill for nine billion dollars for a dam you don't need," commented Bernier, who held the Jarislowsky Chair in Public Sector Management at the University of Ottawa. He added that it was unusual for a government to want to lock up such a large and expensive project so quickly. "There's no emergency to build it," Bernier said in January 2017. "The only emergency in this project is the coming election."

Economist Jim Brander, a professor at UBC's Sauder School of Business, said that BC Hydro's technical staff, not politicians, should have made the decision about the need to fast-track Site C construction. The final call, he said, echoing Neufeld's comments from more than a decade earlier, should have been based on evidence such as electricity demand and Site C's projected rate of return. A Crown corporation's senior management should be arm's length from political issues, Brander pointed out, so that decisions can be made on a technical basis and not for political reasons: "We think that it leads to better management when the managers are able to be managers and not politicians." Any government would want oversight of a project as large and expensive as Site C, but the Premier's Office's direct involvement in media relations for the project, was, according to Brander, "very rare."

Freedom of Information requests revealed that both the Premier's Office and the energy minister's office had directed the timing of various Site C announcements from BC Hydro, including an announcement about the completion of a temporary bridge across the Peace River, which energy minister Bill Bennett did not want BC Hydro to make too close to a scheduled April 2016 increase in hydro rates. The two offices were also involved in the timing for an announcement about the completion of the $470 million lodge for Site C construction workers (with its own movie theatre, gymnasium, cardio studios, and massage therapy services, a lounge called the "River's Bend," and a "Site C Leisure Bus") that cost BC Hydro customers almost as much as Clark's pre-election pledge to spend $500 million on affordable housing projects to help alleviate the Lower Mainland's housing crisis. The government offices also vetted a BC Hydro press release announcing that the Site C turbines and generator contract had been awarded to Voith.

As Bernier pointed out, when a government directs day-to-day communications for a Crown corporation, this can result in decisions being made for political reasons and not because they are in the best interests of the publicly owned company. "For the proper functioning of Crown corporations it should be more independent," he explained. "We do put these organizations further away from politics to make sure the main reason to exist – in this case to produce electricity – is not done for political reasons."

The lines between BC Hydro and the governing Liberal Party also strayed into controversial territory when it came to the corporation's board of directors, most of whom were donors to the party. In September 2015, just after preliminary construction began on Site C, Premier Clark appointed BC Hydro board member Brad Bennett, the son of former premier Bill Bennett, to chair BC Hydro's board of directors. Brad Bennett had spent the entire 2013 election campaign travelling with Clark, who was counting on some of the Bennett dynasty's magic to rub off on her campaign. Most pundits had predicted at the outset that her party would lose. (They were wrong, as it turned out.) As one *Globe and Mail* reporter observed, "While the Liberal Leader delivers her speeches, shakes hands and takes questions from the media, he [Bennett] is just there in the room, the spitting image of his father, lending his family name to the free-enterprise cause."

Brad Bennett was not about to let his new top-dog position at BC Hydro temper either his public support for the BC Liberal Party or his continuing admiration for Clark. In September 2016 the BC Hydro chair himself nominated Clark to run a second time for the Liberals in the riding of West Kelowna. He spoke in her support as she was acclaimed as the candidate and posed with her behind a prominent "Re-elect Christy Clark" banner at the nomination meeting. "We're going to be heading into a[n election] campaign in April," he reminded party and community members at that event, in comments that quickly became motivational. "Our biggest enemy when things are feeling good isn't the NDP necessarily," said Bennett; "it's apathy within our own ranks."

In addition to his duties with BC Hydro, Bennett was the president of McIntosh Properties Ltd., a real estate and private equity investment company that had donated more than $30,000 to the BC Liberal Party between 2005 and August 2015, just before he assumed the BC Hydro chair. A majority of the nine other members of BC Hydro's board of directors also appeared as donors to the BC Liberal Party in the province's online political donations database. The name of another board member was listed as the principal officer for a company that donated to the Liberals. One more board member, Jack Weisgerber, was a former Liberal MLA who had been the energy and mines minister in the Campbell government and who had worked as a BC Hydro consultant on Site C from 2007 to 2014. Brad Bennett took leave from his duties as chair to travel with Clark during the spring 2017 election campaign. It was, indeed, all in the family when it came to Site C. On the campaign trail, Clark made frequent mention of the project that Bennett's grandfather had envisaged and that his father had aspired to build.

Shortly into the month-long campaign, UBC's Program on Water Governance published a detailed study that outlined why Site C was no longer a sound investment and that made the financial case for halting construction. Clark meanwhile told the media that the project, slated to be finished in 2024, would in fact not be completed until 2027. "Site C isn't going to be finished for another 10 years," she said. "So if the electricity isn't needed for 10 years, when do they expect us to start it? Nine years from now? Eleven years from now?" Even BC Hydro had publicly admitted that Site C's power would not be needed in BC for up to forty years. Yet now Clark was telling the electorate – in a widely published and largely unchallenged media interview – that BC would require Site C's power in ten years. Once again, political spin trumped the facts.

BC had only to look east for two cautionary tales about the perils of proceeding with hugely expensive hydro dams when the power was not needed. Construction was well under way on the Muskrat Falls Dam on Labrador's Churchill River and on the Keeyask Dam in northern Manitoba. Muskrat Falls would produce 824 megawatts of electricity while severing a river in the traditional territory of the Inuit and Innu peoples and contaminating fish, one of their main food sources, with methylmercury.

The dam was much too far along to halt when it was revealed that its cost had leapt to $11.7 billion. Stan Marshall, the CEO of Nalcor, the Crown corporation tasked with building Muskrat Falls, publicly admitted that the project was a boondoggle. And that was before the dam's price tag climbed again, to $12.7 billion. Muskrat Falls, a chagrined Marshall confessed, was "not the energy choice for the power needs of this province." "It was a gamble and it's gone against us," he admitted as it was revealed that the dam would tack an additional $1,800 onto the annual hydro bill of every household in Newfoundland and Labrador.

Manitoba did not need electricity from the Keeyask Dam on the Nelson River, more than 700 kilometres north of Winnipeg, any more than Newfoundland needed power from Muskrat Falls or BC needed energy from Site C. Manitoba Hydro planned to ship Keeyask's electricity to Minnesota through a new transmission line (the Great Northern Transmission Line, to be built by Minnesota Power) when the dam was completed in 2021. But Keeysak's comparatively expensive energy would have to compete with the low price of natural gas and the falling price of wind and solar energy in the United States, making for, as one US energy analyst warned, a "risky investment strategy." That strategy had failed miserably even before the first megawatt of Keeyask's electricity came close to reaching Minnesota, as Keeyask's cost suddenly soared by more than $2 billion and Kelvin Shepherd, the CEO and president of Manitoba Hydro, revealed that the economics for the dam had deteriorated. Shepherd admitted that, with "20/20 hindsight," he would have waited to build it, as Manitobans steeled themselves for double-digit hydro rate increases.

WHILE THE LIBERAL GOVERNMENT was busy manufacturing a case for Site C, an Ottawa-based hydro industry association later chaired by BC

Hydro turned its attention to lobbying the federal government. The Canadian Hydropower Association had been founded in 1998, following the rejection of Site C and other large hydro projects, aiming among other objectives to polish Big Hydro's tarnished image. As Jacob Irving, who would become the association's president, once observed, "Trying to get people excited about hydro power can be like advertising oatmeal." "Because it is so well developed and it's been around for so long," he added, "it sometimes fades into the background."

Irving, with his acute sense of strategy and deep understanding of the complexities of both government and industry, was the perfect states-man for the mission. He had joined the association in 2009 after working for the federal government and the petroleum industry, including as the surface rights negotiator and government and public affairs adviser for BP Canada and Devon Canada Corporation. He had also been exec-utive director of the Oil Sands Developers Group, an industry lobby alliance, where his role included government relations. The job af-forded Irving plenty of insights into how the muscles of federal policy were developed and massaged – a skill he ported over to the Canadian Hydropower Association (CHA) with impressive results.

Under Irving's tutelage, the association developed a snazzy website, branding itself blue, the colour of water, and focusing on better ways to "quantify and communicate the undeniable merits of Canadian hydro-power," including through compelling publications and lobby efforts. The message was clear: Canadian hydro was here to stay and indeed was poised for significant expansion. No longer willing to be flayed in the name of the environment and Indigenous rights, Big Hydro was repo-sitioning itself as a friend of First Nations, a harbinger of jobs and eco-nomic development, and an environmental steward. The CHA now successfully marketed hydropower as Canada's "most powerful weapon in the fight against climate change."

A short, animated video on the association's homepage said it all: a chubby water drop with arms, legs, and a big smile alternately donned a yellow hard hat to command a hydro facility and a sword and shield to slay climate change, while a female narrator intoned that "Canada has vast hydroelectric resources, and we could still more than double our current capacity." To capture the attention of anyone who might view hydropower as akin to mushy oatmeal, the original version of the video, posted on the CHA's website, ended with a brief collage of photographs that included scantily clad young women, one revealing her bare buttocks, another showing her backside in a thong, and a third displaying her blue bra and panties. (The ending was later changed.)

Polishing hydro's public image was easy in the broad scheme of things. As Irving soon noted of the CHA's efforts, "Political leaders from all over the country and across all parties are increasingly mentioning hydropower positively when they talk about Canadian energy." Ensuring that environmentally damaging projects like Site C received smooth and timely federal approval was a much tougher slog. So the CHA and its members set about to convince the federal government to knock down some of the major regulatory hurdles facing hydro projects, unofficially embracing a maxim from former BC premier Gordon Campbell: if you don't like the law, change it. With that in mind, the CHA zeroed in on the three top areas of federal interest for the hydropower industry: the Species at Risk Act, the Fisheries Act, and the Canadian Environmental Assessment Act. According to the association, elements of these acts "affected the operations and future growth" of Canadian hydropower and needed to be changed.

Between 2011 and 2016, as Site C progressed through a regulatory review and construction commenced, BC Hydro played an increasingly active role in the CHA. Chris O'Riley, a BC Hydro vice president who later became BC Hydro's president, sat on the CHA's board of directors, as did Edie Thome, a former vice-president of Harmony Airways who was BC Hydro's director of environmental risk management. In 2013, Thome became the CHA board chair, a position she held until June 2017. Over that same period, BC Hydro's representation on the association's busy working groups intensified. The working groups were named after the areas they sought to influence: the Fisheries Act, the Species at Risk Act, Aboriginal relations, public affairs, clean energy, and regulatory processes. Starting in 2013, the working group on regulatory processes, which aimed to "monitor and influence" federal regulatory change, was chaired by BC Hydro. By 2014–15, a BC Hydro representative was sitting on every single CHA working group.

Irving, along with members of various CHA working groups, spent the better part of 2011 working with government stakeholders to underscore the importance, as the CHA explained, of "amending and modernizing" federal legislation affecting hydro projects. That year, the association reported nineteen lobbying communications with federal ministers and their senior staff, including the ministers for fisheries, the environment, and natural resources. Those efforts included meetings in December 2011 and January 2012 with the federal environment minister, Peter Kent, and his staff to discuss Canada's Environmental Assessment Act and to "underscore the CHA priority for 'one project, one assessment.'"

The CHA's efforts had considerable success, Irving noted following the flurry of meetings: "Our efforts to streamline the regulatory review process system have not gone unnoticed." In April 2012, Stephen Harper's natural resources minister, Joe Oliver, announced that the federal government intended to shorten the review process for natural resource projects, shifting to a "one project, one review" policy, thereby eliminating the requirement for a separate federal environmental assessment process. "This approach is reflective of what the CHA has long advocated," said a duly pleased Irving, adding that he was eagerly awaiting details of the implementation. When those details were revealed, they included limitations on the scope of environmental assessments (hydro projects producing less than 200 megawatts of energy were now exempt from federal assessment) and restrictions on public participation in reviews.

Swain referred to the changes as "a complete rewrite of the Act stuffed into the thousand-odd pages of the budget bill." The overhaul, he noted, would make it far easier for Site C to glide through the environmental review process. One change that especially perturbed the panel chair was the federal government's reduced budgets and time frames for environmental reviews. It meant that the Site C panel, as Swain put it, had "very limited resources and very limited time." The condensed timeline precluded the three-person panel from holding hearings on Site C in the heavily populated Lower Mainland or Capital Regional District, a move criticized by First Nations, the Peace Valley Landowner Association, and the Peace Valley Environment Association.

Before Harper's tenure as prime minister, Canada's Fisheries Act had been one of the strongest pieces of environmental legislation in the country. The act left "no stone unturned" when it came to protecting fish and fish habitat, wryly noted the Canadian Electricity Association, a long-standing national forum and voice for the electricity business in Canada, which worked closely with the CHA and whose members included BC Hydro. Habitat protections enshrined in the act included two primary prohibitions: one preventing the destruction of fish for any reason other than fishing, and a second (known by the acronym HADD) that prohibited the harmful alteration, disruption, or destruction of fish habitat.

In October 2011, Irving met with Harper's fisheries and oceans minister, Keith Ashfield, to discuss the CHA's "ongoing concerns" about the Fisheries Act. That meeting took place following the CHA's registered lobbying efforts earlier that year with a deputy minister and assistant deputy minister. One concern the CHA voiced about the Fisheries Act had also been mentioned by the electricity association: the act's focus on protecting the habitat of individual fish species was a "crucial aspect that needs to be revised." The CHA insisted that the level of protection afforded different fish species should be based on their value as part of a commercial, recreational, or Aboriginal fishery, and not on intrinsic biodiversity values, although the association did add that it was committed to environmental sustainability.

Some ecologists called the Harper government's subsequent overhaul of the Fisheries Act the biggest blow to Canadian conservation laws in more than fifty years. Irving called it a "great success on the legislative front," noting that many of the changes "directly reflected positions we've developed and communicated for many years." Instead of protecting the habitat of individual fish species for their intrinsic biodiversity value, the new act focused on habitat protection for commercial, recreational, and Aboriginal fisheries.

The revised act brought more certainty for BC Hydro and other utility companies because it instituted fixed review timelines for approving federal permits such as those required for Site C. Prior to the legislative changes introduced by the Harper administration, there had been no prescribed timelines for permit reviews and approvals, which left much to the minister's discretion. The CHA congratulated the Harper government on changes to the act, pointing out that "authorization processes have been streamlined and the conditions for these same authorizations are now potentially more flexible." The CHA also said it would focus on ensuring that all future amendments and changes to Fisheries Act policies and regulations "moved towards a more streamlined and favourable environment for the hydropower industry."

When the Trudeau government announced a review of the Fisheries Act, pledging to restore "lost protections" while incorporating "more modern safeguards," the CHA (chaired by BC Hydro) and the electricity association made it clear that they supported Harper's legislation; indeed, they called for further changes to the act. Sergio Marchi, the president of the Canadian Electricity Association, wrote to the fisheries minister, Hunter Tootoo, in November 2015, cautioning against what Marchi called a "wholesale and hasty reversal" of changes to the fisheries, navigable waters, and the Environmental Assessment Act. As Marchi noted in his letter, "amendments to the Fisheries Act have been long requested by our membership, and in many aspects helped modernize project approvals for new electricity infrastructure projects." Several months later, Marchi secured meetings with the fisheries minister and his staff to discuss the "efficiencies" of the new regulatory systems as well as "clear and timely approvals."

In briefs submitted to the Trudeau government during a review of the Fisheries Act, the CHA and the electricity association maintained that the act should not revert to protecting habitat for individual fish species. They also called for greater clarity regarding sections of the revised law, such as its definition of "serious harm to fish." *Serious harm,* wrote Irving in his brief, should be interpreted to include fisheries or the habitat supporting them "rather than individual fish or habitats not contributing significantly to the productive capacity of ecosystems."

The Harper government also made a notable change to the Species at Risk Act. The CHA's most pressing concern, shared by the Canadian Electricity Association, was that its members were unable to obtain permits or authorizations under the act for both the construction and operational phases of hydro projects. The CHA wanted "single long-term or renewable incidental harm permits" for hydro activities, as well as a stewardship role for the hydropower industry in conservation agreements. In 2011, a year that BC Hydro sat on the CHA's Species at Risk Act (SARA) working group, the hydropower association lobbied Environment Canada senior officials, including a deputy minister and a senior policy adviser to the minister, to ensure that the CHA's submission on SARA would be well received and that the CHA points would be considered. By the time Harper left office, the Species at Risk Act no longer had mandatory time limits on permits that allowed at-risk species to be harmed. The CHA was "pleased to see" longer permits granted under the act. The goal, in the association's words, was to make the act "a more successful tool to protect species" while allowing what it called responsible development.

Thome, for her part, noted that the CHA had made "tremendous progress" in regulatory affairs and said that engagement in federal regulatory "improvements" would continue to be a core CHA activity. She credited the CHA's new communications and public affairs initiatives for boosting public support for new and developing hydropower, saying, "our industry is growing and so is our voice."

As the newly elected Trudeau government set out to review the Harper government's sweeping changes to the Environmental Assessment, Fisheries, and Navigation Protection Acts, Irving called for the CHA to focus vigilantly on regulatory issues. As he told delegates to the HydroVision convention, "This is something we're going to have to be very involved in." He noted in a CHA annual report that the association would "continue to work relentlessly to ensure the improvements brought by the 2012 amendments are maintained."

While several environmental groups busied themselves asking supporters to send emails to federal cabinet ministers, calling on the Trudeau government to deny Site C permits, BC Hydro, represented by the Canadian Hydropower Association, had already punched well above those groups' collective weight to lay the groundwork to help facilitate their delivery. In the early days of the Trudeau government – on the same day that the prime minister and the thirteen provincial and territorial premiers, including Clark, met in Ottawa to discuss climate change – the CHA ran an advertorial feature in the *Globe and Mail*. Titled "Canada's Unique Climate Change Solution," the page extolled the ability of Canadian hydro to tackle climate change: "Canada boxes far above its weight class when it comes to hydro." The ad read much like a news story, with pithy quotes such as "The world needs low carbon energy and we can deliver." That same month, the CHA joined other renewable energy groups to publish a well-timed report titled "Powering Climate Prosperity: Canada's Renewable Electricity Advantage," in which it urged a shift from fossil fuels to clean electricity, including Big Hydro, and called for increased electricity exports to the United States.

Less than two weeks after the first ministers' meeting, the Canadian Electricity Association – representing BC Hydro and other utility operations – began a new lobbying blitz on Parliament Hill. Over the next eight months, the CEA reported sixty-three lobbying communications, including with the federal departments of natural resources, fisheries, infrastructure, and environment and climate change. Although the subject of these communications was wide-ranging, the Fisheries Act, the Navigable Waters Protection Act, the Species at Risk Act, and the Migratory Birds Convention Act were listed as lobbying topics, "in relation to electricity industry plans to address the need for new infrastructure development to meet growing demand for electricity."

Lobbying efforts focused on a number of designated public office holders, including deputy ministers, assistant deputy ministers, policy advisers, the policy director, chiefs of staff, and a senior adviser to the Prime Minister's Office. As the Trudeau government considered the matter of Site C permits (pressured in one direction by Site C proponents and in the other by First Nations, Peace Valley landowners, and environmental groups) the CEA also reported direct lobbying communications with the fisheries minister, Hunter Tootoo; the natural resources minister, Jim Carr; and the environment and climate change minister, Catherine McKenna.

The announcement about the new Site C federal permits was made on a Friday at the end of July 2016, on the eve of the national August long weekend. In granting BC Hydro a permit to destroy fish habitat, the new fisheries minister, Dominic LeBlanc, who had replaced Tootoo, noted that BC Hydro had engaged in comprehensive consultations with First Nations and other stakeholders and that the utilities company would continue to collaborate with Indigenous groups. To Chief Willson, whose nation was among those fighting Site C in court, the permits were a "spit in the face" from Trudeau. Grand Chief Phillip called the permits a betrayal and pointed out that "the Trudeau Government, like cowardly, thuggish thieves in the dark, quietly issued federal permits before a long weekend to allow for the acceleration of construction."

That Site C fisheries permit from the Trudeau government granted leave for BC Hydro to engage in destructive practices such as the repeated dewatering of fish habitat, the stranding of fish and fish eggs, and the killing of fish trapped in the dam's diversion tunnels and spillways. The permit was also notable for its sweeping timeline: it gave BC Hydro permission to cause harm to fish species in the Peace and its tributary rivers right through until 2064. For the next half-century, there would be no need for BC Hydro to reapply for federal authorization to destroy fish habitat for Site C.

THE SITE C PROJECT was all dressed up for the clean energy ball, but it still lacked a dance partner. As the BC government intensified its search for a market for Site C's electricity, it took a fresh look at its next-door neighbour. As luck would have it, Alberta's new NDP government had promised to untie Alberta from carbon-intensive energy and hitch the province to the renewables wagon. The BC government, supported by some of its clean energy friends, set about to woo Alberta. The first public hint of a potential match came when BC energy minister Bill Bennett mused to a reporter – in a well-timed information drop – that BC could help Alberta transition to clean energy by selling it power from Site C.

To peddle Site C's electricity to Alberta would require a new 600-kilometre transmission line that would cost $1 billion. Somewhat brazenly, Clark asked the Trudeau government to pay part of the bill, in the interest of promoting clean energy across the country. "For us, it's great," an enthused Clark said at the time. "That's profit for BC Hydro, which means it's good for ratepayers. It's also great for Canada because it means we are supplying Alberta with our clean energy so they can get off their coal habit." What Clark *didn't* mention was that Alberta would likely only purchase power from Site C at considerably less than it cost BC to produce it, leaving BC Hydro customers to make up the difference.

The pins continued to fall into place for at least some of Site C's power to be shipped to Alberta. Trudeau and the provinces subsequently agreed to the "Vancouver Declaration," a pan-Canadian framework on clean growth and climate change. Notably for Site C, the declaration included a pledge to develop regional plans for clean energy transmission. At Clark's urging, Trudeau soon said he was open to helping pay for a new grid that would transmit BC electricity to Alberta to help reduce reliance on dirty coal. But as it turned out, Alberta was not going to be such an easy catch. Any prospective deal would come with a quid pro quo. Alberta premier Rachel Notley said she would consider buying some of Site C's power, but only if BC approved a controversial pipeline project to carry diluted bitumen from Alberta's Oil Sands to the BC coast. And while Alberta was Site C's only prospect for a long-term relationship at that point in time, Site C was by no means Alberta's only option for a power partner. "We're a suitor," energy minister Bennett explained. "We're a jurisdiction that has clean inexpensive electricity we'd like to sell to them. They are thinking of a bunch of different options and haven't settled on anything yet."

Clark had a particular, if questionable, use for Site C's power in mind when BC went courting in Alberta. She posited that the electricity could be used in Alberta's Oil Sands, noting that "we could potentially electrify the Oil Sands, which would make the Oil Sands the cleanest oil produced anywhere on the globe." Clark omitted to mention that most of the Oil Sands' toxic legacy is associated with the massive amount of water contaminated in the process. As for using "clean" electricity instead of natural gas as an energy source in Oil Sands processing, the Clark government's original plan had been to use Site C's electricity to develop a liquefied natural gas industry and to encourage maximum natural gas production within BC's borders. The result would not be net carbon reductions but rather a jump in greenhouse gas emissions from LNG.

Clark's unfolding preparations to sell Site C power to Alberta faced other barriers as well. Construction of a new transmission line would have a significant impact on communities along the way. It would also be far more expensive for Oil Sands producers to purchase electricity from Site C instead of using natural gas, according to the Canadian Energy Institute. But Clark wasn't about to give up so easily. BC could swoop in like a white knight, freeing its neighbour from the coils of dirty Oil Sands emissions. Critics might scoff and call the scheme crazy, but Clark and her cabinet were serious.

While the Canadian Hydropower Association helped ease the regulatory burden for hydro projects such as Site C, it also fixed its attention south. If Canadian hydro were to expand, as part of the global army of clean energy amassing to slay the climate change dragon, it would need a far bigger buyer for all the new electricity it would create than Canada could possibly offer. To that end, one of the CHA's strategic priorities was to increase Canadian hydropower exports to the United States. Irving explained that "Americans want to hear the Canadian hydropower story and we are ready to tell it." A new CHA publication, "Five Reasons Americans Should Care about Canadian Hydropower," was made available at Canadian consulates in New York, Boston, Minneapolis, Los Angeles, San Francisco, Chicago, and Seattle. Playing to Americans' fears of relying too heavily on the turbulent Middle East,

the publication lauded Canadian hydropower as the key to energy independence and security. Canada, the world's third-largest producer of
hydro power, had the resources to help the United States free itself from
reliance on unstable and volatile foreign energy sources, the publication
noted. It listed collaboration with Aboriginal communities as one of the
five reasons to buy Canadian power, noting that Canada's hydropower
industry worked "closely with aboriginal communities in the planning,
construction and implementation of new hydropower projects."

In 2013, the year BC Hydro took over the chair of the CHA's board,
the association expanded its outreach efforts to the United States, deepening its messaging with American audiences. During that time, Brenda
Goehring, BC Hydro's manager of regulatory and relationship management, sat on the CHA's Clean Energy Policy working group, the group
leading outreach efforts in the United States.

Irving participated in events that promoted enhancing the ties between the two countries' electricity grids, including gatherings such as
a US-Canada "Hydropower Relationship Celebration," held in Washington in 2011, and another conference, also held in Washington, called
"Celebrating North American Hydro Connections: Clean, Affordable
and Secure Energy." The CHA met with US consular staff in Canada
and regularly took part in activities and meetings with the staff of
Ottawa's American Embassy, in addition to making presentations to
audiences (including those it characterized as "influential Capitol Hill
staffers") on the mutually beneficial hydro relationship between Canada and the United States. When Irving gave an opening speech at
HydroVision International, held in Kentucky in 2012, he drove home
the message that hydropower was a North American resource.

The CHA also made submissions on Canada's hydropower potential
to US federal senate committees and to the US Congress Waterpower
Subcommittee, and it submitted comments on the Obama administration's draft "Clean Power Plan" and on an energy review by the US
Department of Energy. In a statement that would certainly have angered
Peace Valley landowners and First Nations, the association assured
the US Energy Department that Canadian hydropower projects were

developed only after a thorough environmental review and "with the participation of local and Aboriginal communities." The CHA pointed out that Canada and the United States shared more than thirty cross-border interconnections and 200,000 miles of high-voltage transmission lines (the equivalent of travelling all the way across Canada more than sixty times). It said that Canada had the potential to significantly increase its hydropower capacity "to help meet growing American energy demand while supporting clean energy objectives."

Canada was more than open for hydropower business with the Americans – it practically threw itself at its southern neighbour. Irving, wearing a black suit jacket and a striped navy and yellow tie, enthused about the possibilities at a HydroVision convention panel on international issues titled "The Road to Paris and Beyond," where he characterized Canada as the Norway of North America. "We in the North have a lot of potential we could share," he stated. "It means a lot of development. It means a lot of jobs." But Canadian hydro exports to the United States represented only about 1 percent of US electricity consumption, Irving pointed out, before promoting his main message: "We humbly submit that there is room to grow ... Even if we could double it to 2 percent it would mean the world to us. It would be huge. We'd be over the moon if we could go from 1 to 2 percent."

To illustrate the extent to which Canadian hydro was poised for expansion, Irving flashed up a map from the CHA's website. Canada, he declared, could almost double its hydro capacity. BC alone had the potential to develop 32,000 megawatts of electricity, according to the map, more than double its existing capacity. Yukon, which shared the Liard River Basin with BC and the Northwest Territories, had the biggest growth potential in the country, with the ability to accelerate from generating a mere 100 megawatts of electricity to producing 17,600 megawatts – considerably more electricity than was generated in BC during all of 2016.

The hydro association's map raised doubts about former Premier Campbell's promise that Site C would be the last big dam that BC would ever build. In passing the Clean Energy Act, Campbell's government had removed eleven large hydro projects from BC Hydro's long-term radar. Those projects included a fourth hydro dam on the Peace River and three dams on the Liard, the granddaddy river on BC Hydro's 2008 list of potential large hydro projects.

The CHA map raised the question of where, exactly, the 32,000 untapped megawatts of BC electricity would come from if development of other proposed large hydro projects was now legally banned. Only about one-tenth of it could come from small hydro, according to a report commissioned by the CHA. The map served as a poignant reminder that governments come and go and that laws can always be changed, although the increasingly dismal economic optics of Big Hydro projects represent by far the biggest deterrent to any new developments. But poor optics did not hinder the Trudeau government from embracing Big Hydro in a little-known 2016 document that laid out a path for slashing carbon emissions by mid-century and increasing Canada's electricity exports. The document referenced the CHA's assessment of Canada's hydropower potential, noting that a large portion was "economically viable."

As energy ministers from the Three Amigos – Canada, the United States, and Mexico – met in Winnipeg several months after the first ministers' meeting to sign a climate change and clean energy Memorandum of Understanding, the hydropower association wasted no time publicizing Big Hydro's potential role in helping Canada fulfill its commitment. Irving reminded the media that "to fight climate change, strengthen our shared energy systems, and grow a greener economy, we only have to do more of what's already working." When the Three Amigos' heads of state met in June 2016 (the month before the Trudeau government issued Site C permits), each country pledged to get half its electricity from clean power by 2025. And Irving, true to form, was quick to comment that Canada was "very well placed" to play a seminal role in the continent's transition to a clean energy economy.

10

The Renewal Revolution

As Ken and Arlene waited uneasily for Site C to cartwheel its way through the environmental assessment process, they decided to go solar. It was not an easy proposition. Not because the sun didn't shine – summer in the Peace River Valley brought more than seventeen hours of daily sunshine, and winter days were often bright and blue-skied – but because the BC government's energy policies seemed designed to thwart solar installations, not encourage them. Solar had blossomed in other Canadian provinces, and according to the International Energy Agency's website, it was "taking off" around the world. But it had failed to thrive in any meaningful way in BC.

A bizarre illustration on BC Hydro's solar webpage said it all. Titled "Solar Power and Heating for Your Home," it featured a blurry photograph of a man pulling on a sweater, as if to caution viewers that their living rooms might suddenly become uncomfortably chilly if they switched to solar. The same page provided technical information about solar electricity – some of it quite dense – that began with the sombre news that it would take homeowners like the Boons at least twenty years to recoup the cost of a solar installation. "Do your research on the practicality of going solar in B.C.," counselled BC Hydro.

As the Boons and their neighbours soon discovered, going solar in BC was more impractical than in other jurisdictions, where supportive government policies had led to the explosive growth of solar. In just

Ken Boon stands in front of the solar panels he installed on his workshop
at Bear Flat | *Photo by Emma Gilchrist*

seven years – which is how long it took for Site C to pass from Campbell's announcement through the first year of pre-construction work –
Ontario had added solar capacity amounting to more than double the
electricity that Site C would produce. It was an impressive achievement,
but one that many ratepayers in Ontario may not have appreciated
fully because the solar installations came during a time of rapidly rising
hydro prices that had little to do with the arrival of solar. By introducing
policies that made it easy for homeowners and businesses to install
solar, Ontario had quickly become Canada's solar leader. Now, except
for Arizona and California, it was the North American jurisdiction with
the most installed solar capability. The cost to Ontario ratepayers of
going solar was "minimal," according to the Canadian Solar Industries
Association, while the benefits were far more than just financial and
environmental (i.e., carbon-reducing). Besides generating 2,400 megawatts of new energy capacity from solar, Ontario had gained five

thousand full-time solar jobs. In 2009, there had been "virtually no solar in Ontario," explained John Gorman, the president and CEO of the Canadian Solar Industries Association. "It was a question of political will to put the policies in place."

Yet BC's solar prospects remained virtually untapped, despite a provincial government study that pointed to the sunny Peace as a potential solar hot spot. In Ken's words, the benefits of switching to solar were a "well-kept secret" in the province. Gorman pointed out that "BC is just, to the best of my knowledge, not pursuing solar electricity aggressively or contemplating it in any serious way." Gorman, who lived with his family in a solar-powered home in Ottawa and represented Canada on the executive committee of the International Energy Agency, had some sharper words about BC Hydro's submission to the Joint Review Panel claiming that solar in BC was economically unfeasible: "That's just plainly false."

In the United States, the Obama administration's desire to sow solar was reaping a promising harvest for both the economy and the environment. Solar policies achieved a national milestone of one million solar homes in 2016. That year – the same year that the global solar business grew by an astonishing 50 percent – the American solar industry employed 209,000 workers. Eight percent were armed forces veterans, who often found it hard to find reliable employment after leaving the service. By 2017 the American solar industry employed more workers than Apple, Google, and Facebook combined.

In sharp contrast to BC Hydro's solar page, the US Department of Energy's website wooed viewers with a cute graphic of a row of white houses with rooftop solar panels and a compelling message for any homeowner or real estate developer who might be contemplating solar panels. "Solar homes sell for more money," declared the government, citing studies showing that solar adds an average US$15,000 to the resale value of a house. "Just like a renovated kitchen or a finished basement increases a home's value," the page continued, "solar has been shown to boost home valuation and shorten a home's time on the market." For those keen to learn more about how to earn money from solar, all the while helping cut their nation's greenhouse gas emissions, the website contained helpful information about the logistics of transitioning to solar: something like a condensed *Solar for Dummies* guidebook. Solar, according to US government director Rebecca Jones-Albertus, would soon be a standard feature to consider when shopping for a home, "much like central air or granite countertops are today."

The falling cost of solar energy in the United States – by 50 percent in just five years – made it especially attractive to cost-conscious businesses such as Walmart. The retailing behemoth covered the roof of its Mountain View, California, store with solar panels, inspiring US president Barack Obama to drop in to talk about his national energy plan. "More and more companies like Walmart are realizing that wasting less energy isn't just good for the planet, it's good for business," Obama pointed out. "It's good for the bottom line." By the end of 2014, Walmart had installed solar on the roofs of more than three hundred of its stores and distribution centres – enough solar panels to power about twenty thousand American houses – becoming the single largest commercial generator of solar in the country. And it planned to double its solar capacity by 2020 as part of a solar revolution expected to satisfy more than one-quarter of the prodigious appetite for energy in the United States, which has only 5 percent of the world's population but consumes one-quarter of all the world's energy. The International Energy Agency, for its part, has stated that solar could meet one-quarter of the globe's energy needs by 2050.

In tandem with plummeting prices, a spate of new inventions made the decision to go solar a practical one as well. Tesla has begun marketing new solar roofs – rooftop shingles made of textured glass that convert sunlight into solar energy for homes and electric vehicles. The company says its solar roofs cost less to manufacture and install than a traditional roof, look more attractive, and last twice as long, never mind the savings on electricity bills. "Electricity," explained Tesla CEO Elon Musk, "is just a bonus."

Then there is the smartflower, a mobile "flower" developed in Austria, billed as the "world's first all-in-one solar system." The flowers, available in eight different colours, have photovoltaic petals that track the sun, opening with the dawn and closing with the dark or during inclement weather. The portable solar technology can be installed in public places like squares and parks, or in your garden. Solar flowers are ideal for renters, and you can take them with you if you move.

IN 2010 THE BOONS purchased fourteen solar panels from a company in Red Deer, Alberta, the closest solar provider they could find at the time. Ken installed the panels on the roof of the farm shop where he ran a log cabin-building business, contracting an electrician to do the final hookup for a total investment of $17,000. "Prices have come down since that time," Ken noted in 2017, "and now you can put in a bigger system than you need and receive an annual cheque for surplus." With solar panels on the roof of just one of their farm buildings, the Boons' hydro bills were sliced in half.

Others in the valley soon followed suit. Guy Armitage, a beekeeper and hotel manager who lived with his wife and elderly father in a bungalow on a Peace River cliff bank in Hudson's Hope, installed so many solar panels that BC Hydro paid him for his surplus electricity, rather than the other way around. Through an energy co-op in Dawson Creek, a two-hour drive from Hudson's Hope, Armitage arranged for the delivery and installation of fifty solar panels, as many as he could squeeze, in soldier-like rows, onto the south-facing side of his roof, facing the future Site C reservoir that would eat away a sizeable chunk of his backyard. A machine the size of a hot plate, fastened to the wall of his laundry room, tracked hourly, daily, and lifetime production of energy from the panels.

The family's smart meter recorded how much energy the home used as well as how much electricity the solar panels fed to the common grid. In the first full year that Armitage's solar panels operated, while most British Columbians faced higher and higher bills for electricity (hydro rates were scheduled to increase 28 percent over a five-year period even before Site C), his family's annual hydro bill came to zero. (They paid a twelve-dollar monthly administration fee to BC Hydro for their private

Guy Armitage looks after his bees. Armitage, a beekeeper and hotel manager who installed solar panels on his roof, lives in Hudson's Hope, a community that will lose four dozen properties to Site C | *Photo by Garth Lenz*

solar set-up.) The gregarious Armitage liked to show visitors a photo-copy of his first annual cheque from BC Hydro: $758. "Solar is the way of the future," he said. "They are doing it all over the world. But we're locked into hydro power."

Hudson's Hope, like municipalities around the province, viewed its escalating municipal hydro bills with considerable alarm. The district's annual hydro bill had more than doubled, from $68,000 in 2000 to $172,000 in 2016. And the hydro tab was poised to climb even higher despite concerted efforts at energy conservation, such as installing LED lights in the town arena (often the biggest energy guzzler for municipalities).

In early 2017, Hudson's Hope tendered a contract to install 1,580 photo-voltaic panels on municipal buildings. From solar-powered curling to solar-powered sewage treatment, the district soon became a "real, honest-to-goodness twenty-first-century solar community," in the words of the Dawson Creek energy co-op that installed the panels. Because BC Hydro had capped the amount of power it would allow from any single solar installation, the co-op worked with the district to spread out the panels for maximum effect. Funded by a $1.37 million grant from the federal gas tax fund, solar went up in more than half a dozen locations, including the rooftops of the public works shop, the municipal building, the curling rink, and the arena – with the help of five local high school students, who were given summer jobs and training. A bank of panels was also installed next to the sewage treatment lagoons that would be flooded out by Site C.

Hudson's Hope mayor, Gwen Johansson, who would lose her riverside bungalow and property to the Site C reservoir, said that the solar installations would save the district an estimated $70,000 in annual hydro bills. "Over 30 years, that amounts to savings of more than two million dollars. If hydro rates go up, the savings will be even greater." The town's curling club now produces 100 percent of its electrical needs; the arena will meet just over half of its energy demand through solar. "We know electricity bills are going to continue to rise," explained Johansson. "It's purely a financial decision. It's a pragmatic cost saving."

In countries like Germany, government programs support the purchase of solar panels by individual households, and utility companies spread the cost of the panels over many years so that the average homeowner can afford them. In BC, under the Liberal government, you had to dig deep to find and interpret information about what BC Hydro called its Net Metering Program. The Boons and Armitage described the "net metering" program – it was hardly a catchy name – as "not publicly promoted at all." Armitage said he had been told that BC Hydro, which employed 5,350 people, had just one employee working on net metering before 2016, when it added an assistant.

If Armitage and the Boons lived in Ontario, the cost of going solar would have been significantly less. Ontario had adopted what Gorman called the "European model" for solar, where utility companies sign purchase agreements with homeowners to buy their solar energy over decades, guaranteeing set rates in a graduated formula. BC Hydro was telling homeowners it could take twenty or even twenty-five years to recoup an investment in solar panels; Ontario homeowners needed only seven to earn back the $15,000 cost of a typical home solar installation, according to Gorman. After that, the solar benefits became even more enticing. After seven years, Gorman pointed out, the average solar homeowner in Ontario could pocket an average of $2,000 a year selling rooftop electricity to the grid.

Other municipalities besides Hudson's Hope were demonstrating how solar could help meet the province's energy needs. From solar-powered trash compactors, solar pedestrian signals, and bus shelter solar in Fort St. John to solar-heated hot water in Dawson Creek's high-use municipal buildings, cities were introducing new policies to encourage solar installations. More than 1,000 kilometres away, on BC's coast, the municipality of Richmond installed solar panels on the roof of a community centre, on three fire halls, and on other municipal buildings. The installations were part of a broader clean-energy strategy intended to wean the city off carbon and demonstrate, according to long-time city councillor Harold Steves, that Site C's power was not needed. What was needed, he said, were BC government policy changes to encourage new energy sources that were not just clean but also green – energy sources that would also create long-term employment and more prosperous communities than the boom-and-bust economy attached to large dam construction.

As plans to build Site C waxed, the Liberal government's support of other renewable energy solutions waned. SolarBC, an initiative funded by the BC and federal governments to invest in renewable energy "while increasing energy security and saving money," wound down in 2013, even though BC receives more annual sunshine than Germany, a country at the forefront of the global march to solar. Just three years earlier, in a statement that proved unfortunately premature, SolarBC's executive director, Nitya Harris, had proclaimed that "there really is a solar revolution going on in BC." The defunct SolarBC initiative provided financial incentives for installing solar rooftop panels and solar-powered hot water tanks (heating water accounted for about 15 percent of energy use in an average BC household) and partnered with TD Canada Trust to offer a zero-interest loan.

West Moberly First Nations became BC's first Aboriginal community to be officially designated a "Solar Community" by SolarBC in 2009. The initiative provided funding for an energy plan to reduce greenhouse gas emissions and transition to solar: "to tread lightly on the Earth," as the band's vision stated, with "clean, renewable and low-impact energy," including the installation of solar hot water systems.

BC's showcase solar installation, the SunMine project in Kimberly, a small town in the Rocky Mountains, also received BC government funding and support from BC Hydro. The project, which saw ninety-six solar trackers stationed on the site of the former Sullivan lead and zinc mine owned by mining giant Teck, received a million dollars from the Innovative Clean Energy Fund, launched by the Campbell government to promote clean energy initiatives.

Under the Clark government, according to the Liberal government's website, the fund's focus shifted to "clean energy vehicles, clean air and clean water." Solar, geothermal, and wind energy initiatives were conspicuously absent when Premier Clark dished out almost $12 million from the fund in March 2016. Much of the fund that year went to help some of BC's more affluent consumers purchase electric vehicles worth up to $77,000 apiece. The subsidy was publicly lauded by the New Car Dealers Association of BC, the third-largest donor to the BC Liberal Party from 2005 to 2015, giving more than $1.3 million in political donations.

JOHN WRIGHT COULD BE called a herder in the renewable energy business. It was a small measure of Wright's success that when he brought politicians to tour the site of a planned pumped storage hydro project in Marmora, Ontario, the local hardware store, grocery store, and garage, along with other businesses, changed their signs to say "Support Marmora pumped storage project" and "Let's Make It Happen: Marmora Pumped Storage." Wright works with Northland Power, a Toronto-based independent power producer with solar, wind, hydro, and natural-gas-fired cogeneration projects in Canada and Europe. But it was his education as a landscape architect that shone in October 2016 as I stood with him on the edge of a precipice near Marmora overlooking an abandoned iron ore mine.

Far below us, five times the drop of Niagara Falls, was an oval pit with sheer limestone walls. The water it held was almost the same blue colour as the crisp and cloudless sky. Close up, the water was crystalline and fit to drink; groundwater had seeped in between a wide ribbon of limestone and the harder rock. From our vantage point, atop football fields of iron-streaked waste rock and crunchy gravel, it looked like a glistening lake that would beckon for a swim if it weren't so impossibly far below. The appeal of the water and off-white cliffs was accentuated by fall foliage buttered onto the landscape in every direction: green forest coloured with bunches of burgundy, red, orange, and amber. Even though it was mid-October, the mercury had climbed to twenty-three degrees, another reminder of the urgent need to unbuckle ourselves from fossil fuels.

Wright gazed across the pit at the Group of Seven landscape and remembered how he had driven the provincial energy minister to the site a few years earlier, along the same rough access road we had just taken through a moonscape of rock heaps piled high. "John, I'm not quite seeing the appeal," the minister had said as they trundled along. "Give it a few minutes," Wright advised. When they reached the top of the slag heap where we stood, the minister turned to Wright. "You don't need to say anything more about the tourism potential," he said. "I get it."

A short distance down the road, atop a second bluff hemmed in by random heaps of rock and gravel, we found the missing slice of the panoramic view. Through the canopy of trees below, a kilometre distant, we glimpsed the brick and clapboard houses and church spires of Marmora, once a hardscrabble mining town where the main employer was the Marmoraton Mining Company, a subsidiary of Bethlehem Steel. The last bit of profitable ore had been dug out in 1978 after twenty-seven years of operation, leaving 300 people out of work. As with so many older shut-down mines, responsibility for clean-up was firmly in the hands of the province.

For decades, seventy million tons of waste rock had lain untouched, with one exception: a gravel operation run by Aecon, one of Canada's largest construction and infrastructure development companies, which crushed the waste rock to produce gravel for highway construction. "This was just a scar on the landscape with absolutely no prospect of being repaired," said Wright. Prospects for repair came more than three decades after the mine closure, when Aecon invited the CEO of Northland Power, John Brace, to come and have a look at the man-made lake adjacent to their gravel-crushing operations. Brace saw what needed to be done. Instead of mining the pit for ore or gravel, Northland would mine it for megawatts.

Mother Nature and Bethlehem Steel had created a near-perfect site for pumped storage hydro, a flexible and green way to produce electricity. Pumped storage is often viewed as the third musketeer on the renewable energy grid, filling gaps when the wind doesn't blow and the sun doesn't shine. Like a hydro dam, a pumped storage facility holds electricity for when it is required, operating much like a battery. In pumped storage hydro, though, water circulates back and forth between two reservoirs at different heights. Water can be pumped to the upper reservoir at night, when electricity prices are low, and released during the day, when energy is needed and prices are higher. Pumped storage works much like conventional hydro, with the force of the water driving turbines. It can either provide a set amount of electricity daily or store it ready for the moment it is urgently required, such as during a cold snap or heat wave.

Pumped storage is a new concept for most Canadians. In 2017, only one small pumped storage project was operating in the country, at Niagara Falls. Yet the technology, developed more than a century ago in Switzerland and Italy, is tried and true. There are more than sixty pumped storage facilities around the world, each of them capable of generating at least 1,000 megawatts of electricity. In North Wales, the

Dinorwig Power Station in Snowdonia National Park can ramp up more than two-and-a-half times Site C's energy output in a matter of minutes. When an entire nation turns on its teakettles at the end of an instalment of *Downton Abbey* or during halftime Premier League soccer, Dinorwig, built on the site of former slate quarries, releases water into turbines to meet demand. In Virginia, the Dominion Virginia Power pumped storage project produces a whopping 3,000 megawatts of electrical capacity, almost three times the capacity of Site C. When the project first came online in the mid-1980s, it sent so much electricity onto the grid so rapidly that the price of electricity trading prices spiralled down. Operators subsequently had to negotiate when to come online, and by how much.

Northland has secured the rights to the 2,000-acre former mining site from Aecon, to carve an upper reservoir from the seventy million tonnes of waste rock, lining it with asphalt or plastic. The Marmora pumped water project also had something else going for it: it was only 8 kilometres from a major transmission line servicing the Golden Horse-shoe, which could absorb more electricity.

But Northland's plan was far more ambitious than even this. Led by Wright, who had been a commissioner in the Ontario city of Brampton before he dove into the renewable energy field, the company conceived a multifaceted project – "like a Swiss Army knife," Wright put it – that would involve and benefit the entire community. "It's not a one trick pony," he explained. He reached out to Loyalist College in Belleville, forty-five minutes away by car, and soon had students working on a video about the project, which Northland then used to promote the site to investors, the media, and the public. Sir Sandford Fleming College in nearby Peterborough had Ontario's largest heavy-equipment operator training program; Wright envisioned two or three classes of students apprenticing during the four to five-year construction phase of the project. With funding from the Ontario government, a consulting firm fleshed out a plan to use the pumped storage project to attract tourists keen to see a clean energy project in action, while taking in the panoramic view and hiking, cycling, and cross-country skiing on an expanded local trail system. Also, a small mining museum would showcase rock samples and pay tribute to miners.

Wright saw an even larger benefit emerging from pumped storage. What if future mines close to the grid could be designed with the knowledge that they would become pumped storage projects after all the ore or nickel or other metals had been extracted? Instead of piling waste rock in random heaps, as was the case at Marmora, during mining operations the rock could be placed to form a reservoir; this would bring down the cost of pumped storage and the time it took to develop a site. Marmora, said Wright, was a project that would keep on giving. "It's a pretty good use of a natural resource, the ultimate use in my point of view."

Even though a report commissioned by BC Hydro revealed pumped storage to be a viable, cost-effective option for the province, one that would leave a pinky toe of an environmental footprint compared to large dams with their prodigious reservoirs, the government did not consider it an energy option. "The focus has shifted to Site C," commented Wright. "Everything else has fallen by the wayside."

A report written by the consulting firm Knight Piésold over a scant six weeks, after Campbell's big Site C announcement, focused solely on pumped storage options in southwestern BC. After eliminating any potential pumped storage sites in terrestrial parks and on salmon-bearing rivers, Knight Piésold concluded that there were almost two hundred potential pumped storage sites in southwestern BC. As the study explained, "the abundance of small lakes in combination with the steep topography, give south-western British Columbia a high potential for freshwater pumped storage development." On Vancouver Island, the study only included sites capable of producing 500 megawatts of electricity. In the Lower Mainland, that threshold was 1,000 megawatts, about the same amount of energy that would be generated by Site C. Of those sites, Knight Piésold identified forty-five as the cheapest to develop. A second report commissioned by BC Hydro in 2012 found that BC's north coast also had strong potential for pumped storage hydro. This report identified more than thirty freshwater pumped storage sites, each capable of producing 500 to 1,000 megawatts of electricity.

Other jurisdictions are not nearly as blinkered to the appeal of converting derelict mine sites into clean energy. In 2017 the Commonwealth of Virginia passed legislation to spur the development of pumped storage hydro projects at abandoned Appalachian coal mines. That same year in Australia, an abandoned Canadian gold mine near the northern Queensland town of Kidston was poised to become not just a pumped storage project but also an integrated solar farm, capable of generating 450 megawatts of electricity. Projects to turn abandoned mine sites into pumped storage facilities are also in the works in New York State's Adirondacks, where an iron mine that shut down in 1971 could be converted into 240 megawatts of pumped storage capacity, and in the German state of North Rhine–Westphalia, where an abandoned coal mine will generate 200 megawatts of electrical capacity, enough to power 400,000 German homes on demand.

IN MARCH 2017, while Ken and Arlene were witnessing the clear-cut logging and mulching of the family's forest at Cache Creek, sixty-one state-of-the-art wind turbines whirled to life at the province's newest and largest wind farm, just 200 kilometres distant. The Meikle Wind Project, built by the independent power company Pattern Development with strong support from Treaty 8 First Nations, has the capacity to pump enough electricity onto the grid to power the equivalent of 54,000 BC homes.

Located just north of the coal-mining town of Tumbler Ridge, surrounded by forest scarred by the mountain pine beetle and a landscape replete with dinosaur footprints and fossils, Meikle's turbines represent "another step forward in the evolution of wind technology," according to Robert Hornung, president of the Canada Wind Energy Association. The turbine blade tips are up to 170 metres long, and each turbine can adjust itself for varying wind speeds, sheer, and turbulence.

BC has lavish wind resources – "world class," according to Jean-François Nolet, vice-president of the Canadian Wind Energy Association. The province's potential for generating electricity from wind farms like Meikle is enormous. BC Hydro estimates the province's wind capacity at a whopping 16,000 megawatts, the equivalent to almost fifteen Site C dams (and that's just *on*shore capacity – it doesn't include BC's offshore potential). According to BC Hydro's own calculations, wind has the potential to blow the equivalent of all the power generated in BC onto the grid. Even without building any costly new transmission lines or other infrastructure, wind installations could quickly whistle up almost three Site C's worth of electricity capacity. And unlike Site C, whose power would come online all at once, capacity from wind developments can be added to the grid only as required.

Wind, whose cost is dropping rapidly, is widely viewed as the perfect complement to hydropower. Hydropower peaks during the spring freshet when meltwaters pour into the Peace and other rivers. Wind power peaks in the winter, when hydro's capacity is reduced. Elsewhere in the world, wind power is taking off. In 2015, as China began to transform itself from a climate villain into a green energy superpower, it added a new wind turbine to its renewable energy fleet every single hour. That same year, the Province of Quebec boasted five thousand full-time jobs in wind development. The Obama administration, for its part, set the stage for wind turbines to add the equivalent of 170 Site C dams in energy capacity to the American power grid.

Wind farms made up more than half of Europe's new power in 2016, with Germany setting the pace by coming online with the newest wind energy. That same year, France, Finland, the Netherlands, Ireland, and Lithuania all set records for wind farm installations. At the same time, Northland Power was busy constructing the North Sea's largest offshore wind farm – one of the biggest offshore wind installations in the world. After just two years of construction, the Gemini wind farm will supply the Netherlands with 600 megawatts of electricity capacity, reducing that country's annual greenhouse gas emissions by 1.2 million tonnes. A second Northland North Sea wind farm, Nordsee, off the coast of Germany, will have the capacity to generate almost as much power as Site C once all three phases are complete.

As with solar, new wind power technology is advancing at head-shaking speed. If you live in India, for the cost of an iPhone you can buy a wind turbine the size of a ceiling fan that, depending on the weather, will generate enough annual power for an average home. Two brothers from the Indian state of Kerala, Arun and Anoop George, invented the turbine. Their start-up company, Avant Garde Innovations, was among the ten Indian enterprises featured on the UN's clean energy investment opportunity directory. News of the invention came at around the same time as the Kerala state government's announcement that the Athirapally waterfalls, the largest natural waterfalls in Kerala, would be destroyed to create 163 megawatts of hydropower, submerging tribal settlements, compromising an irrigation system that provides water for 8,000 hectares of farmland, and eradicating a 140-hectare forest that provides habitat for tigers, Asiatic elephants, the Great Indian Hornbill, and the Malabar Giant Squirrel.

THE GEORGE BROTHERS SAID their goal was to introduce affordable energy solutions that would take "renewable energy self-sufficiency and energy empowerment to the next level through a distributed and decentralized approach." Another term for the same concept is prosumer – someone who produces energy as well as consuming it.

Producing energy locally, rather than sending it long distances over transmission lines, has many benefits. Ultimately, it costs consumers far less. And when households produce their own energy, there is very little waste, for 5 percent of electricity is lost when power is shipped through long-distance transmission lines in BC and an additional 5 percent is lost through local transmission lines.

Even though BC lags far behind other parts of the world, Gorman and other energy experts are confident that Canadians will soon make the move from simply consuming energy, over which most people "now have no control," to becoming prosumers, whom Gorman described as "consumer[s] with the ability to manage and generate electricity." Some players in the renewable energy sector, such as Steve Wenke, who works for the South Carolina–based utilities consulting firm AAC, predict that the upcoming transformation will throw the traditional power-delivery model into disarray. "The system is going to radically change," Wenke told colleagues gathered at the HydroVision conference.

The death spiral for today's typical power model, with energy consumers and producers cleaved apart, is now well under way in Germany. More and more German households are producing all or some of their own electricity, and 16 percent of German businesses are now energy self-sufficient. As more businesses and households start to produce electricity, the traditional model is being dealt another blow. When the capital cost of renewable energy decreases and prosumers multiply, households and businesses that only *consume* energy pay higher electricity costs, and this provides even more incentive to become energy self-sufficient. Meanwhile, one technology journalist has noted that global outlook for large utilities is "somewhat grim" as they face being "stuck with a growing pile of stranded assets."

After BC Hydro announced that the province would not require any additional wind power until at least 2030, Northland Power withdrew proposals for two wind farms, one near Prince George and the other near Summerland, with the combined capacity to generate half as much electricity as Site C. The proposals were already winding their way through BC's environmental assessment process when the company decided to pull up stakes and seek a more welcoming jurisdiction.

A few months before Northland's departure in May 2016, the Canadian Wind Energy Association had also retreated from the province. Citing a lack of opportunity to develop new wind projects in BC, the association pulled out its regional director and said it would focus for now on provinces friendlier to wind power – namely, Alberta and Saskatchewan. BC lacked a "vision of short-term opportunities" for wind power, said Nolet. Vancouver energy lawyer David Austin pointed out that Site C threw "a terribly dark shadow over the renewable sector in BC ... There has to be a reasonable prospect of a market" if clean renewables are to set up shop in the province.

The wind association was far from the only renewable energy advocate to encounter a lacklustre reception in BC. The government had rolled out the red carpet for Site C. Alison Thompson, the president of the Canadian Geothermal Energy Association, received a far less enthusiastic welcome when she provided the BC government with studies showing that geothermal could provide five times as much energy as Site C and create 1,900 long-term jobs.

Canada is the only country in the Pacific Ring of Fire – a horseshoe-shaped geological zone with intense volcanic and seismic activity – that does not use its geothermal resources to produce commercial-scale energy. The recurrent claim by Site C proponents that geothermal is an unproven technology is belied by its routine use in countries such as the United States, Italy, New Zealand, and Iceland. Iceland, for instance, grows bananas and salad greens in geothermal-heated greenhouses that supply much of the country's produce. It even uses geothermal energy to make ice cream in its capital city, Reykjavik, which is itself heated entirely by geothermal. Hot water is piped from Iceland's largest geothermal energy plant, Hellisheidi, and circulated throughout the city for district heating.

Closer to home, the United States is the world's top geothermal energy producer, and Mexico ranks fourth. Why can't BC, which is brimming with geothermal activity, follow suit? According to the geothermal association's website, BC is "Canada's lowest hanging fruit geothermal resource base." Widespread natural gas drilling in northeastern BC has already provided data on where to tap into the subsurface's abundant heat sources, and the association has mapped the hot sedimentary aquifers around the province that can provide low-impact geothermal energy.

Thompson said only one thing has prevented BC from becoming a geothermal powerhouse: a lack of political will. Had the BC government treated geothermal as a priority, and not as an afterthought, geothermal could have provided reliable energy starting in 2018, at a lower cost than Site C and with far less of an environmental footprint. As Thompon's association pointed out in a statement to the Joint Review Panel, "BC Hydro has not properly informed themselves about the geothermal option and continues to perpetuate the just-ain't-so information to the public."

The BC government was not alone among the provinces in snubbing geothermal. As a geochemist with Natural Resource Canada's Canadian Geological Survey stated, "We have enormous potential for geothermal energy in Canada ... well over a million times what Canadians actually use." The survey calculated that Canada could meet all its electricity needs with as few as one hundred geothermal projects. But as Thompson points out, even though Canada has an incredible high-quality resource, "we can't even get out of the starting gate."

When the BC Utilities Commission reviewed Site C in the early 1980s, it advised BC Hydro to examine geothermal with an eye to using it to meet future electricity demand if technological advances significantly improved its relative cost. But "little was done," according to the Joint Review Panel. Geothermal potential was all but ignored by BC's Liberal government, even though its own Clean Energy Act included a directive to support renewable energy resources. The Joint Review Panel laid the blame for BC Hydro's failure to investigate geothermal firmly at the feet of the government. BC Hydro's "lack of performance" on geothermal, the panel said, was due to a lack of geological exploration funding. The panel lamented the lost opportunity: "A failure to pursue research over the last 30 years into BC's geothermal resources has left BC Hydro without information about a resource the BC Hydro thinks may offer up to 700 megawatts of firm, economic power with low environmental costs." CanGEA maintained that the geothermal potential in BC was considerably higher than BC Hydro's estimates. The equivalent of five Site C dams – or 5,500 megawatts of electricity – could be tapped for energy, the association said.

The Rocky Mountain town of Valemount also glimpsed a clean and green energy future in geothermal. Once a typical northern forestry town, Valemount decided to tap into geothermal energy generated from the nearby Kinbasket Canoe Reach hot springs. In tandem with a company called Borealis, the town planned a future in which geothermal would fuel an "eco-village" or "geo-park" of businesses, including an existing microbrewery, fish farms, and greenhouses to extend the town's relatively short growing season and offer fresh produce any month of the year. Michael Lewis, owner of the local Three Ranges Brewery, explained that geothermal "has the potential for being a really ticketable showcase" for clean energy.

BC Hydro told the Joint Review Panel that it had looked at alternatives to Site C, including wind and solar, and found that they were more expensive. Energy experts disputed that claim, as did the heads of Canada's national wind, solar, and geothermal associations. Deloitte LLP, one of the country's leading auditing firms, found that an alternative resource portfolio – primarily wind and geothermal – could provide as much clean energy as Site C at a comparable or lower cost. Through a Freedom of Information request, lawyers for the Peace Valley Landowner Association spent many months trying to get Cabinet documents and related background materials outlining the cost of renewable energy alternatives to Site C. When they finally did get it, so many pages had been redacted that it was useless.

In the seven years following Campbell's Site C announcement, the cost of solar tumbled by 74 percent, while the cost of wind fell by 65 percent. "The day of the megaproject has passed," declared American energy economist Robert McCullough, who was hired by the landowners' association to examine Site C. A blustery man with an encyclopedic knowledge of continental energy trends, McCullough warned that there were fundamental flaws in BC Hydro's business case for Site C, which he called an "expensive luxury." The project was dramatically more expensive than other renewable energy options, said McCullough, adding that "only an idiot would be building a very expensive project in Canada instead of buying power on the open market."

As Karen Bakker and other academics pointed out, in tandem with McCullough's and Swain's comments, BC Hydro had based its projections about the cost of Site C relative to other clean energy sources on dubious premises. Essentially, BC Hydro had assumed that the price of wind and solar would not fall after 2012, even though international energy experts concurred that the costs of wind power would fall substantially, from a 25 percent reduction by 2025 or 2030 to up to 40 percent by 2040. Solar, for its part, was "set to decline dramatically" from current prices, Bakker and other academics pointed out in an April 2017 report. The report concluded that Site C's business case was so weak the project should be immediately put on hold and that it would be cheaper to cancel it than to continue with construction.

The report also revealed that BC Hydro had been incrementally scaling back its energy conservation programs – programs that encouraged energy conservation through voluntary measures such as retrofitting buildings, switching to energy-efficient appliances, and turning off lights in unoccupied rooms – effectively driving the need for new electricity. The public utility had even failed to meet the reduced energy conservation targets it had set for itself. Before cutbacks, BC Hydro's Power Smart program was so successful that, in fiscal 2014, it had saved almost the same amount of energy that Site C would produce, the equivalent of meeting the annual needs of more than 440,000 homes.

By reducing its energy conservation programs, BC Hydro saved between $50 and $100 million a year on its books. But those were false savings when compared to the cost of Site C. Bakker and her colleagues concluded that Site C's electricity would cost about three times as much as reducing demand through energy conservation. Energy conservation measures alone could meet any excess demand for a decade, and in the meantime, as Bakker pointed out, "it would allow us to explore other cheaper and less environmentally damaging renewables." The report also showed that Site C's power would not be needed even if future LNG developments required electricity and BC set about to decarbonize its economy, such as by putting more electric vehicles on the road.

If something entirely unforeseen shifted dramatically, and BC did indeed need more energy, there were easier and less expensive ways to get it than Site C. On the north shore of Port Moody, just east of Vancouver, stands BC Hydro's mothballed gas-fired Burrard Generating Plant. Built in 1963, the plant was refurbished in the 1990s to become the cleanest standby natural-gas-fired plant on the continent. It can generate 950 megawatts of power, almost as much power as Site C. But because of its comparatively high greenhouse gas emissions, and in response to deepening concerns about air pollution in the Lower Mainland, the plant was used only as standby electricity during cold snaps, and even then only for emergencies – when ice jams on the Peace River curtailed electricity generation or heavy snows toppled transmission towers on Vancouver Island. Burrard Thermal, explained Port Moody resident Elaine Golds, was "like the twenty-year-old car that's only been used to drive to church on Sundays."

The BCUC, acting in the public interest, wanted the Burrard plant to continue to function as electricity insurance. For a maintenance cost of $20 million a year, the plant could provide emergency backup power if it was ever needed. But the Liberal cabinet decided to close Burrard Thermal, thereby helping to justify the need for Site C. During the Joint Review Panel hearings, Swain and other panel members heard repeatedly from northern residents that the political decision to close Burrard Thermal had opened the gates for Site C. Swain put it bluntly to BC Hydro during the Joint Review Panel hearings: "We're trading air pollution in the Lower Mainland for a set of environmental consequences up here plus $8 billion." The district of Hudson's Hope pointed out that it would take only $1 billion to retrofit the Burrard plant to bring it into compliance with the Clean Energy Act. But for the Liberal government, doing so was never an option. In the spring of 2016, Burrard Thermal quietly shut its doors.

Another way to acquire new electricity for BC, should it ever be needed, was to claim the Canadian entitlement for power produced on the Columbia River. Under the terms of the 1964 Columbia River Treaty signed by Canada and the United States, BC had built three dams on the Columbia River – the Mica, Revelstoke, and Keenleyside dams – while the United States constructed the Libby Dam in Montana. Canada retained the rights to have the downstream power generated by the Libby Dam, whose operations were only possible because of the BC dams upstream. That amounted to roughly the same amount of power as Site C would produce. Swain pointed out: "To say we will not consider our entitlement under the Columbia River Treaty is inexplicable." Either country could pull out of the treaty with ten years' notice, which was, Swain noted, considerably less time than it was taking for Site C to proceed through regulatory review and construction.

Under the terms of the Columbia River Treaty, BC accepted delivery of the power and immediately sold it back to the United States at spot market prices. In the years leading up to the start of Site C construction, the province sold the power for $100 to $300 million a year. In the two years after Site C was announced, from 2010 to 2012, the province received about $30 per megawatt hour for the power. That compared favourably with the projected cost of Site C's power, which Swain pegged at $120 per megawatt hour in early 2018 (by comparison, Alberta bought new wind power in late 2017 for $37 per megawatt hour). "Why not just use our own inexpensive resources instead of selling them off for so little?" asked Philip Raphals, an energy analyst hired by the Treaty 8 Tribal Association to provide expert testimony during the Site C hearings.

The nonsensical reason BC did not consider the Columbia River entitlement as an alternative to Site C circled back to the Campbell government's Clean Energy Act, which mandated that BC must be self-sufficient in electricity. The act prohibited BC from accepting Columbia River electricity generated in the United States. In other words, BC could import its cars, computers, and steel, but it could not increase electricity imports. Rejecting geothermal, new wind power, vastly expanded solar, pumped storage, a Burrard Thermal plant refurbishment, and Canada's entitlement under the Columbia River Treaty left only one option: Site C.

11

Fight or Flight?

As Arlene harvested grapes and corn from her family garden in late August 2016, the Boons received a package from BC Hydro. It was a draft offer to buy most of the couple's property, the cover letter explained, and to do so without prejudice, meaning that BC Hydro would not be beholden to the terms if the case wound up in court. The letter was adroitly worded. It sounded more like a polite invitation to an event than an ultimatum.

The letter mentioned nothing about compelling the Boons to sell, or what would happen if they declined the offer. "BC Hydro requires the acquisition of the rights for the re-alignment of Highway 29 by the end of this year," it simply said. Signed by Thomas Brent, BC Hydro's new property representative, the buyout offer was in the Boons' inbox when they returned to the house after harvesting barley and oats and checking on their Bear Flat campground, where BC Hydro's plan called for the new highway to run right through the cook shack and shower buildings.

For several weeks, the offer lay dormant in the computer on the Boons' shared desk in their little office adjoining the kitchen. If they reached out the office window, they could almost touch the centreline of the planned new highway, next to their woodshed. From the window, Arlene could see the renovated schoolhouse where her mother had lived, and just beyond that, the apple and pear trees in a corner of her garden,

Ken and Arlene sit at their kitchen table looking at BC Hydro maps of their third-generation family farm, expropriated for Site C | *Photo by Louis Bockner*

fenced to keep out the deer, moose, and elk. A few months earlier, her mother, Caroline Bentley, had decided she did not want her final years to be shrouded in uncertainty and tension and had moved to Fort St. John. Arlene worried about her mother, who had spent the past sixty years living on farms. But there was nothing she could do to dissuade her from the move. Listening to noisy drilling rigs, and watching a seemingly endless parade of BC Hydro contractors flow past her kitchen and living room windows, as workers spent weeks testing the geological properties of the family farm and marking out the new highway's centre-line, had taken its psychological and emotional toll.

For the first time, the Boons were unsure what to do. They had always known what to do before: fight Site C. Write letters. Stay informed. Speak out. Resist. They had asked BC Hydro many questions about the highway relocation, and months later they were still waiting for most of the answers. So many things were up in the air. But the Boons knew one thing for certain: they could not ignore that letter.

The landowners were informed that they had two options for expropriation. They could sign an agreement called a Section 3, which would
give BC Hydro the opportunity to announce that it had reached agreement with the Cache Creek property owners over expropriation terms,
or they could refuse to sign. Either way, they would lose their home.
Refusing to sign a Section 3 expropriation agreement could leave the
Boons in an even more compromised position, their lawyer warned,
for they might forfeit any say in the terms of any residential and farming lease that could allow them to remain in their home and farm for
another season.

Arlene wondered if they would have enough money to buy another
farm, even one that did not have expansive views of the valley and a
microclimate that allowed her to harvest strawberries and grapes at the
tail end of September. Her next grandchild was on the way, providing
yet another compelling reason to stay close. The Boons might be able
to move somewhere farther uphill in the valley, out of the reservoir and
sloughing zones, and buy property owned by another family member
or a neighbour. But what would it be like to live so close to the reservoir,
to see the valley inundated, to witness the destruction of so many things
dear to them? Noise from the angle of the new highway might be very
disruptive, and no one could predict what living next to the reservoir
would be like as the river banks collapsed, fomenting waves and dust.
For safety reasons, BC Hydro had said that people would not be able
to venture near the lip of the reservoir for years after its creation. There
were so many unknowns. "We're kind of on the cusp now," Ken said.
"It's not a rosy picture, that's for sure."

The civil lawsuit had stopped the Boons from granting permission
to valley residents, First Nations members, and others to camp on their
land to block work on the new highway. It would have been much easier
to set up a camp like the Rocky Mountain Fort protest on their side of
the valley, close to food and shelter. It would also have been much more
visible, especially in the summer. But the Boons worried they would
face criminal records and even jail time if they agreed to let others stage

a protest on their land. The $420 million in potential damages stemming from the civil suit was constantly on their minds.

Arlene admitted to being tired, and it was not the kind of tired that can be fixed with a few good nights' sleeps, but the bone-deep exhaustion of living with acute stress and uncertainty for far too many years. The fight had been gruelling. Now she had to consider the prospect of flight.

The following month, in September 2016, the Peace Valley Landowner Association lost its Site C appeal in the BC Supreme Court. The ruling was a bit of a head-scratcher, according to Ken. He also called it a "dangerous precedent" and "pretty scary." The landowners had argued that the BC government had failed to consider key recommendations made by the Joint Review Panel, including that the project be examined by the BC Utilities Commission. But the court ruled that the government was not bound to consider that panel's recommendations.

The ruling raised the sticky question of why the BC government was devoting considerable time and money to environmental assessments in the first place, if there was no requirement for it to heed the resulting conclusions and follow the key recommendations. "This one comes right out of left field and leaves one wondering what good is the environmental assessment process," commented Ken. "It really turns out to be a rubber stamp process if government doesn't have to consider key recommendations."

The Boons had little time to digest that news, however, before another pressing issue swept them up. Two weeks before the court decision, BC Hydro had filed a notice in a local paper, the *Alaska Highway News*, advising the public that it had applied to the provincial Ministry of Forests, Lands and Natural Resource Operations (FLNRO) for another "license of occupation" to cut and clear forest and vegetation. In keeping with procedure, BC Hydro's application for a licence of occupation was made to FNLRO's FrontCounter BC division, a "single window service for clients." Once again, a Crown corporation that took its marching orders from the provincial cabinet had applied to a government

ministry that also took its marching orders from cabinet, requesting
a permit it would undoubtedly receive.

Ken tracked down a map of the application area. Yellow lines demar-
cated the next zone on the Site C chopping block. The lines indicated
that clear-cutting and bulldozing would soon take place all the way from
what the locals called Eagle Island, just upstream from the Rocky Mountain Fort site, right up to the Boons' property line at Cache Creek, about
20 kilometres distant. The application – one of many staged applications
for Site C clear-cutting – covered 1,225 hectares of Crown land along
the banks of the Peace River, an area six times the size of Vancouver's
West End. It included known nesting areas for migratory bird species
vulnerable to extinction, like the Canada Warbler, and three of the rare
tufa seeps.

BC Hydro said the clearing was necessary to prepare for any flooding
that might ensue three years later, in the fall of 2019, when the Peace
River was scheduled to be diverted through tunnels to dry out the river-
bed so that work on the dam structure could begin. The application for
a licence of occupation required a public comment period, and the
Boons and many others dutifully outlined their concerns about the
impact the logging would have on the tufa seeps, rare and endangered
wildlife, and the valley's First Nations and farming community. But the
licence, as expected, was duly granted. The public comment period had
been merely a formality. UBC professor Karen Bakker said that while
she didn't want to seem overly cynical, she could only conclude that "BC
Hydro and the provincial government want to be seen as going through
the motions, and this is going through the motions."

For the Boons, it was another punch among so many. Even if the
landowners, working in tandem with First Nations leaders, managed
to postpone the highway relocation or succeeded in switching the route
to the other shortlisted one, the family would soon be looking across
the Peace River at clear-cuts instead of at the green quilt of old-growth
forest that had been set aside to become part of the Peace–Boudreau
protected area. Along the terraces on the Boons' side of the river, immediately downstream from their farm, a necklace of small ponds of

varying sizes, a magnet for migratory birds surrounded by Saskatoon and chokecherry bushes, stood little chance of being spared. Above the ponds was an overgrown path that had been the former road to Charlie Lake. Once a First Nations trailway, the path offered broad views of the looping river below and the forest beyond.

As the Boons absorbed the magnitude of the next extended valley clear-cut, they found themselves in the middle of a painful and protracted negotiation with BC Hydro, with lawyers as intermediaries on both sides, over the terms of their farm expropriation. In the absence of a framework agreement – the agreement that had been denied by BC Hydro – the Boons and their neighbours had to negotiate with Hydro individually, without a common baseline to determine a dollar value for everything from their homes to their arable land to their lost access to parts of their properties that BC Hydro did not plan to expropriate. The landowners decided to work together with a lawyer and communicate among themselves despite the lack of a formal agreement, an initiative that, Ken noted, "did force BC Hydro to treat people the same."

The Boons and other valley landowners believed that the assessed value of their properties had been depressed because of the longstanding Site C flood reserve, the fact that BC Hydro had become a major valley landowner over the years, and the uncertainties surrounding Site C. Except for land sales to BC Hydro, which had picked up after construction began in 2015, Site C had killed much of the valley's real estate market.

The issue of a gravel deposit deep under the Boons' property offered a revealing glimpse of how land prices are set when you have only have one buyer and you know you have to sell. Buried under 3 metres of topsoil in the Boons' riverside fields was a layer of gravel, deposited thousands of years earlier by a departing glacier. Gravel was expensive, besides being a necessary component of the new highway. The couple had long suspected that BC Hydro might want to extract the gravel below their bottom fields for the highway or for other construction related to Site C, although BC Hydro did not say that to them. The gravel lay several metres below the topsoil and would be costly to extract, but shallower gravel beds existed in places along the highway realignment. Extracting gravel close to the new highway would save the province's transportation department the time, and BC Hydro the cost, of trucking tons of gravel in from elsewhere. So the Boons sent a note to BC Hydro asking them to include the value of the gravel in their appraisal. But BC Hydro replied that it was not interested in the gravel and could not include it in the assessment. The Boons could do nothing. BC Hydro would ultimately set the price for their land, and the couple could challenge that price only by going to court. Once BC Hydro owned the property, it could do whatever it wanted with both the topsoil and gravel. Even while home sellers in Vancouver and Victoria were benefiting from bidding wars, with modest homes selling for tens and even hundreds of thousands of dollars above asking prices, valley landowners sitting on some of the most productive farmland in the province faced a BC Hydro monopoly that pushed land values down, not up.

THE CABIN WHERE Caroline Bentley had lived sat near the edge of the field where Richard Hebda had found the taiga vole skeletons. In late September, when I visited, hay bales were scattered asymmetrically around the field. The nearly empty cabin's kitchen window was framed with a bouquet of freshly picked sunflowers and kale. Arlene was still harvesting potatoes, carrots, kale, and squash even though October was knocking at her door. The chirrupy barn and cliff swallows were gone, a week into their migration south, as the Peace River Valley prepared for its winter snooze. The valley grass was still green and leaves still clothed many trees, but the weather forecast warned that up to 20 centimetres of snow was on its way.

In the rosy late afternoon sunlight, three generations of Arlene's family gathered in the garden to put it to bed for the winter. The week had been sun-filled and mild, and Arlene's strawberry patch still blushed with fruit. Purple grape bunches hung upside down from the monkey bar of a trellis. Most of the vegetables had been harvested two days earlier, before a heavy frost, but stragglers still popped up as Arlene and her youngest son, Derrick, and daughter-in-law Brenda tugged out rows of corn stalks, shaking black earth from their roots: a cucumber, a handful of green beans, a garland of cherry tomatoes, half-red, half-green. Waist-high dill had gone to seed in frilly clusters. The air smelled like fresh dill pickles.

Arlene heard the birds before anyone could see them. They flew in three tight V-formations, honking, the needle of their flock's compass pointed south. They knew what Arlene knew: a significant snowfall was on its way to the Peace. She squinted at the sky. It likely wouldn't affect the valley, she said. With her finger, she drew a snow line on the cliffs downstream from the farm, cliffs coloured five shades of pink by the falling sun. "We have our own microclimate here," she reminded me.

A niece and two young grandnieces from Fort St. John joined the work party. No one spoke of Site C. No one talked about the new high-way that would run right through the garden. The corn's departure un-covered rows of fat green pumpkins, all shapes and sizes. These were piled into wheelbarrows to be carted to a cold room, where they would turn orange and become puree for pies and dinner. Caleb, Arlene's four-year-old grandson, would choose one for Halloween. He dragged corn stalks into a pile; he was the fifth generation of his family to harvest this land. He had bright blue glasses and curly blond hair. In one fist Caleb gripped the tip of a pale yellow ear of corn, its missing kernels in his belly. The other fist clenched a carrot streaked black by the soil. For Arlene, there was no illogic in the garden. There were no ultimatums, and no threats. There was only earth and a buffet of bright-coloured vegetables and fruit, and a task that had a clear beginning and end.

The next morning brought a thick, cold rain. Snow had fallen during the night, but the white line stopped halfway down the cliffs on the Fort St. John side of the valley, just as Arlene had predicted. At the top of the cliffs, clearly visible from the Boons' farm, lay a good six inches of snow. Down at the farm, the grass was still green, the hayfields golden. In Fort St. John, Arlene's friends posted Facebook photos of snowmen and measured heaps of snow on backyard picnic tables. Arlene placed a long dish of freshly picked strawberries, grapes, and tomatoes on her outside railing and snapped a photo with the green valley in the background, a reminder to her Facebook friends that microclimates were not to be taken for granted.

A short while later, sitting at her kitchen table, Arlene suddenly cocked her head and said, "Here come the robins." We jumped up to see dozens of migrating robins parachuting onto the grass and the garden fence. Soon more arrived, seeking refuge from the snow. And more. By mid-afternoon, when I had to leave, hundreds of robins were spiralling around the farmhouse. Other birds also landed in quick succession: cowbirds, ravens. A flock of smaller birds I could not identify circled over a river-side field of sunflowers, like a school of fish in the grey sky. But it was the robins that enchanted me. They dangled from the trees like Christmas ornaments and claimed haystacks as round as their summer bellies.

AS THE BOONS DELIBERATED about their two options for expropriation, BC Hydro was ever present. October 5 marked the fifty-sixth day that the family had to contend with BC Hydro workers on their property. That month, valley landowners and First Nations launched the Yellow Stakes Campaign to raise money for ongoing First Nations court cases against the dam. Each stake marked a $100 donation to support First Nations court cases against Site C. The stakes mimicked the ones that BC Hydro contractors had hammered into the ground throughout the Cache Creek area to mark the new highway centreline. As the number of yellow stakes and public scrutiny of Site C grew like two parallel climbing lines on a graph, the Boons received even more distressing news from their lawyer. BC Hydro, the lawyer informed the couple, had advanced its deadline for acquiring the Cache Creek properties. The utility company now required the Boons to sign over their farm and other properties by October 31, two months earlier than the previous deadline. Clara London, Arlene's younger sister, would have to do the same.

When the landowners challenged the new deadline, BC Hydro said it had to acquire their properties earlier so that Cache Creek clear-cutting could be completed that winter, to avoid destroying songbird nests. The

Ken Boon and Bob Fedderly, a Fort St. John oil and gas contractor, pound in yellow stakes near the Boon's house. The stakes mark the planned centreline for the new Site C highway | *Photo by Louis Bockner*

Boons and their neighbours were incredulous. They were even more disbelieving when news stories circulated that same week saying that the BC government was trying to drive up demand for electricity because of a surplus. Once again, Premier Clark was talking about shipping power from the Site C dam to Alberta's Oil Sands, again underscoring that the electricity was not needed in BC. "It just makes your blood boil," Arlene commented. "To lose low elevation bottomland farmland to electrify the Oil Sands does not seem very ethical. To think that we're going to lose our home and land to that is very disturbing to us."

As the stressful negotiations continued, BC Hydro moved the expropriation deadline to November 4, then to noon on November 10. It was finally set at one p.m. on November 21, leaving landowners scrambling under intense pressure to settle the terms for handing over their properties. As the deadlines shifted, the Boons felt like hostages on their own land. There was little they could do. The number of days before the final deadline shrank, and the number of yellow stakes grew. BC Hydro's apparent insensitivity to the stress placed on the landowners by the repeatedly shifting deadline, combined with increased awareness of and opposition to Site C around the province, nudged the Boons to a clear decision overnight. They had put up with far too much to give up now.

The couple refused to sell their property to BC Hydro as a Section 3 expropriation, even though they faced far greater personal and financial risks as a result. Ken said they knew they might get "hung out to dry." But at the end of the day, he said, "there was no way we were going to sign it over to them." Arlene's sister Clara and her husband, who owned 7 hectares of adjacent farmland that BC Hydro also wanted for the highway, also refused to sign. Their loss, noted London, was "pretty small" compared to what Ken and Arlene faced.

Once BC Hydro learned that the Boons had refused to sign the Section 3 expropriation papers, bargaining began in earnest. The Boons said they wanted to be able to farm their bottom fields for two more years, and BC Hydro acquiesced. They said they wanted to stay in their house over the winter, and BC Hydro consented. But the final agreement, like so much else to do with Site C, came at a price. In it, BC Hydro stipulated that the family's riverside fields, which had been used for more than a decade as the pullout spot for the annual Paddle for the Peace and post-paddle barbecue hosted by First Nations, could only be used for agriculture and not for camping or gatherings. BC Hydro would let the Boons stay in their home until the end of May, but only if the couple signed a legal agreement saying they would not prevent work on Site C from taking place. Clearly, the government did not want images of farmers booted from their land circulating before or during the provincial election campaign in April and early May. In what was called a No Interference document, the Boons were obliged to consent "not to directly or indirectly impede or obstruct the Project or any Project activities."

The Boons felt they had no choice but to sign. If they were ousted from their home before the provincial election, it would demoralize other valley landowners as well as First Nations, environmental, church, and community groups all over the province who were now campaigning to stop Site C. Their departure, they believed, would give the government and BC Hydro yet another reason to point to the project being past the point of no return. The Boons now clung to what at the time was a faint hope that the May 9 provincial election would bring in a new government that would terminate Site C. The decision to sign the document and stay in their home for another six months brought fleeting relief and eased some of their stress, even though, as Arlene said, "It's going to be a roller coaster, I know."

The expropriation, when it happened, underscored just how few rights Canadian landowners have once any level of government decides their property is needed for the "greater good." Canada is a democratic country, yet homeownership does not grant the Boons (or any other Canadians, for that matter) security of tenure on their private property. Property rights are not enshrined in the Canadian Constitution – something that places the country out of step with most other industrialized nations. Over the years, Canadian families have been forced to relinquish their property or homes to corporations and governments for everything from a kitty litter mine to hydro transmission line corridors. "We didn't even realize the expropriation process had happened," recalled Arlene. "We were the little peons at the other end of the pile of paperwork. We never signed a thing."

The person who signed the expropriation paperwork was Bill Bennett, the energy minister. He did so on December 8, from his hometown of Cranbrook, never having met the Boons or set foot on their farm. The Boons received the documents from their lawyer a few days after Bennett affixed his signature. The notice invoked Queen Elizabeth: "Take notice that her Majesty the Queen, in right of the province of British Columbia, as represented by the Minister of Energy, Mines and Minister responsible for Core Review, has approved the expropriation."

The expropriation stripped the Boons of 130 hectares of land. It left them with full ownership of 33 devalued hectares of land flanking the new highway corridor and with 25 hectares of land over which BC Hydro said it would place a statutory right-of-way. No buildings would be permitted on the right-of-way, which meant that even though the Boons still held legal title, they would have limited use of their land. They were left with 4 hectares of farmland in two separate pieces. The small chunks might suit a different type of farming operation – growing organic vegetables near a major city, for example – but the Boons farmed large crops like hay and barley with large equipment like combines that needed bigger fields even just to turn around. "We're not sure if we even have a viable piece left to make a farm," said Arlene.

The amount of money BC Hydro had determined the property was worth suddenly appeared in the Boons' bank account. This would have serious implications for the couple in terms of their income taxes, and on top of that, the way in which BC Hydro had carved up their property presented them with other headaches and potential financial liabilities. Because BC Hydro had subdivided their property, their remaining land might now be taxed as a residential lot instead of as farmland. The Boons consulted a lawyer and hired an accountant to try to untangle the mess.

Following the expropriation notice, the Boons thought – mistakenly, as it turned out – that they would have some peace and quiet for a while. The Christmas season brought a new baby into the family. A welcome distraction, Arlene said. Baby Rene, a sister for Caleb, arrived just in time to celebrate Christmas with the extended family. Four generations of the Boons and the Bentleys gathered on their land for what could be their last Christmas in the farmhouse, a time to laugh together and share meals and memories.

The New Year began jarringly for the Boons. On January 3 they received notification from BC Hydro that in three days' time, geotechnical crews would be arriving to drill test holes along the centreline for the new highway on the west side of the house, right outside their kitchen window. Just four months earlier they had received a notice saying that all the drilling on their property had been completed. The place slated for drilling was the spot where BC Hydro crews had already drilled a geotechnical test hole. It was also the exact spot where five hundred yellow stakes had been driven into the ground and where hundreds more would soon be added. BC Hydro informed the Boons that the new geotechnical work would take between five and ten days to complete. Also, the yellow stakes – photos of which were circulating widely on social media – would have to be moved. (After much discussion, the drilling contractor conceded that drilling beside the stakes would yield sufficient results and that it would not in fact be necessary to extract them from the frozen ground.)

The "Cooperation Agreement" the Boons had signed with BC Hydro stipulated that they, as tenants, "may peaceably possess and enjoy the Premises" during the agreed term. But there was no chance of either peace or enjoyment for the couple. What ensued was so disruptive that the Boons wrote a public statement titled "The Landlord from Hell," stating that BC Hydro's actions "smelled of harassment" and were "not a very classy way to treat us." From seven-thirty a.m. to six p.m., the drilling machine roared outside their farmhouse windows. Arlene was thankful her mother was no longer living there to suffer through the racket and intrusion. On her Facebook page, she posted a video clip of the drilling machine and the insufferable noise – like a jet taking off in close proximity.

As the end of January approached, the Boons' extended family gathered once again. Twenty-nine adults and children, mostly family members, hiked up Cache Creek in the snow and had a wiener and marshmallow roast outdoors. Arlene posed for photos with her two sisters in some of the same places where they had played as children.

Early in the New Year, BC Hydro applied to the Ministry of Forests, Lands and Natural Resource Operations for another licence of occupation. This time, the licence sought permission to clear-cut the Cache Creek Valley bottom and slopes and most of the Bear Flat area – not just the property needed for the highway relocation but the forest all the way to the top of the reservoir line. Watson Slough, the sprawling complex of wetlands at Bear Flat, just upstream from the Boons' property, was included in the application.

News of BC Hydro's imminent logging plans for the slough came as communities around the world celebrated World Wetlands Day and Australian scientists embarked on a experiment using tea bags to measure the considerable amount of carbon stored in wetlands worldwide. The planned logging, according to wildlife biologist Mark Phinney, would eradicate habitat for about twenty bird species that nested in trees and shrubs around the wetland, including the Western Tanager, Least Flycatcher, and Yellow Warbler. Many species would no longer be found around the slough if logging proceeded, Phinney said: "They'll come back and their habitat will be gone."

BC Hydro's plans to log the slough riled the broader Peace community well beyond anyone who would lose land to Site C. The slough had long been the community's outdoor skating rink, and many a game of pick-up hockey had been played there over the decades. Ross Peck publicly challenged BC Hydro executives to a hockey duel to determine the future of the slough. The Peace River Regional District, encompassing seven municipalities and four electoral areas, voted to ask BC Hydro to postpone the wetland logging. The slough was not needed for the highway relocation, and Site C's reservoir would not flood it for at least another seven years.

Karen Goodings, the regional district director who represented the area that included the slough, described the wetland as an irreplaceable landmark in the valley. The regional district said it had not been given BC Hydro's mitigation plans for the slough, which BC Hydro was required to circulate to the district and others for comment as a condition of Site C's environmental certificate. BC Hydro countered that the mitigation plans had been included in a six-hundred-page mitigation and monitoring plan for vegetation and wildlife that it had released in 2015. That plan, however, did not include specific mitigation options for the slough.

In February, while BC Hydro was considering the regional district's request, logging machinery and security crews arrived at Bear Flat. An operations camp was established across the highway from Watson Slough. The Boons did what many would not have had the strength or the stomach to do: they watched as the forest their family had protected was destroyed. "The creek bottom with those large trees was valuable wildlife habitat, and we chose to leave it that way," the couple pointed out. The logging crew clear-cut Cache Creek first – Ken took a photo of a felled cottonwood with a Red-Tailed Hawk nest that the contractors left until last, as if reluctant to destroy it in plain view of Ken – and then the machinery rumbled up the broad-bottomed creek.

Industrial wood mulchers spewed black diesel as they chewed up the large cottonwoods, poplars, and birches. It took thirty minutes for one machine to mulch a large cottonwood, calculated Ken, and a mulcher burned about 1,000 litres of diesel fuel per shift. "If there is a more expensive and dirty way to clear the valley, BC Hydro has not found it," wrote the couple. "Those mulchers are literally mulching dollar bills." In their haste to complete the work, BC Hydro's contractors mulched Arlene's brother's fence posts, destroying the enclosure that kept his cattle contained and compelling BC Hydro to pay another contractor to build him a new fence. Arlene's sister Clara wrote to the local newspaper after the trees on what had been her property were mulched. For three generations, London said, the family had protected and respected the land, only to see the logged trees, including merchantable timber, discarded and then shredded. Landowners, she said, had been "treated with great disrespect."

As the crew cleared Cache Creek, along with strips of valuable moose and bird habitat on the opposite side of the highway, closer to the river, BC Hydro took out an ad in the local newspaper. "Watson Slough: We're Listening," said the headline. BC Hydro, the ad asserted, was committed to being a good neighbour and partner. The ad announced that Hydro had made changes to the Watson Slough clearing plan to "prolong the productivity of the wetland area." Only 10 percent of the slough area would be logged that winter, leaving the rest intact for another seven years or so, until the winter before scheduled flooding. It was a small victory for the Boons and other valley residents, in the face of many defeats.

As the legal bird-nesting window approached on March 31, the machinery near the Boons' house fell silent. BC Hydro had informed the Boons and other valley residents, through an information bulletin, that people "living in the vicinity of the reservoir area will experience visual changes as a result of clearing." That was quite the bureaucratic understatement for what the Boons referred to as an "ecological disaster." The wide Cache Creek Valley had been shaved bare. Logging extended well up the valley, covering 40 hectares in all. It even reached around two feeder creeks, Red Creek and Chicken Creek. BC Hydro crews had left no riparian zones at all. "It is a fricking mess," Ken declared when the spring rains arrived. "Big dams of mulch with water are flowing through on their way into Cache Creek. In other areas down there, where water is lying in the mulch [and] is not flowing, the water looks like tea now." That spring, the Boons did not hear the annual symphony of boreal chorus frogs calling in the valley bottom. While Watson Slough itself had not been logged, the clear-cut right behind the slough looked like a straw-coloured, four-lane highway, fringed by trees.

Downstream, the Rocky Mountain Fort site now resembled a charcoal-grey-and-black open-pit mine as the Site C waste rock dump grew. Nothing remained of the flank of old-growth forest and the dense forest understorey that had been left intact the previous year, when the eagles had built their nest and incubated eggs before the bird nesting window, putting a temporary halt to clear-cutting. A few kilometres upstream from the fort site, every single tree on Eagle Island, named for its eagle nests long admired by valley residents, had been cut down.

But one thing from the Rocky Mountain Fort camp still stood tall: the civil lawsuit that BC Hydro had launched against the Boons and four other valley residents, along with Jane and John Doe. The suit served as a financial and emotional deterrent for anyone else who might be thinking of setting up another Site C protest camp or blockading a road.

Despite the despoliation, almost 90 percent of the Peace River Valley remained intact in the summer of 2017. The clear-cuts had blighted some of the valley, whose greenery was still featured in local tourism promotions, but as Ken and Arlene pointed out, the forests would eventually return, although it would take hundreds of years for the majestic cottonwoods and spruce to reappear.

The May provincial election resulted in a virtual tie that kept the Boons and the rest of the province on tenterhooks for many weeks. The Liberals did not earn enough seats to form a majority government, but neither did the opposition New Democrats. Three Green Party MLAs, including Andrew Weaver, the party leader, held the tenuous balance of power. For almost two weeks, no one knew which party the Greens would support. In the middle of the political suspense, only days before the legal deadline to leave their home, the Boons and their neighbours received a one-month extension from BC Hydro, until the end of June.

Almost two weeks after the election, while Arlene was driving home, she heard on her car radio that the Greens and the NDP had reached an agreement to form an NDP minority government. She pulled over and stopped at the lookout on the contoured cliff downstream from her farm, with its expansive view of the Peace River below and the valley beyond. "I cried and cried," she said. The Greens had promised to cancel Site C outright, but the NDP had taken a more tempered approach during the campaign, pledging to send the project to the watchdog utilities commission for a quick review.

Below Arlene, the Peace River ran past the intact tufa seep directly opposite the Boons' bottom fields, trickling thousands of years of natural history down the embankment. The annual Paddle for the Peace was approaching. The election results had given the landowners, First Nations, and others in the community the courage to ignore BC Hydro's insistence that the Boons' bottom fields no longer be used for any gatherings, and posters had shot up in the valley boldly advertising Bear Flat as the location for the Paddle pullout and community barbecue. Despite the clear-cuts in and around Cache Creek, the fields all around the Boons were ten shades of green. The sun shimmered warmly. Each early dawn brought a raucous tangle of bird song from the tens of thousands of migrating songbirds and waterfowl that had found spring purchase in the valley one more time.

No matter what happened politically, BC Hydro could not burn, bulldoze, or lift the Boons' farmhouse onto a trailer and ship it out of sight for several more months. A pair of brown-bellied barn swallows had built a mud nest just above Ken and Arlene's bedroom window, a tiny protective shield for the house. A pair of blue-backed cliff swallows darted in and out of one of the painted birdhouses that perched on the garden fence, safeguarding the garden as well. BC Hydro might have legal authority to dismantle the Boons' family home, but it was illegal for the Crown corporation to wreck the two nest cups before the young swallows had fledged.

The swallows were not the only birds whose homing instincts drew them back to Cache Creek while the Boons awaited the new government's verdict on Site C. On a deliciously warm and sunny day at the end of May, a Red-Tailed Hawk, thought to be one of the same pair whose cottonwood nest tree in Cache Creek had been logged, flew in circles above the farm, seemingly searching for a place to nest. Only days earlier, the Boons and Ross and Deborah Peck, who had dropped by to buy animal feed, had spotted what they thought was a Golden Eagle, arcing above Cache Creek. For reasons the Boons did not fully understand, the loggers had left a few potential raptor nesting trees on the opposite side of Cache Creek, along the chosen highway route. The Pecks and the Boons had squinted at the Golden Eagle as it soared on its steady wings. "Stay, stay," they called out to the bird.

Arlene turned away from the sheared and brown Cache Creek Valley to embrace the green Peace River vista. Yes, she thought, no matter what happened, the fight was far from over.

The Decision

For months, Arlene rode an emotional rollercoaster, her hopes dashed and airborne once again. The long-awaited BC Utilities Commission report, released on November 1, 2017, partially lifted the veil of secrecy that had shrouded Site C under the BC Liberal government. It equipped the NDP government with plenty of ammunition to terminate the project.

Despite the persistent mantra from the Liberals that Site C was "on time and on budget," the three-month investigation revealed that the project had fallen behind schedule and faced escalating costs only two years into a nine-year construction timeline. The final price tag could top $12.5 billion. The review also revealed that the project had encountered serious and unresolved geotechnical issues on the north bank, where the dam structure would be anchored (BC Hydro called the problems "tension cracks"). BC Hydro had also run into troubling financial and legal problems with Site C's major civil works contractor. The sole Canadian partner in the civil works consortium, Calgary-based Petrowest, had slipped into receivership several months earlier, and the remaining two partners were suing BC Hydro for more money. Finally, the commission concluded that BC Hydro had systematically overestimated energy demand. It found that Site C's electricity could be generated for the same price or more cheaply by clean energy sources such as wind and geothermal.

Former BC Hydro CEO Marc Eliesen, who had suspected from the outset that the NDP's restricted terms of reference for the review stacked the deck in favour of continuing with Site C, was taken by surprise by the commission's strongly worded concerns about the project. After reading the report, he called the decision to terminate the project a "slam dunk." "What the commission has come forward with in terms of their recommendations are such that no sensible, rational person could take any other decision than to terminate Site C." Given that the report had been written by commissioners appointed by the former Liberal government, the Boons and many others wondered what more evidence the NDP could possibly need to cancel the project.

Premier John Horgan, who had allowed Site C construction to continue while the project was being reviewed, announced that cabinet would make a final decision by the end of the year. Until then, the government said it would permit the Boons and their neighbours to remain in their homes.

As the 2017 December holiday season approached, valley residents struggled to engage in traditional festivities. The Peace Valley Environment Association launched "Home for the Holidays" cards on social media that featured photographs of the Boons and other families who would lose their homes to Site C. Caroline Beam, a teacher from Hudson's Hope whose great grandparents' house and ranch had been submerged by the Bennett Dam, appeared on one of the cards with her husband and three sons, aged seven, eleven, and thirteen. Beam said that waiting for the decision had taken an emotional toll on her children, who had been given Christmas wish pyramids. "I peeked in, and sure enough, out of all the things my kids could be wishing for at Christmas time, they are wishing for Site C to be stopped," she said. "They love their home, they love the valley, they love the river ... I'm pretty much just doing the best I can to hold it together ... If Site C moves forward right now, what does that say about our system and our politicians?"

The events that transpired revealed quite a bit about the political system in a province the *New York Times* had dubbed the "Wild West of Canadian political cash" based on its astonishing lack of restrictions

Caroline Beam and her family on the banks of the Peace
River. The Beams would lose their home to Site C | *Photo
by Louis Bockner*

on political donations. Following the release of the BC Utilities Commission report, construction trade unions that had donated generously
to the BC NDP launched a public relations blitz in a concerted attempt
to discredit some of the commission's key findings. Working through the
Allied Hydro Council, an umbrella trade union group that had been
virtually shut out of the Site C job site by the Clark government, the
unions widely promoted Site C as a job-creation scheme that was also
urgently needed to fight climate change. They also claimed that terminating the project would unnecessarily burden ratepayers.

Stealing a verse from Clark's chorus sheet, one prominent lawyer
and NDP insider representing the Allied Hydro Council told reporters
at a well-attended press conference at Victoria's posh Empress Hotel that
Site C was needed to "keep the lights on in BC." That news conference,
along with an Allied Hydro Council press event in Vancouver the previous week that had also pushed for Site C's completion, was shepherded
by NDP insider Bill Tieleman, a columnist, media commentator, and
former NDP strategist who had also been a communications director
for former NDP Premier Glen Clark. Tieleman served as a registered
lobbyist for nine trade unions, including four Allied Hydro Council
members. Once the NDP had been sworn into office, Tieleman registered
to lobby Horgan and a slew of cabinet ministers on behalf of those council members, on numerous issues, including "the creation and protection
of private sector jobs, economic development and fair labour laws in
regard to BC Hydro, Site C dam project and other infrastructure."

The Boons and other valley landowners, who had no ongoing access
to the Premier's Office and key ministers, or money to hire lobbyists,
were disconcerted to learn of this behind-the-scenes manoeuvering.
They were deeply perturbed when friends in Vancouver told them that
other NDP insiders with ties to the construction trade unions were also
pushing hard for Site C's completion. Ken found it frustrating that the
lobbyists had come out "in full force: paid lobbyists who get access to
the key ministers and Horgan."

On December 11, 2017, Horgan's office summoned the media to a late-
morning announcement about the Site C dam. Reporters and television
cameras congregated in the BC Legislature's marble library rotunda,
which had been hastily stripped of festive tinsel and a Christmas tree
made from stacked hardcover books. Against a backdrop of five BC flags,
in the same spot Clark had chosen three years earlier to make her "good
news" announcement that the Liberal government had given the green
light to Site C, Horgan told reporters that the NDP had made the difficult
decision to complete the project.

Energy minister Michelle Mungall and environment minister George
Heyman stood on either side of Horgan. When they were members of

the opposition, both politicians had spoken out strongly against Site C. They now appeared solemn and grim-faced, as did Horgan. As BC political columnist Les Leyne observed, "It's not exactly the kind of chipper, can-do attitude you'd like to see in a government that's setting out to spend billions more dollars on the biggest project in B.C. history. If president John F. Kennedy had started the space program in this frame of mind, they'd barely be getting chimps into orbit by now."

Horgan said the Site C project should never have begun, but he claimed the BC Liberals had recklessly pushed it past the point of no return, just as Clark had vowed. The NDP government, said Horgan, could not in good conscience saddle British Columbians with a tab for billions of dollars for what he called "nothing in return." Site C's price tag had surged again. Horgan now pegged the project's cost at $10.7 billion, an increase of more than $4 billion since the day, seven years earlier, when Campbell had announced the project. When asked if he could guarantee that there would be no further cost overruns, the premier dodged the question by saying it was in the best interests of British Columbians to "make better a bad situation." The NDP conceded that Site C's energy would be surplus and sold on the spot market for less than it cost to produce it.

The Boons, along with First Nations members and other valley residents, heard about the decision through the media. No government or BC Hydro representative, much less an elected official, called to deliver the news. Nor did they in the days that followed. Arlene texted a message to everyone who contacted her: "With the announcement today I am too upset to answer." Yvonne Tupper and Helen Knott told friends that the decision had broken their hearts.

Grand Chief Phillip, calling the decision an "absolute outrage," said in a media statement that the day of the announcement would go down in the annals of history as "black Monday" for the NDP. He warned that both the NDP and the Greens, who spoke out against the decision but did not threaten to bring down the government in a future non-confidence vote because of it, would suffer the consequences. In a statement made on New Year's Day, the grand chief referred to the coming year as "Battleground 2018" for BC's Indigenous peoples. He noted that Site C and other highly destructive resource projects were proceeding without their free, prior, and informed consent and that there could be no justice for Indigenous peoples without climate justice.

The Liberals had spun Site C as a project that would fight climate change, keep the lights on in BC, and create ten thousand construction jobs. Horgan wisely sidestepped the issue of job creation. At that time, in the middle of a cold, snowy winter, hundreds of Site C construction workers had been laid off, and work on the site had largely halted. Horgan astutely left others to wave the indefensible clean-energy banner for Site C. This time around, the government justified Site C by using reverse logic: it claimed that cancelling the project would add $4 billion dollars to the province's debt, due to $2 billion in sunk costs and $1.8 billion that BC Hydro said would be needed for reclamation. Terminating Site C, according to Horgan, would put "at risk our ability to deliver housing, child care, schools and hospitals for families across BC."

Yet only three months earlier, in fulfillment of an election campaign promise directed at the Lower Mainland, the government had removed tolls on two Lower Mainland bridges, essentially stripping $3.5 billion from the province's coffers. The NDP's new justification for Site C – the latest in a string of rationalizations that had changed so many times that valley residents, in their lighter moments, were amused – made no sense at all to the Boons and many others. In essence, the government had stated that, in order to pay for capital projects such as schools and hospitals, it would be willing to violate basic human rights, sidestep treaty rights protected under the Canadian Constitution, destroy a valley and its communities, remove the largest chunk of land in history from the agricultural land reserve that a previous NDP government had created, and eradicate critical habitat for more than one hundred species vulnerable to extinction (even as it pledged to introduce a new law to protect endangered species). But the government was not willing to maintain tolls on two bridges in the Lower Mainland, its support stronghold, to save the valley and protect all British Columbians from a boondoggle down the road. Most of Site C's costs would not hit the books until the power came online in 2024 or 2025, by which time another government would likely be in power to absorb the fallout from rising hydro rates.

Horgan's claim that terminating Site C would lead to an almost immediate 12 percent hydro rate hike (adding $198 to annual household hydro bills) was immediately refuted by Marc Eliesen and three other project-financing experts, Harry Swain, Robert McCullough, and Eoin Finn, a retired partner at KPMG, one of the world's largest auditing firms. All four had harsh words for the premier and his cabinet. Eliesen referred to the government's arithmetic and rationale for Site C cancellation costs as "completely erroneous," McCullough characterized them as "deeply flawed," Finn stated they were "pure financial fiction," and Swain argued that they were based on "appalling" reasoning. McCullough, who had been an officer for a major hydroelectricity facility in Oregon, in addition to his other expertise, pointed out that the NDP could easily choose to spread Site C's sunk costs out over many decades, thereby keeping with standard practice for North American utility companies that abandoned projects, as they sometimes did. Swain said Site C's sunk costs could be paid off over thirty years "without any heavy breathing at all."

McCullough also pointed out that the $1.8 billion in reclamation costs that BC Hydro had claimed as part of the $4 billion could immediately disappear from BC Hydro's books if the government declared the disturbed area a park. After all, part of the cleared area had already been slated to become part of the Peace-Boudreau protected area. Chief Willson said BC Hydro should make the site safe and just "go home," leaving nature to regenerate the land.

As for the NDP's claim that terminating Site C would prevent investment in new schools and hospitals, the cost of trucking bull trout past the dam could instead pay for nine new elementary schools in the Lower Mainland.

Rob Botterell, legal counsel for the Peace Valley Landowner Association, called on the government to disclose, in detail and un-redacted, all information and advice received by cabinet concerning hydro rate

increases arising from Site C's termination, but no such transparency
was forthcoming. The landowners' association and the Peace Valley Environment Association hand delivered a letter to Carol Bellringer, the
auditor general of British Columbia, requesting that her office launch
an urgent examination of the government's figures and their impact on
British Columbians.

Ten days after Horgan's announcement, BC Hydro said that it had
selected a preferred proponent for the next big Site C civil works contract: building the dam's generating station and spillways. The four-
corporation partnership had signed a project labour agreement with
three unions, two of which belonged to the Allied Hydro Council. On
its Site C webpage, the government posted the Allied Hydro Council's
press release, which claimed that the BC Utilities Commission's report
was "fundamentally flawed." In response, McCullough quickly pointed
out that information on which the press release had been based had
either been submitted to the commission and rejected or not been presented to the commission for independent scrutiny.

After reacting to Horgan's announcement with tears and anger,
many valley residents fell silent, retreating into shock and grief. But
then they reemerged to continue the fight for their homes and land.
Ken said they had put up with far too much "to throw in the towel now."
Christmas was far from merry for the Boons, who spent a quiet few
days at home with their two youngest grandchildren. But they were
used to chaos and uncertainty at that time of year. Clark had made her
announcement in mid-December 2016. The Liberal government had
expropriated the couple's home and property only days before the 2017
holiday season. And now this news.

As Canadians rang in 2018, the civil lawsuit against the Boons and
other Rocky Mountain Fort campers remained in place. BC Hydro's
vexing issues at Bear Flat continued. The Cache Creek bridge design
still contravened BC Hydro's environmental assessment certificate, and,
in any case, the highway bridge that would affect the First Nations sweat
lodge and burial grounds could not proceed without an agreement from

West Moberly First Nations and Prophet River First Nation on appropriate mitigation measures.

News from Brazil in early January underscored the environmental, financial, and social folly of Big Hydro projects. The Brazilian government signalled that it was reconsidering its contentious plans to open half the Amazon to hydroelectric development. A senior Brazilian government official said hydro projects needed to be re-thought in the face of environmental issues, Indigenous opposition, and growing public unease. "The Brazilian government's announcement validates what scientists, indigenous activists and economists have long known," responded Kate Horner, the executive director of International Rivers, a nonprofit organization that works to protect rivers and the communities that depend on them. "These costly, corrupt hydropower projects are destroying lives, livelihoods and the vibrant ecosystem of the Amazon, the lungs of the planet. Brazil can meet its energy needs without mega-dams, and now it will finally get the chance."

But no such chance arose in British Columbia. On January 16, 2018, West Moberly First Nations and Prophet River First Nation announced that they had filed notices of civil action on the grounds that Site C, along with the two existing Peace River dams, unjustifiably infringed on their constitutional rights under Treaty 8. Legal scholars pointed out that the question of whether Site C violated treaty rights had not yet been tested in the courts. Based on a settlement awarded to the Cree after the James Bay Project had flooded their lands, lawyers for the two Treaty 8 First Nations said the lawsuit could cost BC and federal taxpayers $1 billion. The Boons and other valley landowners understood that the First Nations lawsuit, which would seek an injunction to stop work on Site C, could be the last chance to save the valley and their homes.

On the same day that lawyers for the First Nations announced the civil action, BC Hydro summoned the Boons and other Cache Creek landowners to what Arlene described as another frustrating meeting in Fort St. John. BC Hydro said it wanted to consult with landowners about a potential new highway route, one tucked back against the hills, even though the previous route remained an option. The Boons noticed in new documents BC Hydro gave them that the timeline for constructing the new route would allow them to stay in their home until 2020. Arlene pointed out that their lease with BC Hydro had expired and that they were now squatters in their own house.

Outside her kitchen window, the snow lay thick on the ground, but Arlene found hope in planning for the spring: "I'm planting a garden and ordering seeds."

Acknowledgments

The idea for this book emerged in the fall of 2015 after a summer trip to the Peace River Valley. I had heard many stories from valley residents about the Site C dam's impact, and I couldn't shake them. Throughout my writing journey, I met many remarkable people who gave this project wings.

Chief among them are Ken and Arlene Boon, who had no idea they would become central characters in the book when they graciously welcomed me onto their farm. They spent countless hours talking with me, sharing their vast knowledge of the valley, showing me the land, searching for documents and photographs, and tolerating my pestering questions, large and small. Words fail me when I think of their generosity, kindness, and good spirit.

Other Rocky Mountain Fort campers shared their time, wisdom, and perspective on numerous occasions. Helen Knott, Yvonne Tupper, Lynn Chapman, Verena Hofmann, and Rhoda Paquette, you have my enduring thanks and gratitude.

George Smith convinced me that I should visit the valley, and for that I will be forever grateful.

For immeasurable hospitality in Fort St. John, I thank Danielle Layman, who so kindly put me up in her warm home and helped in so many other ways. Diane Culling lent me winter gear and showed me the Rocky

Mountain Fort site through the eagle eye of a wildlife biologist. Andrea Morison from the Peace Valley Environment Association was unfailingly at the end of the phone line or email to answer questions and root out information.

I owe a special debt to scientists who made time for my questions; helped me navigate through the hazardous shoals of field observations, reports, and terminology; and offered important suggestions and corrections. Thanks to Curtis Björk, Claudia Copley, Purnima Govindarajula, Richard Hebda, David Langor, Erica Wheeler, and Eveline Wolterson.

A very special thank you to Esther Pedersen, Ross Peck, Deborah Peck, Renee Ardill, Guy Armitage, Caroline Beam, Art Napoleon, Bob Fedderly, Clarence Willson, Clay Peck, Katy Peck, Della Owens, Colin Meek, Leslee Jardine, Don Hoffmann, Jack Askoty, Chris McDonald, Steve Ogle, Bess Legault, Rod Backmeyer, David Mullan, Rob Botterell, Sean Holman, Mae Burrows, and Eliza Stanford. Mark Meiers took me out in his jet boat to tour the Peace and Halfway rivers. Maryann and Blane Meek pulled my rental car out of a steep driveway when it was spinning on ice and then fed me lunch. Gwen Johannson was a constant source of warm hospitality, thoughtful conversation, and helpful history.

Chief Roland Willson of West Moberly First Nations generously offered his time and knowledge. I am very grateful to him for inviting me to visit the caribou-penning project his nation runs with Saulteau First Nations, and I thank West Moberly First Nations for welcoming me to cultural camps at Bear Flat. I wish to thank Saulteau First Nations biologist Naomi Owens for taking me to the caribou project and patiently answering my questions. I extend my thanks as well to Chief Marvin Yahey for inviting me to a Blueberry River First Nations cultural camp. A heartfelt thank you as well to Alex Neve and David Suzuki.

I owe a considerable debt to Bruce Muir, Harry Swain, Marc Eliesen, Robert McCullough, Richard Bullock, Harold Steves, Jason Gratl, Craig Benjamin, Chris Tollefson, Scott Hamilton, Maegen Giltrow, and John Wright for generously offering their time and for providing instructive comments. Thank you as well to staff at the Fort St. John North Peace Museum, the Hudson's Hope Museum, the Legislative Library of BC, the UBC Herbarium, and BC Archives.

Any errors in the book are mine, and mine alone. I thank anyone in advance who spots something I have missed, and I invite you to contact me with any corrections.

Just as it takes a village to raise a child, it takes an extended, enthusiastic, supportive, and inquisitive community to raise a book. My Sunday hiking buddies – Charlie Cartwright, the late and dearly missed Mary McCartney, Kim Parker, Brian Parker, and Don Stewart – somehow knew just when to ask questions and when to hold back, allowing me peaceful time in nature before another writing spree. Valentina Cambiazo, Robin June Hood, Maeve Lydon, the late John Shields, and Tricia Roche provided ongoing encouragement and assisted with everything from title brainstorming to parsing complex energy issues. Valentina read an early draft of the book's chapter on agriculture and alchemized it into an elegy in iambic pentameter, which found its way into a book of her poetry published by Ekstasis Editions.

Among the very first to offer encouragement and sound advice was Stephen Hume, whose wise counsel proved invaluable. Vicky Husband offered a willing ear from the start and assistance in many appreciated ways. Bob Peart was also deeply helpful and encouraging. Yvon Chouinard, Andy Wright, Joy Illington, Michael Nation, Penny Goldrick, and Pippa Blake were keenly supportive from the get-go, and I thank them for their faith in this project and for their abiding interest in the Peace. The Willow Grove Foundation generously provided a grant to assist with travel and research costs. My mother, Lynn Spink, was big-hearted and hugely supportive throughout, as was my sister, Rachel Cox. DeSmog Canada inadvertently helped fund this book through Site C assignments, and for that I thank the fearless Emma Gilchrist and Carol Linnitt. DeSmog Canada's revealing coverage of Site C began long before most other media outlets showed an interest, and this online magazine continues to dig deep into Site C issues of public importance that might otherwise never see the light of day.

I am especially grateful to everyone at UBC Press, with a big thank you to James MacNevin for seeing the promise in an unwieldy manuscript. Two mystery UBC Press reviewers provided insightful comments on a draft. Lesley Erickson was the best kind of editor, providing top-notch counsel and good cheer, and this book is very fortunate to have had her on its team. Thanks also to Laraine Coates and Kerry Kilmartin. I am deeply appreciative to Garth Lenz, Louis Bockner, Reg Whiten, the Yellowstone to Yukon Conservation Initiative, and Don Bain and the Union of BC Indian Chiefs for photographs.

My everlasting thanks go to my enormously supportive and thoughtful partner, Ben, whose enthusiasm for this project never waned, even when the book ate up sunny long weekends and the dining room table. I also thank our respective daughters, Charlotte and Kali, for their patience, understanding, and keen interest in Site C. They belong to the millennial generation who will pay for Site C long after our current politicians have turned out the lights.

Notes

Chapter 1

7 **"$1,000 for lanyards and name badges"**: Wendy Stueck and Ian Bailey, "BC Hydro Spends $360,000 to Showcase Dam Project," *Globe and Mail*, September 8, 2010.

8 **"It was a significant announcement"**: Ian Bailey, "Premier's Charter-Jet Trip to Announce Hydro Project Support Cost Nearly $9,000," *Globe and Mail*, June 11, 2010.

8 **"got to be kidding"**: Personal communication with Arlene Boon, September 21, 2017.

8 **as the third in a string of five dams**: Later, seven dams were proposed.

8 **"best source of supply"**: BC Utilities Commission, "Site C Report," May 3, 1983.

9 **Eliesen added that Site C's**: Rod Nutt, "Hydro Runs Up $10 Billion Spending Bill: Peace River Site C Dam Dead," *Vancouver Sun*, November 30, 1993.

9 **"ever be advanced in the future"**: Personal communication with Marc Eliesen, January 9, 2018.

11 **"I take issue with the fake news crowd"**: "Powering up the Province," *NewNorthBC*, May 2, 1917.

11 **a treaty their ancestors had signed in 1900**: Treaty 8 was signed in Alberta in 1899. Eight Dunne-Za Indian leaders signed the treaty at Fort St. John in May 1900.

12 **lose sixty-eight properties to Site C**: The homes include properties already owned by BC Hydro.

13 **"They'll sing you a song"**: Personal interview with Renee Ardill, November 9, 2015.

15   **"Either you let me in or arrest me"**: Personal communication with Leigh Summer, September 22, 2017.

15   **"I will not give you permission to come on my land for anything"**: Lloyd Bentley to BC Hydro, "Site C Project, Property Matters, June 10, 1982," Fort St. John North Peace Museum archives.

16   **"resent being exploited for the benefit of the Lower Mainland"**: "Site C Project, Property Matters, June 10, 1982," Fort St. John North Peace Museum archives.

16   **"by way of threatening gestures & verbal warnings"**: Ibid.

16   **"We have a somewhat irate and anxious group"**: Ibid.

18   **If you added the adjoining pipelines**: Peter G. Lee and Matt Hanneman, "Atlas of Land Cover, Industrial Land Uses and Industrial-Caused Land Use Changes in the Peace Region of British Columbia," Global Forest Watch, 2012.

21   **"cowboys and Indians, working together"**: Personal interview with Chief Roland Willson, July 12, 2016.

22   **"suffocating its critics in a blizzard of paper"**: Vaughn Palmer, "Hydro Deferral 'Rat' Keeps Getting Bigger," *Vancouver Sun*, August 7, 2016.

22   **"behaving like old Mister Grinch"**: Larry Pynn, "Timing and Location of Site C Dam Public Hearings Criticized," *Vancouver Sun,* November 11, 2013.

23   **McDonald ... had served as Campbell's deputy minister**: While McDonald had no experience in the energy sector, her job as head of BC's public service entailed managing thirty-six thousand employees and overseeing an annual budget of $40 billion.

Chapter 2

27   **"the country abounds in beaver"**: Royal BC Museum website.

28   **"exuberant verdure"**: Sir Alexander Mackenzie, "The Discovery of the Canyon," *Peace River Chronicles* (Vancouver: Prescott Publishing Company, 1963), 23.

28   **along with the remains of a fireplace**: David V. Burley, J. Scott Hamilton, and Knud Fladmark, *Prophecy of the Swan: The Upper Peace River Fur Trade of 1794–1823* (Vancouver: UBC Press, 1996).

28   **archaeologists had neither the time nor the resources**: Personal interview with Scott Hamilton, January 7, 2016.

28   **five or more First Nations lodges**: K.R. Fladmark, "Early Fur-Trade Forts of the Peace River Area of British Columbia," *BC Studies* 65 (Spring 1985): 49.

29   **"gone forever if this project proceeds"**: According to BC Hydro, the archaeologists it contracted in 2015 had searched for evidence of Aboriginal

encampments in the immediate area of Rocky Mountain Fort and found some cultural materials thought to be possible indicators of Aboriginal presence. The areas were marked with flagging tape and paint on trees, and heavy machinery was not permitted in those zones when they were cleared. Final archaeological excavation work at Rocky Mountain Fort was planned for the summer of 2016.

30   **"It sounds like an airport, with beep, beep, beep"**: Personal interview with Esther Pedersen, November 12, 2015.

33   **"We're ordinary people"**: Personal interview with Mark Meiers, January 14, 2016.

34   **The First Nations argued that Site C had been green-lighted**: They were appealing both federal and provincial court decisions that had gone against them, and also awaiting a BC Supreme Court decision on a petition to have provincial permits overturned.

35   **at a cost of $22,000**: It took valley residents two years to raise the money to pay the helicopter bill.

38   **She did not agree with the direction**: Mike Carter, "Internal Strife Ignites Saulteau First Nations," *Alaska Highway News*, July 29, 2015.

40   **"Waking up to stoke the woodstove in the shack"**: Helen Knott, blog post, December 28, 2016.

45   **"to see big names like Suzuki and the grand chief come up, it was a relief"**: Personal interview with Helen Knott, January 14, 2016.

46   **only place in the entire province where two other warbler species ... hatched their young**: Two other threatened warblers, the Canada Warbler and the Mourning Warbler, were thought to nest only in the Peace River Valley in BC until some individuals were also detected in a very small zone north of the valley.

49   **"This is what we were instructed"**: Personal interview with Helen Knott, February 2, 2016.

49   **She said that BC Hydro**: Personal interview with Yvonne Tupper, January 22, 2016.

50   **"I think there's a real effort"**: Personal interview with Craig Benjamin, March 3, 2016.

Chapter 3

52   **"In this moment I am heartbroken"**: Helen Knott, blog post, "Site C: Elusive Justice in the Pursuit of Existence," January 24, 2017.

52   **"feeling helpless and feeling frustrated"**: Personal interview with Verena Hofmann, January 13, 2016.

53 **Notably, BC Hydro refused to divulge the amount of money**: A Freedom of Information request made by the author, requesting the total amount of money BC Hydro had spent on legal fees related to Site C, was answered with a few sentences, which said the total expenditure was subject to legal privilege and that, consequently, "BC Hydro is withholding the records sought by your request."

57 **"There is no question that the lawsuit ... has served to intimidate some of its opponents"**: Colleen Brown, "SLAPP Suits: Another Tool in the Developer's Kit?" *Alaska Highway News*, February 29, 2016.

58 **"articulate, passionate and highly educated young woman"**: Andrew Weaver, blog post, "Eleven Days and Counting: Hunger Strike against Site C," March 24, 2016.

58 **"fiscally reckless"**: Personal interview with Andrew Weaver, March 16, 2016.

58 **"to cover the lights with bags"**: Johnny Wakefield, "BC Hydro Seeks to Remove Site C Protest Camp Outside Vancouver Office," *Alaska Highway News*, April 8, 2016.

59 **Julia Ratcliffe, "They're saying there's graffiti"**: Ibid.

59 **"You just killed how many animals"**: Personal interview with Kristen Henry, July 13, 2016.

60 **"it has some of the hallmarks of a SLAPP"**: Personal interview with Chris Tollefson, May 16, 2016.

60 **"think twice before they talk"**: Personal interview with Josh Patterson, May 23, 2016.

66 **"we're going to lose all"**: Personal interview with Rod Backmeyer, February 4, 2016.

Chapter 4

70 **1,100 megawatts of energy, less than one-third the combined output**: When Campbell announced that Site C would proceed to a regulatory review, he said the dam would create 950 megawatts of power. BC Hydro said 1,100 megawatts would power the equivalent of 450,000 homes.

71 **If the communist brass was worried ... they didn't show it**: The dam was dynamited by retreating Red Army troops during the Second World War. The resulting wave of water killed thousands of people.

73 **An international toad rescue**: The spray toad was reintroduced to the wild in 2013, and it was not known if populations would survive.

73 **"The rangers found monkeys"**: Jacques Leslie, *Deep Water: The Epic Struggle over Dams, Displaced People, and the Environment* (New York: Farrar, Straus and Giroux, 2005), 125.

74   "our mightiest rivers ... do not reach the sea": World Commission on Dams, "Dams and Development: A New Framework for Decision-Making," November 2000, ii.

75   It decided to bow out: Nicholas Hildyard, "Dams on the Rocks: The Flawed Economics of Large Hydroelectric Dams," Corner House Briefing 08, August 28, 1998. Web.

75   "priming B.C.'s economic pump": Rod Nutt, "Hydro Runs Up $10 Billion Spending Bill: Peace River Site C Dam Dead," *Vancouver Sun*, November 30, 1993.

76   In Hungary, people risked reprisals: Patrick McCully, *Silenced Rivers: The Ecology and Politics of Large Dams* (London: Zed Books, 1996), 290.

77   Pressured by the "environmental resistance of the Cree": Karl Froschauer, *White Gold: Hydroelectric Power in Canada* (Vancouver: UBC Press, 2000), 101.

78   "We're stuck in a 1950s mode": Jacques Leslie, "Large Dams Just Aren't Worth the Cost," *New York Times*, August 22, 2014.

78   Even with this new focus: *International Rivers*. Web.

78   "big dams have instead become symbols of the destruction of the natural world": McCully, *Silenced Rivers*, 308.

79   As the world scrambles: Bruce Barcott, "Big Bad Hydro," *Forbes*, June 19, 2008.

79   It joined big hydro dams: Belo Monte was finished in 2015, flooding almost 700 square kilometres of lowlands and forest and displacing twenty thousand people, many of them Indigenous. In 2017, plans were also afoot to build forty-three dams on the Tapajós River, an Amazon tributary.

80   "We needed to develop power lines and generating stations everywhere": Roger Keene, *Conversations with W.A.C. Bennett* (Toronto: Methuen Publications, 1980), 107.

82   "tampering with the security and welfare of future generations": Paddy Sherman, *Bennett* (Toronto: McClelland and Stewart, 1966), 221–22.

82   "Swedish Columbia": Ibid., 226.

82   BC Electric "didn't have the vision for the kind of growth our province needed": Keene, *Conversations with W.A.C. Bennett*, 114.

83   "The Peace is the only reason ... there has been some real action on the Columbia": David J. Mitchell, *W.A.C.: Bennett and the Rise of British Columbia* (Toronto: HarperCollins, 1983), 283.

84   Bennett "hopped aboard a giant belly-dump Caterpillar": Mitchell, *W.A.C.*, 372.

86 **had kept plans for Site C "shelf-ready"**: Neufeld later became BC's energy minister, after the Reform Party unofficially merged with other right-of-centre political parties to become the BC Liberal Party, which had no connection to the federal Liberal Party other than its name.

86 **"You have to look at the markets and see if we can sell it"**: "Neufeld Says Site C Dam on Agenda; Could Be Built within the Next 10 Years," *Alaska Highway News*, April 6, 2004.

86 **BC Hydro had filed a blueprint document … and Site C had been included as an option**: Richard Macedo, "Neufeld Won't Speculate on Site C Timeline," *Alaska Highway News*, April 6, 2004.

86 **"leadership to take the project through to the approval stage"**: Scott Simpson, "BC Hydro Boosts Plans to Build Controversial Site C Dam," *Vancouver Sun*, September 15, 2005.

87 **BC Hydro said it did not want people "to think this is a done deal by any account"**: Ibid.

88 **"We want British Columbia to become a leading North American supplier"**: BC Government, news release, "New Act Powers B.C. Forward with Clean Energy and Jobs," April 28, 2010.

Chapter 5

90 **"bodies are usually laid to rest, so that they have a view"**: Personal interview with Chief Roland Willson, August 17, 2017.

91 **Highway 29 hugged the north side**: The valley highway connected the Alaska Highway to Highway 97, the longest provincial highway in Canada, which snaked from the US border to Yukon.

92 **"blatant hypocrisy" and "racist double standards"**: Union of BC Indian Chiefs, press release, "UBCIC Denounce BC Hydro's Tactics at Proposed Site C site," January 23, 2016.

94 **"You're going to flood out a lot of traplines up that way"**: Bouchard and Kennedy Research Consultants, "Blueberry River First Nations Traditional Land Use Study: Site C Clean Energy Project," November 1, 2011, 158.

95 **"ruin our hunting, our trapping"**: Ibid., 159.

97 **The spectre of a third dam**: The Blueberry River First Nation later withdrew from the tribal association, leaving six members.

98 **"a united front"**: Personal interview with Art Napoleon, March 24, 2017.

99 **"social consequences were catastrophic"**: WAC Bennett Dam Visitor Centre display text.

100 **"everybody turned to alcohol"**: Shawn Bell, "Tsay Keh Get Cash for Bennett Dam," *Slave River Journal*, July 7, 2009.

100 described living conditions among the Tsay Keh Dene as "the most primitive I've seen": Vaughn Palmer, "Four Decades On, Deal for Redress Reached with Flooded-Out Bands," *Vancouver Sun*, December 9, 2006.

100 "pinepole-and-plywood cabins scattered over three kilometres": Terry Glavin, "The People of the Mountaintops," *Vancouver Sun*, May 1989.

101 their electricity came from diesel generators: Dennis Izony and Hadi Dowlatabadi, "Opinion: B.C. Hydro and Duty of Care," *Vancouver Sun*, September 29, 2016.

105 Saulteau First Nations had told the Joint Review Panel that the nation remained "gravely" concerned: Saulteau First Nations, "Written Closing Comments," Joint Review Panel, February 3, 2014.

106 The [McLeod] band said it had reached an agreement: Matt Preprost, "Two First Nations Withdraw from Fight against Site C Dam," *Alaska Highway News* (reprinted in *Business in Vancouver*), July 20, 2015.

106 "Members could not trap, hunt or fish": McLeod Lake Indian Band, submission to Inquiry Respecting Site C, British Columbia Utilities Commission, Prince George Hearing, September 29, 2017.

107 "All we're trying to do": Larry Pynn, "Treaty 8 First Nations Split over BC Hydro's Site C Dam," *Vancouver Sun*, December 8, 2013.

109 hired by the Peace River Partnership: The companies were ACCIONA Infrastructure Canada Inc., Petrowest Corporation, which later went into receivership, and Samsung C&T Canada Ltd.

110 No press release or media advisory was issued: A few media outlets, including *DeSmog Canada* and the *Alaska Highway News*, heard about the event from community members and registered to attend through an online form sent to First Nations communities and local politicians.

112 "They are just doing the same thing all over again": Personal interview with Della Owens, June 9, 2016.

112 "We can't change that; we can't bring it back": Personal interview with Emil McCook, June 9, 2016.

113 Willson and Tzakoza failed to obtain a satisfactory answer ... about protecting the burial grounds: Email from Dave Conway, BC Hydro's Site C community relations manager, to DeSmog Canada, November 23, 2016.

Chapter 6

118 The health impacts of methylmercury: Azimuth Consulting Group Partnership, prepared for BC Hydro, "Site C Clean Energy Project," Volume 2 Appendix J, Part 1, *Mercury Technical Synthesis Report*, 2012.

119   **unknowingly consuming levels of mercury**: ERM, prepared for West Moberly
       First Nations, "Aboriginal Health Risk Assessment of Mercury in Bull Trout
       Harvested from the Crooked River, British Columbia," March 2015.

119   **simply had no strategy ... for tracking mercury**: Justine Hunter, "BC Hydro
       to Test Fish for Mercury after First Nations Voice Concerns," *Globe and Mail*,
       May 13, 2015.

120   **permanent loss of Aboriginal knowledge of choice fishing sites, preferred
       species, and cultural attachment to specific sites**: Report of the Joint Review
       Panel, Site C Clean Energy Project, BC Hydro, May 1, 2014.

123   **"It's important to our people"**: Elaine Anselmi, "Caribou Recovery Program
       a Success," *Alaska Highway News*, July 11, 2014.

129   **"In Amnesty International's view"**: Amnesty International, "The Point of
       No Return: The Human Rights of Indigenous Peoples in Canada Threatened
       by the Site C Dam," August 2016.

133   **"a consultation process with a determined outcome is not consultation"**:
       Matt Prepost, "Site C Hearings, Day 2: Process Has Been Unfair, Say First
       Nations," *Dawson Creek Daily News*, December 10, 2013.

133   **"let us blow off steam"**: Roy L. Hales, "The Treaty Canada Wants to Forget,"
       ECOreport, March 14, 2016.

Chapter 7

134   **what we today call the Peace River Valley**: This description is from soil sci-
       entist Eveline Wolterson, personal communication with author, January 13,
       2018.

137   **"Nobody new how to fight city hall"**: Personal communication with Harold
       Steves, October 22, 2015.

138   **"flooded for hydroelectric power"**: Geoff Meggs and Rod Mickleburgh,
       The Art of the Impossible (Vancouver: Harbour Publishing, 2012), 73.

139   **"equal, if not slightly better"**: Personal interview with Eveline Wolterson,
       October 14, 2015.

139   **They concluded ... that the Peace**: Wendy Holm, "Diminished and Dis-
       missed," submission to CEAA/EAO Joint Review Panel, BC Hydro Site C
       Clean Energy Project, Environmental Impact Statement (EIS) Potential
       Project Impact on Agriculture, January 14, 2014.

139   **"That's a conservative estimate"**: Personal interview with Wendy Holm,
       November 23, 2015. The BCUC final report on Site C quoted a 1980 BC
       Hydro study stating that Site C would reduce the Peace Valley land base
       with vegetable potential from approximately 9,000 hectares to 6,700 hectares
       and sand alluvial soil from approximately 4,300 hectares to 2,500 hectares.
       The panel supported the conclusion of the BC Hydro study that Site C would

not preclude development of a vegetable industry in the valley. The panel found that "there still remains ample land in the Peace River Valley to develop a vegetable industry if it is considered viable."

140 **Class 2 and Class 3 farmland**: BC Hydro, Response to Working Group and Public Comments on the Site C Clean Energy Project Environmental Impact Statement: Technical Memo, Agriculture, June 4, 2013.

141 **The landowners' association had hired an expropriation lawyer**: The same lawyer had recently leveraged better deals for landowners whose property stood in the way of BC Hydro's $300 million DCAT transmission line between Chetwynd and Dawson Creek, built to service the oil and gas industry.

141 **"affected by the highway re-alignment"**: Sarah Cox, "BC Hydro Tells Farmers Fighting Site C Dam to Vacate Property by Christmas," *DeSmog Canada*, June 15, 2016.

141 **"It's divide and conquer"**: Personal interview with Arthur Hadland, June 9, 2016.

143 **"It is important that Hydro consider the position of the ranchers"**: "Site C Project, Property Matters," June 10, 1982, Fort St. John North Peace Museum archives.

144 **when the total cost ... was estimated at $15 million**: "Site C Project: Property Matters," June 10, 1982, Fort St. John North Peace Museum archives.

144 **spent more than $20 million quietly buying up valley property**: In 2007 and 2008, several years before the Campbell government announced it would seek regulatory approval for Site C, Hydro spent close to $2 million on land purchases for the dam. In 2011, prior to the appointment of the Joint Review Panel that examined Site C, Hydro dished out more than $11 million to buy land, followed by another $8.7 million over the next two years. In 2015, after Site C had been given the final green light, the Crown corporation doled out another $3.7 million in land purchases.

145 **owned almost 1,000 hectares of Peace Valley**: BC Hydro, "Site C Clean Energy Project Environmental Impact Statement," January 25, 2013.

145 **"This land can grow anything"**: The author attended the event and heard the speech.

146 **"a lengthy formal application"**: Report of the Joint Review Panel: Site C Clean Energy Project, BC Hydro, May 1, 2014, 148.

147 **"Am I pissed off?"**: Personal interview with Richard Bullock, October 30, 2015.

148 **"We grew corn, melons, field tomatoes"**: Personal interview with Katy Peck, November 11, 2015.

149 **The increase in precipitation would be most noticeable**: Impacts on farmland are outlined in RWDI AIR Inc., prepared for BC Hydro, "Site C Clean Energy Project," vol. 2, Appendix K, Technical Data Report: Microclimate, December 7, 2012.

149   **Almost 6,000 hectares of valley farmland was in that zone**: BC Hydro also did not include an additional 1,125 hectares of farmland (an area about the size of four Stanley Parks) that it said would be lost only on a "temporary" basis, even though its topsoil would be eroded by landslide-generated waves when the reservoir was filled. BC Hydro also did not count 506 hectares of agricultural land at the dam site as permanently lost farmland, even though topsoil would be removed to excavate gravel. Nor did it count 109 hectares of farmland that would be lost on what it said would be a "temporary" basis for the relocation of 30 kilometres of Highway 29. A further 38 kilometre stretch of land with "agricultural activities," including private farmland and land with active grazing leases and licences, would also be lost in the short term when a new transmission line was constructed to connect Site C with the existing Peace Canyon Dam substation. And even though close to another 40 hectares of farmland would be out of commission for construction access, BC Hydro dismissed that loss as well, claiming it would only be temporary.

151   **"With flooding, slumping, and erosion we question if there would be anything left"**: Personal interview with Ross Peck, November 9, 2015.

151   **Landslides were a familiar sight**: BGC Engineering Inc., "BC Hydro, Site C Clean Energy Project: Preliminary Reservoir Impact Lines," November 30, 2012.

152   **"I expect BC Hydro will think we should relocate"**: Personal interview with Renee Ardill, November 9, 2015.

153   **[California's] susceptibility to drought**: Brent Mansfield, *Wake Up Call: California's Drought and B.C.'s Food Security* (Vancouver: Vancity Credit Union, 2014).

154   **"So many agricultural regions"**: Cultivating our own food also brings health and environmental benefits. It's fresher, which means it packs a higher nutritional value. And Steves pointed out that most imported food is grown as monocrops, using hefty doses of carbon-intensive fertilizers, herbicides, and pesticides, whereas most BC farms are family-owned and have a far lighter touch when it comes to the use of pesticides and herbicides. BC farmers also widely practise crop rotation, regardless of whether their farms are organic, resulting in healthier soils that require fewer chemical inputs.

154   **"We are running down our stock of fertile topsoil"**: David R. Montgomery, *Dirt: The Erosion of Civilizations* (Berkeley: University of California Press, 2007), 3.

155   **"Fifty years from now every hectare ... will be crucial"**: Ibid., 244.

155   **Site C's impact on farming in BC would be "negligible"**: Report of the Joint Review Panel, Site C Clean Energy Project, BC Hydro, May 1, 2014.

156   **"I came back to work on the family farm from the oil patch"**: Personal communication from Colin Meek, December 16, 2015.

Chapter 8

158 **had taiga voles fossils been discovered**: Richard J. Hebda, James A. Burns, Marten Geertsema, and A.J. Timothy Jull, "AMS-Dated Late Pleistocene Taiga Vole (Rodentia: *Microtus xanthognathus*) from Northeast British Columbia, Canada: A Cautionary Lesson on Chronology," *Canadian Journal of Earth Science* 45 (2008): 611–18.

159 **"it's not only the rare and the beautiful"**: Erica Wheeler, "A Tale of Two Plants from the Banks of the Peace River, BC," *Newsletter of the Biological Survey of Canada* 34 (Winter 2015): 14.

159 **outliers are the flashing beacons**: Personal interview with Richard Hebda, April 27, 2016.

162 **"reduced to about one-half of its potential to support certain wide-ranging species"**: Yellowstone to Yukon Conservation Initiative, news release, "Site C Dam Would Harm Species in Peace Region," January 15, 2014.

162 **at-risk species like the fisher**: R.D. Weir, "The Status of the Fisher in British Columbia," prepared for the BC Ministry of Water, Land and Air Protection and the BC Ministry of Sustainable Resource Management, March 2003. The fisher is a blue-listed species in BC, meaning that it is vulnerable to extinction and a number two priority for conservation after red-listed, or endangered, species. Females give birth to one to three kits in winter, and their survival rate is low.

162 **"You don't get those classic giant trees"**: Personal interview with Rod Backmeyer, February 4, 2016.

163 **"that are poorly understood"**: Personal interview with David Langor, October 21, 2016.

163 **as "incomplete"**: "2015 Biological Survey of Canada Bio-Blitz: Peace Region, British Columbia June 22-26, 2015," information sheet.

163 **nothing but dragonfly collections**: Personal communication with Claudia Copley, October 24, 2016.

165 **"It's the only place"**: Personal interview with Claudia Copley, February 25, 2016.

169 **slough as a wetland conservation project**: The federal government contributed to the conservation project through its Canada Millenium Partnership Program and AgriFood Canada. The provincial government's contribution came through the Ministry of the Environment.

169 **Ironically, as the BC government is preparing to destroy**: Larry Pynn, "Environmental Group Ramps up Protection Effort for Western Toads Threatened by West Kootenay Logging," *Vancouver Sun*, June 1, 2016.

172 **"Any well-seasoned botanist would do a 'woo-hoo'"**: Personal interview with Curtis Björk, March 22, 2016.

173   **What the folder doesn't say**: Joint Review Panel report. The daisy was not included in BC Hydro's lengthy list of plant species that would be affected by the dam. Nor was a plant called persistent sepal yellowcress, expected to become locally extinct to Site C. When questioned by the Joint Review Panel, the Crown corporation excused this omission by saying that neither plant had been assigned a listed status when it wrote the Site C environmental impact statement.

176   **Site C's impact on ... tufa seeps will be "permanent and irreversible"**: Report of the Joint Review Panel, Site C Clean Energy Project, BC Hydro, May 1, 2014.

177   **"We checked this many times"**: Carol Linnitt, "Site C Project Far from Clean and Green, Finds New UBC Report," *DeSmog Canada*, July 18, 2016.

177   **The projects against which these scholars compare Site C**: Other projects include Oil Sands projects in Alberta such as Shell Canada's Jackpine project and the Lower Churchill hydroelectric generation project in Quebec.

177   **the authors of a 2016 UBC report found that**: Program on Water Governance, University of British Columbia, "Comparative Analysis of Site C Greenhouse Gas Emissions versus Alternatives," July 2016.

177   **US scientists, working with colleagues from around the world**: Chris Mooney, "Reservoirs Are a Major Global Source of Greenhouse Gases, Scientists Say," *Washington Post,* September 28, 2016.

178   **"there are no reliable and economical means"**: Thurber Consultants Ltd., "Site One Development Environmental Impact Study, a Report to the British Columbian Hydro and Power Authority, September 1973.

178   **"How could they re-create tufa seeps?"**: Personal communication with Curtis Bjork, October 19, 2016.

179   **Yet there was no doubt that Site C was good business**: Johnny Wakefield, "Who's Getting Direct Award Contracts on Site C?," *Dawson Creek Mirror,* August 9, 2016.

180   **The trap-and-haul facility**: Graham Long and Dan Ohlson, Compass Resource Management Limited, prepared for BC Hydro, "Volume 2, Appendix Q2, Fish Passage Management Plan, Attachment A, Fish Passage Alternatives Assessment," 47.

181   **"bull trout seem more reluctant to enter these non-natural traps"**: Personal interview with Ryan Kriener, March 30, 2016

181   **The leaflet points out that BC contains**: "Bull Trout in British Columbia: A Species of Concern," accessed from the BC Ministry of the Environment website, July 2, 2017.

181   **A different government publication singles out**: Jay Hammond, "Bull Trout," accessed from the BC Ministry of the Environment website, July 2, 2017.

182 **The red-listed coral hairstreak ... would lose so much habitat**: Already endangered butterfly species that will be affected include the Alberta Arctic, Assiniboine skipper, coral hairstreak, great-spangled fritillary, and striped hairstreak.

Chapter 9

185 **Campbell administration's directive to BC Hydro to sign contracts with independent power producers**: Independent power producers donated $615,000 to the BC Liberal Party between 2005 and 2015, according to Integrity BC, a nonprofit organization dedicated to restoring accountability and integrity to BC politics. Independent power producers donated $45,000 to the BC NDP over the same period, according to Integrity BC.

185 **"the strangest thing is [the company] is making more money"**: Judith Lavoie, "EXCLUSIVE: BC Hydro Paying Millions to Independent Power Producers to Not Produce Power Due to Oversupply," *DeSmog Canada*, April 5, 2016.

186 **pegged BC Hydro's loss**: Ibid.

186 **"Everything is being massaged"**: Richard McCandless and Harry Swain, "Comment: Hydro Pricing – What the Minister Didn't Tell Us," *Times Colonist*, August 23, 2016.

187 **"strongly disposed to listen"**: Personal interview with Harry Swain, March 30, 2017.

190 **"There's no emergency"**: Personal interview with Luc Bernier, January 13, 2017.

190 **"We think that it leads"**: Sarah Cox, "Besties? BC Hydro and Premier's Office Too Close for Comfort, Experts Suggest," *DeSmog Canada*, January 30, 2017.

190 **Any government would want oversight**: Brander also said at the time that he believed Site C's energy would eventually be needed.

190 **The government offices also vetted**: Freedom of information requests were made by the author.

191 **"For the proper functioning"**: Ibid.

191 **"While the Liberal Leader delivers her speeches"**: Justine Hunter, "A Political Scion Lends Christy Clark a Hand," *Globe and Mail*, April 21, 2013.

191 **"Our biggest enemy ... it's apathy"**: Barb Aguiar, "Clark to Run Again in Okanagan," *Daily Courier*, September 14, 2016.

192 **"Site C isn't going to be finished for another 10 years"**: Michael Ruffolo, "B.C. Could Save $1.6-Billion by Cancelling Site C: UBC Report," *Globe and Mail*, April 19, 2017.

193 **Muskrat Falls ... was "not the energy choice"**: Terry Roberts, "It's Official: Muskrat Falls a Boondoggle, Says Stan Marshall," *CBC News*, June 24, 2016.

193   **as one US energy analyst warned**: "Manitoba Hydro's Keeyask Dam Was 'Risky Investment Strategy' Says U.S. Energy Expert," *CBC News*, December 26, 2016.

193   **Shepherd admitted**: Kristen Annable, "What Manitoba Hydro's Gamble Means for Your Rates," *CBC News*, February 19, 2017.

194   **"Because it is so well developed"**: Michaela Rosano, "13 Things You Didn't Know about Energy," *Canadian Geographic,* June 1, 2013.

194   **an industry lobby alliance**: After a 2013 rebranding, Oil Sands Developers Group became the Oil Sands Community Alliance.

194   **"the undeniable merits of Canadian hydropower"**: Canadian Hydropower Association, "Report of Activities 2014," 4.

195   **ended with a brief collage**: Canadian Hydropower Association website, https://www.youtube.com/watch?v=qi7bCYGxSyo, accessed August 2016.

195   **"Political leaders from all over the country"**: Canadian Hydropower Association, "Report of Activities 2014," 4.

195   **these acts "affected the operations and future growth" of Canadian hydropower**: Canadian Hydropower Association, "Report of Activities 2011–2012," 7.

196   **By 2014–15, a BC Hydro representative**: BC Hydro's manager of regulatory environmental risk, West Virginia graduate Greg Scarborough, chaired the CHA's regulatory processes working group starting in 2012; and BC Hydro also chaired the CHA's Aboriginal Relations Working Group from 2011 to 2015.

196   **to underscore CHA priority**: Canadian Hydropower Association, "Report of Activities, 2011–2012."

196   **"one project, one assessment"**: Ibid., 8.

196   **"Our efforts to streamline the regulatory review process"**: Ibid., 4.

196   **Swain referred to the changes as "a complete rewrite of the Act"**: Zoe Ducklow, "Q&A: Dr. Harry Swain, Former Site C Panel Chair Becomes Outspoken Opponent," *Alaska Highway News*, July 8, 2016.

197   **the CHA's "ongoing concerns" about the Fisheries Act**: The CHA's 2011–12 Report of Activities listed two BC Hydro representatives on its Regulatory Process Working Group.

197   **"communicated for many years"**: Canadian Hydropower Association, "Report of Activities 2012–2013," 4.

198   **"authorization processes have been streamlined"**: Ibid., 5.

198   **"moved towards a more streamlined and favourable environment"**: Canadian Hydropower Association, "Report of Activities, 2014," 5.

198   **to discuss the "efficiencies"**: From an Access to Information Request filed by the author.

199   "single long-term or renewable incidental harm permits": Canadian Hydro-
       power Association, "Report of Activities, 2011–2012," 7.

199   The CHA was "pleased to see" longer permits granted: Canadian Hydro-
       power Association, "Report of Activities, 2012–2013," 5.

199   Thome, for her part, noted: Canadian Hydropower Association, "Report of
       Activities, 2014–2015," 3.

200   continue to work relentlessly: Canadian Hydropower Association, "Report
       of Activities, 2016," 3.

200   the CEA reported sixty-three lobbying communications: The CEA was
       unwilling to discuss either the meetings or its role, if any, in promoting
       Site C. Calls requesting an interview with its president, Sergio Marchi, were
       not returned.

201   "like cowardly, thuggish thieves in the dark": Union of BC Indian Chiefs,
       press release, July 29, 2016.

202   "That's profit for BC Hydro": Claudia Cattaneo, "How a Pipelines-for-Hydro
       Deal Could Save Alberta's Pipelines and B.C.'s Site C Dam," Financial Post,
       April 1, 2016.

203   "we could potentially electrify": Johnny Wakefield, "Justice Minister, Courts
       Won't Derail Site C, Christy Clark Says," Alaska Highway News, April 7, 2016.

203   "Americans want to hear the Canadian hydropower story": Canadian Hydro-
       power Association, "Report of Activities, 2014," 4.

204   the group leading outreach efforts in the United States: Canadian Hydro-
       power Association, "Report of Activities 2012–2013," 4, 10.

205   "to help meet growing American energy demand": Canadian Hydropower
       Association, pamphlet, "Five Reasons Americans Should Care about Can-
       adian Hydropower," n.d.

206   Only about one-tenth of it could come from small hydro: Natural Resources
       Canada Hydraulic Energy Group, "Emerging Hydropower Technologies
       R&D in Canada: A Strategy for 2007–11," December 2007, accessed from
       webcache, September 16, 2016.

206   a large portion was "economically viable": Government of Canada, "Canada's
       Mid-Century, Long-Term, Low-Greenhouse Gas Development Strategy,"
       2016, 24.

Chapter 10

208   Ontario had added solar capacity: Torontonians pay nearly double what
       Vancouverites pay for electricity. A Globe and Mail article in January 2017
       noted that Ontario's higher electricity costs reflect repayment costs for nuclear
       power investments from the 1980s and 1990s, upgrades to aging hydro

infrastructure, and numerous fixed twenty-year purchase agreements with private companies to provide new sources of power, including natural gas. Adrian Morrow and Tom Cardoso, "Why Does Ontario's Electricity Cost So Much?" *Globe and Mail*, January 8, 2017.

208   **Besides generating 2,400 megawatts**: Later, Ontario made national headlines for its high hydro bills, but these were largely the result of the astronomical cost of refurbishing aging nuclear plants, which still provided more than one-half of the province's energy.

209   **"It was a question of political will"**: Personal interview with John Gorman, August 17, 2016.

209   **Eight percent were armed forces veterans**: The number of jobs in American solar increased by 20 percent in each of the three years prior to 2016, and continued to grow.

210   **much like central air**: Personal communication with Rebecca Jones-Albertus, August 19, 2016.

210   **it planned to double its solar capacity**: Christopher Helman, "How Walmart Became a Green Energy Giant, Using Other People's Money," *Forbes*, November 23, 2014.

210   **but consumes one-quarter of all the world's energy**: In the United States, in sharp contrast to the policy in BC, once Site C was officially approved, the government promoted borrowing tools to "unlock new ways to go solar" through special financing programs and other initiatives. These included a federal tax credit that refunded 30 percent of the cost of installing a solar system, solar energy loans with below-market interest rates, and the opportunity to slash household energy bills by leasing rooftop solar energy systems owned by solar companies: an especially attractive deal for renters.

210   **explained Tesla CEO Elon Musk**: Tom Randall, "Musk Says Tesla Solar Singles Will Cost Less Than a Dumb Roof," *Bloomberg Technology*, November 17, 2016.

212   **"Solar is the way of the future"**: Personal interview with Guy Armitage, July 11, 2016.

212   **its escalating municipal hydro bills**: So many municipalities expressed concern about Site C's financial impacts that the Union of BC Municipalities – representing the majority of British Columbians – voted in favour of supporting a moratorium on dam construction until the project was reviewed by the BCUC, a vote the government ignored.

212   **The district's annual hydro bill had more than doubled**: Personal communication with Gwen Johansson, October 2017.

213   **"We know electricity bills"**: Personal interview with Gwen Johansson, April 17, 2017.

213 **its Net Metering Program**: Gorman pointed out that net metering does not fully value the electricity that solar contributes to the grid, because it is based on average electricity rates rather than higher electricity rates during the daytime, when solar kicks in.

216 **"You don't need to say anything more about the tourism potential"**: Personal interview with John Wright, October 12, 2016.

219 **A report written by the consulting firm**: Knight Piésold, "BC Hydro Evaluation of Pumped Storage Hydroelectric Potential: Screening Assessment Report," November 30, 2010.

220 **More than thirty freshwater pumped storage sites**: Knight Piésold, "Evaluation of Pumped Storage Hydroelectric Potential in the North Coast Region of British Columbia," prepared for BC Hydro, March 15, 2012. However, the report cautioned that the North Coast potential for pumped storage was "slightly less than in the Lower Mainland and Vancouver Island, primarily due to the relatively undisturbed nature of the landscape and the lack of many existing hydropower and other man-made reservoirs suitable for use as part of a pumped storage facility" (8).

220 **German homes on demand**: The average Canadian household uses two to three times as much power as a typical European home.

220 **According to Robert Hornung**: Judith Lavoie, "B.C.'s Biggest Wind Farm Just Came Online – But Future of Wind in Province Bleak," *DeSmog Canada*, March 6, 2017.

220 **lavish wind resources ... according to Jean-François Nolet**: Trent Ernst, "Canadian Wind Energy Association Disbands BC Caucus," *Tumbler Ridge News*, February 17, 2016.

221 **Wind, whose cost is dropping rapidly**: Canadian Wind Energy Association, "BC Climate Policy Goals: The Contribution of Wind Power," September 13, 2015. A significant component of wind power's expense is the high price of turbines. But as worldwide production increased and technology improved over a seven-year period from 2008 to 2015, the price of wind turbine generators tumbled by almost one-third, and it is poised for a further fall.

222 **"energy empowerment to the next level"**: Avant Garde website.

222 **"consumer[s] with the ability"**: Drew McKibben, "The Rise of the Prosumer," *Solutions*, Fall-Winter 2013.

223 **"stuck with a growing pile of assets"**: Stephen Lacey, "This Is What the Utility Death Spiral Looks Like," *Greentech Media*, March 4, 2014.

223 **Northland Power withdrew**: Nelson Bennett, "Done with the Wind," *Business in Vancouver*, February 15, 2016.

223   BC lacked a "vision of short-term opportunities for wind power": Ibid.

223   "a terribly dark shadow": Wendy Stueck, "Two B.C. Wind Farm Projects Halted with Huge Site C Dam in Wings," *Globe and Mail*, May 25, 2016.

224   Had the BC government treated geothermal: Environmental issues related to geothermal can include the release of hydrogen sulfide gas (at low levels it smells like rotten eggs) and potential low levels of toxic materials in some geothermal fluids that require safe disposal.

225   "out of the starting gate": Carol Linnitt, "Canada Has Enormous Geothermal Potential: Why Aren't We Using It?," *DeSmog Canada*, April 27, 2016.

226   "a really ticketable showcase": Carol Linnitt, "Meet the Forestry Town Striving to Become Canada's First Geothermal Village," *DeSmog Canada*, August 18, 2016.

226   "only an idiot would be building": Timothy Renshaw, "Stalled Power Outlook Not Slowing Site C Dam," *Alaska Highway News*, February 16, 2016.

226   As Karen Bakker and other academics pointed out: Richard Hendriks, Philip Raphals, and Karen Bakker, "Reassessing the Need for Site C," Program on Water Governance, University of British Columbia, April 2017.

227   meeting the annual needs of more than 440,000 homes: BC Hydro, "2008 Long Term Acquisition Plan, Appendix L1, Site C – Stage 1 Completion Report," 2.

227   "it would allow us to explore": Carol Linnet, "B. Scales Down Energy-Saving Measures to Manufacture Demand for Site C: UBC Report," *DeSmog Canada*, April 20, 2017.

228   "like the twenty-year-old car": Dawn Paley, "Burrard Thermal: A Victim of Private Power?," *Georgia Straight*, December 9, 2009.

228   "To say we will not consider our entitlement": Emma Gilchrist, "The Forgotten Electricity That Could Eliminate Need for Site C Dam," *DeSmog Canada*, May 28, 2015.

229   "Why not just use our own inexpensive resources": Ibid.

Chapter 11

241   from a kitty litter mine to hydro transmission: In the case of one Nova Scotia family who lost their Christmas tree farm, the "greater good" was a gold mine.

244   "They'll come back and their habitat will be gone": Personal interview with Mark Phinney, February 6, 2017.

246   "It is a fricking mess": Personal communication with Ken Boon, April 17, 2017.

Chapter 12

250   "no sensible, rational person could take any other decision": Personal interview with Marc Eliesen, November 30, 2017.

250   "out of all the things my kids could be wishing": Personal interview with Caroline Beam, December 8, 2017.

250   "Wild West of Canadian political cash": Dan Levin, "British Columbia: The 'Wild West' of Canadian Political Cash," *New York Times*, January 13, 2017.

251   unions that had donated generously to the BC NDP: A search of the BC government's political donations database revealed that the Allied Hydro Council had donated almost $100,000 to the party between 2005 and 2014. Individual construction trade unions donated far more. The International Union of Operating Engineers, for instance, donated almost $500,000 to the BC NDP between 2005 and 2017. In total, almost $14 million was gifted to the BC NDP by a variety of unions – including construction trade unions – between 2005 and 2015. The International Association of Heat and Frost Insulators and Asbestos Workers, representing workers involved in BC's insulation industry, donated more than $22,000 to the NDP in 2016 and 2017 alone. The Construction and Specialized Workers' Union, for its part, handed over $122,500 to the party between 2005 and 2017, and the Ironworkers Union gave $45,000 between 2005 and 2015. During the same period, the BC Liberals raised almost $80 million from corporations, unincorporated businesses, and business associations. Total amounts are from Gordon Hoekstra, "Big Unions Are Big Donors to NDP, but Amendable to Banning Their Contributions," *Vancouver Sun*, February 13, 2017.

252   "the creation and protection of private sector jobs": Office of the Registrar of Lobbyists for BC, website.

252   "paid lobbyists who get access to key ministers": Personal interview with Ken Boon, December 5, 2017.

253   "getting chimps into orbit": Les Leyne, "Past Point of No Return, Says Premier," *Times Colonist*, December 12, 2018.

253   Grand Chief Phillip ... said in a media statement: The BC Greens were not willing to bring down the government on a future vote of non-confidence because they had their eye on the big prize of a promised referendum on proportional representation, which would help ensure their continuing electoral success if passed.

255   "completely erroneous," "deeply flawed," "pure financial fiction," and "appalling": Personal communication with Marc Eliesen, January 7, 2018; Robert McCullough, December 14, 2017; Eoin Finn, December 13, 2017; and Harry Swain, December 13, 2017. Swain was the former CEO of Hambros Canada Inc. and a former board member of Hambros Bank Ltd. of London.

256 **a project labour agreement with three unions**: The two unions are the International Union of Operating Engineers, Local 115, and the Construction and Specialized Workers Union, Local 1611. Tieleman lobbied on behalf of both unions.

257 **"These costly, corrupt hydropower projects"**: International Rivers newsletter, January 11, 2018.

258 **"I'm planting a garden and ordering seeds"**: Personal interview with Arlene Boon, January 19, 2018.

Selected Bibliography

Barcott, Bruce. *The Last Flight of the Scarlet Macaw: One Woman's Fight to Save the World's Most Beautiful Bird.* New York: Random House, 2008.

Bowes, Gordon E. *Peace River Chronicles: 81 Eye-Witness Accounts of the Peace River Region of British Columbia.* Vancouver: Prescott Publishing Company, 1963.

Brody, Hugh. *Maps and Dreams: Indians and the British Columbia Frontier.* Vancouver/ Toronto: Douglas and McIntyre, 1981.

Burley, David, Knut R. Fladmark, and J. Scott Hamilton. *Prophecy of the Swan: The Upper Peace River Fur Trade of 1794–1823.* Vancouver: UBC Press, 1996.

Cannings, Richard, and Sydney Cannings. *British Columbia: A Natural History of Its Origins, Ecology, and Diversity with a New Look at Climate Change.* Vancouver: Greystone Books, 2015.

Cannings, Sydney, JoAnne Nelson, and Richard Cannings. *Geology of British Columbia: A Journey through Time.* Vancouver: Greystone Books, 2011.

Fladmark, K.R. "Early Fur-Trade Forts of the Peace River Area of British Columbia." *BC Studies* 65 (Spring 1985): 48–65.

Froschauer, Karl. *White Gold: Hydroelectric Power in Canada.* Vancouver: UBC Press, 1999.

Hebda, Richard J., James A. Burns, Martin Geertsema, and A.J. Timothy Jull. "AMS-Dated Late Pleistocene Taiga Vole (Rodentia: *Microtus xanthognathus*) from Northeast British Columbia, Canada: A Cautionary Lesson on Chronology." *Canadian Journal of Earth Science* 45 (2008): 611–18.

Keslie, Jacques. *Deep Water: The Epic Struggle over Dams, Displaced People, and the Environment.* New York: Farrar, Straus and Giroux, 2005.

Kolbert, Elizabeth. *The Sixth Extinction: An Unnatural History.* New York: Picador, 2014.

Lee, Peter G., and Matt Hanneman. "Atlas of Land Cover, Industrial Land Uses and Industrial-Caused Land Use Changes in the Peace Region of British Columbia." *Global Forest Watch,* 2012.

Leonard, David W. *The Last Great West: The Agricultural Settlement of the Peace River Country to 1914*. Calgary: Detselig Enterprises, 2005.

Mansfield, Brent. *Wake Up Call: California's Drought and B.C.'s Food Security*. Vancouver: Vancity Credit Union, 2014.

Meggs, Geoff, and Rod Mickleburgh. *The Art of the Impossible: Dave Barrett and the NDP in Power, 1972–1975*. Madeira Park: Harbour Publishing, 2012.

Mitchell, David J. *WAC Bennett and the Rise of British Columbia*. Vancouver: Douglas and McIntyre, 1983.

Montgomery, David R. *Dirt: The Erosion of Civilizations*. Berkeley: University of California Press, 2007.

Pearkes, Eileen Delehanty. *A River Captured: The Columbia River Treaty and Catastrophic Change*. Victoria: Rocky Mountain Books, 2016.

Pollon, Christopher, and Ben Nelms. *The Peace in Peril: The Real Cost of the Site C Dam*. Madeira Park: Harbour Publishing, 2016.

Pollon, Earl K., and Shirlee Smith Matheson. *This Was Our Valley*. Calgary: Detselig Enterprises, 2003.

Reisner, Marc. *Cadillac Desert: The American West and Its Disappearing Water*. New York: Penguin Books, 1993.

Ridington, Robin, and Jillian Ridington, in collaboration with elders of the Dane-Zaa First Nations. *Where Happiness Dwells: A History of the Dane-Zaa First Nations*. Vancouver: UBC Press, 2013.

Stanley, Meg, for the BC Hydro Power Pioneers. *Voices from Two Rivers: Harnessing the Power of the Peace and the Columbia*. Vancouver: Douglas and McIntyre, 2010.

Tyabji, Judy. *Christy Clark: Behind the Smile*. Victoria: Heritage House, 2016.

Urban Systems. "A Review of the Proposed Site C Clean Energy Project: Exploring the Alternatives." Prepared for the District of Hudson's Hope, 2014.

Wilkinson, Charles. *Peace Out: Adventures on the Road to Green Energy*. Markham: Red Deer Press, 2015.

World Commission on Dams. "Dams and Development: A New Framework for Decision-Making." November 2000.

Index

Sarah Katharine Cox is an award-winning journalist who specializes in energy and environmental issues. Her work has appeared in numerous magazines, online publications, and provincial and national newspapers. *Breaching the Peace* is her first book. She lives in Victoria, British Columbia.